THE MYTHIC FOREST,

THE GREEN MAN

AND

THE SPIRIT OF NATURE

THE MYTHIC FOREST,

THE GREEN MAN

AND

THE SPIRIT OF NATURE

The Re-Emergence of the Spirit of Nature from
Ancient Times into Modern Society

Gary R. Varner

Algora Publishing
New York

ISBN-13: 978-0-87586-434-1 (trade soft)
ISBN-10: 0-87586-434-1 (trade soft)
ISBN-13: 978-0-87586-435-8 (hard cover)
ISBN-10: 0-87586-435-X (hard cover)
ISBN: 0-87586-351-5 (ebook)

Library of Congress Cataloging-in-Publication Data —

Varner, Gary R.
The mythic forest, the green man and the spirit of nature : the re-
emergence of the spirit of nature from ancient times into modern
society / by Gary R. Varner.
    p. cm.
Includes bibliographical references and index.
ISBN-13: 978-0-87586-435-8 (hard cover: alk. paper)
ISBN-10: 0-87586-435-X (hard cover: alk. paper)
ISBN-13: 978-0-87586-434-1 (trade soft: alk. paper)
ISBN-10: 0-87586-434-1 (trade soft: alk. paper)
[etc.]
    1. Green Man (Tale)—History and criticism. 2. Trees—Folklore.
3. Sacred groves. 4. Tree worship. 5. Nature worship. I. Title.
GR75.G64V37 2006
398'.368216—dc22
                                        2006000115

Printed in the United States

Other Books by This Author:

Sacred Wells: A Study in the History, Meaning, and Mythology of
    Holy Wells & Waters (2002)
Water of Life — Water of Death: The Folklore and Mythology of
    Sacred Water (2004)
Menhirs, Dolmen, and Circles of Stone: The Folklore and Magic of
    Sacred Stone (2004)

These then are the spirits of the trees, whose very virility is linked with their capacity to destroy. For the tree, like every other important symbol, is a meeting of opposites. On one side it is the place where the dead haunt with hungry spirits, demanding the sacrifice of life, but on the other it is the very essence of life itself. The central meaning of the tree is rebirth. And this rebirth requires also a dying.

- Jyoti Sahi[1]

1. *The Child and the Serpent.* Sahi, Jyoti. London: Arkana 1980, p. 153.

For Lady Raglan, Kathleen Basford, and William Anderson, the first to study the Green Man, and to Dione Fortune, who was the first to give him a name in popular literature.

TABLE OF CONTENTS

Table of Contents

FOREWORD

Nature. We live with it, in it, around it. Some of us take deep delight in hiking through the woods with others or solitary walks along deserted beaches. Others enjoy weekend bird watching events and some of us are employed to take accurate counts of wildlife and to protect it.

Others see nature in an entirely different way. To them, nature is to be dominated and exploited. Entire species of animal and plant life have been destroyed, and continue to be destroyed, by humans who hunt them to extinction or have obliterated the habitats that allowed them to thrive. If man originally hunted to survive, now the profit motive is often the ultimate reason for these acts of destruction. Others simply seem to derive some satisfaction from the very act of destruction.

Humankind has altered the environment around the globe and has been responsible for both deliberate and unintentional acts of destruction since we first started to stand upright. However, humans have also known that nature, in both its obvious details and the mysterious "laws of nature" that man has always struggled to comprehend, are vital to our survival — as individuals and as a species.

Mankind has given a recognizable face to the awesome and impalpable forces of nature in the image of the Green Man and the nature spirits that this book will explore. The ways in which different societies and different craftsmen have depicted these spirits display the wide creative range of the human imagination, but their persistence suggests that in all their many facets these "spirits" represent a deep, primordial sense that humans have shared since civilization

1

began. For the very origin and message of these images have remained the same, even if somewhat altered over time. The message of all the "sacrificial" gods throughout time is one of hope, rebirth, renewal and life ever after.

The Green Man is a paradox and filled with many meanings. I think my friend David Catherine sums it up best: "the face staring out from *behind* the foliate Green-Man sculptures, whether smiling or distorted, might just represent (or offer reflection on) the very leaf-fresh nature staring or dwelling *within* oneself: the very *Breath* this suffocating and dehydrated society is either denying or reaching out for."[1]

Kathleen Basford, who wrote the first scholarly analysis of the Green Man, said, "the secular use of the foliate head ha[s] not yet been extensively studied."[2] This book is the start of that study.

I have been interested in the Green Man for several years; but only when I discovered images of the Green Man in American architecture that rivaled those in England and the Old World did I embark on this study. However, the Green Man is more than just a carved image. The image of this mysterious creature is an ancient one, tied directly to ancient gods and goddesses and to the original concept of life, death and the rebirth of spirit. I have searched out the Green Man from Great Britain to Oregon — finding his image in many unexpected locations, created in many different times, but carrying the same message.

It is hoped that this book will instill a sense of wonder and a desire in the reader to search for the Green Man and his at times obscure meaning. This work touches on history and philosophy, folklore and religion. It is written in two parts. The first, The Spirit of Nature, deals with our perceptions of nature over time, how the Christian Church has influenced contemporary thought, and various aspects of the folklore and mythology associated with nature — trees in particular. The second part is about the Green Man specifically, the origins and the mythic symbolism of the Green Man, how he appears in American culture, and how this archetypal figure together with other ancient symbols can serve to keep contemporary humankind in balance and in touch with the spirit of the earth. In addition, several previously unpublished photographs of Green Men in England, Wales, Ireland, New York, Iowa, California, and Oregon are presented.

---

1. Catherine, David. "The Green Fingerprint: Exploring a critical signature in the quest for the authentic self". Unpublished paper copyright 2004 by Ufudu Medicinal Arts, South Africa, 1.

2. Basford, Kathleen. *The Green Man.* Cambridge: D.S. Brewer 1978, 21.

Special thanks to David Catherine of Natal, South Africa, for providing a copy of his unpublished paper *The Green Fingerprint: Exploring a critical signature in the quest for the authentic self.* Thanks also to Ellen Lissard for the photos of the Green Men and Green Dragon of Manhattan. Unless otherwise noted, all other photographs were taken by the author.

— Gary R. Varner
South Beach, Oregon

INTRODUCTION
THE NATURE OF THE PROBLEM

The "problem" is the very question of just "what is the Green Man?" Is the foliate head a result of contemporary creation? Alternatively, is it a relic of an age long past?

The research and writings of many of the early folklorists such as Sir James Frazer and Margaret Murray have been discredited as Victorian and Romantic recreations of something that never was. Their writings espoused the vision of a wonderful albeit violent world of spirits, talking trees and Faeries, and sought to show that our contemporary traditions are rooted in ancient paganism and nature worship. There is substantial evidence that Murray distorted her information to support her theories of an organized Witch Cult — leaving out any data that ran counter to the conclusions she wished to prove. "Murray," write Jones and Pennick, "was driven simply by a deep personal need to believe in the continuation of pagan religion...and so created 'evidence to prove [her] case."[3] "But in fact," they continue, "no more evidence was needed to prove the continuation of pagan customs and attitudes. The work of Sir James Frazer...had already provided that."[4]

I am probably one of few contemporary writers who regard Frazer, at least, as a researcher to be respected and, while I may disagree with some of his conclusions, I find little fault in the majority of his voluminous research. His docu-

---

3. Jone, Prudence & Nigel Pennick. *A History of pagan Europe.* New York: Barnes & Noble, Inc. 1999, 207.
4. Ibid.

mentation of ancient pagan traditions continuing into the modern age is priceless.[5] It is true that many of the customs and rituals we may believe to be of ancient origin are quite frankly relatively "new" creations. They fill a need that modern humans have to link their troubled *present* with a past that is both mystical and meaningful — even though that *past* may be an invented one.

The Green Man has taken many forms over the years and has been viewed by some as simply a decorative motif rather than a symbol of the spirit of nature.[6] At the same time, the attraction that people have toward the foliate figure seems to express a human need. What is the link between our existence and the mysterious hybrid human-plant creature that can be found on both ecclesiastical buildings and secular ones? What is this attraction?

I think each of us may answer the question in our own way. However, it is clear that humans feel a necessity to link themselves to the natural and supernatural world in many ways. In modern times, some of these ways are simply recreated folkways; but folklore is a fluid and evolving body of cultural representations and it is not frozen at any particular time, place or event. Folklore continues to evolve and unfold in our contemporary society and it is as meaningful as the lore and traditions that are as old as time itself. The Green Man and all of the other creatures that inhabit our minds and souls exist because we create them, and we create them because we need them. There is nothing wrong with this and the process should not be discredited. We create the image of our gods for our own understanding. It is important to create and establish our own relationships with both the natural and supernatural world, as well as the other things that we find meaningful.

Some have claimed that all of the vegetation gods of humankind are the Green Man. While these deities represent many common elements, such as fertility, renewal, rebirth and the continuation of life after death, it is incorrect to equate or amalgamate all the vegetation gods into one. At the same time, it would be fair to say that all of the elements they represent are aspects of the

---

5. Derided as an "armchair anthropologist," Frazer must be acknowledged as one of the first to explain the development of religion and the universality of many of the myths, rituals and traditions found around the world. He also must be credited for his explorations into the hidden psyche of the human spirit and the previously unexplored worlds of metaphor and psychic image.

6. "Decorative motifs" are normally representative of ancient symbols. Be they spirals, zigzags, vegetable or animal images they are derived from symbols that were important in earlier cultures. To dismiss the Green Man image as simply a "decorative motif" suggests a shallow concept and understanding of the history of religion and humankind.

character of "god" in the broadest sense; the first god of humankind was perhaps nature itself. The Green Man includes all of the individual characteristics of these gods and more. The Green Man is an embodiment of the heart and soul of the mystery of nature, the cyclical character of life and death, and where we as individuals fit within this cycle.

I have written about many nature gods and spirits of nature in this book. While others may disagree, I believe that the Green Man is an ancient symbol but one that is molded by the human psyche to fit within the structure of each society and time it resides in. The meanings change over time — as they should. He is at once a symbol of lust and evil as illustrated by his images in Christian churches as well as an ancient woodland spirit watchful of human trespassers. He is what we make of him. To say that the Green Man is no more than a bit of decoration to fill in a blank spot on a wall is the same as saying that the ankh is symbolic of an Egyptian death-cult. There is much more to be told.

The foliate head has a long history around the world and it was created for specific reasons. The image appears to flourish in a cyclical manner, and there would appear to be some reason for its periodic boost in popularity among the "common folk."

In this book, we will explore the various vegetation deities throughout time and space in a broader context. We will also examine how they culminated in the mysterious and mystical motif still found around the world. I have examined the Green Man from various angles to show his history, his travels to other nations and continents, and his various possible meanings. Ultimately, the real meaning of this fascinating image is up to the reader to determine.

PART ONE

The Spirit of Nature

Chapter 1. The Gods of Nature

To understand the nature of the Green Man fully we must look at the other gods of nature that humans have revered over the centuries. Water sprites, fairies, Bacchus, Pan and Dionysus are all gods and supernatural beings closely associated with nature. They represent the spirits of everything — including plants, animals, stones, trees, the winds and all other aspects of this "natural" world and the Otherworld. Early cultures expressed their traditions and beliefs orally, in the form of myths. Modern day society regards these myths as tales of fantasy and, even though some of them undoubtedly were the basis for Judeo-Christian lore, they are relegated to a "primitive" and "fairytale" category. The dominant culture or leadership always discredits the traditions of others. As scholar John Bierhorst said, "myths are what others have; we ourselves have 'scripture' or 'history'."[7] These "myths" are as solid in their meanings as the Biblical versions of history and they should not be considered inferior. Myths were used to transmit actual events in non-literate cultures and were important for the way that they preserved the memory of these events from generation to generation. These early stories are the basis for modern day religious constructs and the difference between these myths and other "scriptures" goes little further than the change in the names of the heroes and gods.

---

7.   Bierhorst, John. *The Mythology of Mexico and Central America.* New York: William Morrow and Company, Inc. 1990, 1.

The dominant religions today regard animism as a primitive form of ancestor worship, worth little more than a footnote in the history of religion. Religious historians and scholars such as Fred Skinner take the view that "primitive people, ancient or modern, make no distinction between the natural and the supernatural...They have no knowledge of natural laws or natural causation. Speculation among the ancients could not take an intellectual or rational form; it had to be poetic or imaginative."[8]

I disagree with this analysis. The "knowledge of natural laws or causation" does not diminish the feelings of awe that we experience when confronted by the forces of nature, the unseen forces that cause massive storms or earthquakes or volcanoes. It does not matter that a scientist can "explain" how something happens; the event is still caused by forces that are beyond the scope of the average person's understanding or control. Much of the scientific theory current today was also understood thousands of years ago — by those same people who worshipped the Old Gods and recognized the spirits of nature. To know that something exists or happens "because" of certain forces does not explain those forces or displace the wonder felt toward those forces — nor should it. Nor do technical details help us to understand those occurrences that science has yet to explain and which therefore strike us as "supernatural."

The notion that "cults" are less valid than a "religion" is a continuation of that ethnocentric mind-set marked down by the Jewish religion in Exodus 20:1-5 and aggressively promoted during the early Christian era. At one time, the Eleusinian Mysteries dominated religion throughout the Mediterranean region. For over 2000 years, the Mystery Rites of Dionysus inspired philosophers, scholars and ordinary people from Egypt, Rome, Greece and other Mediterranean countries — until the early Christian church ruled these rites a "cult" and set out to destroy it. The followers of Mithra met with the same fate. Today we know that Mithraism was the basis for much of the Christian faith. Mithra had twelve followers, sat at a last supper, performed baptisms (in bulls' blood) and was resurrected from the dead — promising eternal life. Emperor Constantine declared this, too, a "cult," just in time to prevent it from becoming the dominant religion, almost surpassing the new religion of Christianity.

Some scholars are blatant in their ethnocentrism and Judeo-Christian biases. Harvard anthropologist William Howells wrote, "it is quite true that we

---

8. Skinner, Fred Gladstone. *Myths and Legends of the Ancient Near East.* New York: Barnes and Noble Books 1970, 8.

know their gods do not exist and their magic is hollow...."[9] It is not clear what level of logical and academic rigor one can expect from Harvard if an anthropologist means to suggest that one might prove or disprove whether *any* god or gods exist. Neither does anyone have a right to say that a god or gods do or do not exist for a particular individual or group of people. Today's dominant religions each espouses the view that it is the only true religion, and each points to some ancient record as the proof. Ironically, these ancient records can be shown to be compiled from the lore and mythology of older belief systems, religions which had suffered conquest, absorption or annihilation at the hands of an invading and dominant religion and culture.

The annihilation of the goddess-centered and life-espousing nature oriented cultures came at the hands of nomadic warrior societies that replaced the Earth Goddess traditions with those of a patriarchal form. The goddess created life from within (the Earth). In a profound move, the warrior societies replaced the Earth Goddess with a Sky God who created life from without (heaven) — this was the impetus that changed humankind's perceptions and relationships with nature, or was an expression of that change in perception. These nomads not only dealt physical devastation but also cultural impoverishment to the societies they over-ran.[10] "Now everywhere," writes Riane Eisler, describing this transition, "the men with the greatest power to destroy — the physically strongest, most insensitive, most brutal — rise to the top, as everywhere the social structure becomes more hierarchic and authoritarian. Women — who as a group...are most closely identified with the old view of power symbolized by the life-giving and sustaining chalice — are now gradually reduced to the status they are to hold hereafter: male-controlled technologies of production and reproduction.

"At the same time the Goddess herself gradually becomes merely the wife or consort of male deities, who...are now supreme."[11] Nature has become an adversary of man, to be defended against, exploited and abused — not nurtured and respected. The ancient Hebrews continued this attack as they entered the "Land of Milk and Honey." Not simply shepherds, the Hebrews did not just wander into a vacant paradise but took it by force from the Canaanites, killing

9. Howells, William. *The Heathens: Primitive Man and His Religions.* Garden City: Anchor Books 1962, 6.

10. Eisler, Riane. *The Chalice & The Blade: Our History, Our Future.* San Francisco: HarperSanFrancisco 1987, 52.

11. Ibid., 53.

all living things, whether plant, animal, man, woman or child. The Canaanites were followers of the Goddess Asherah, also known as the Queen of Heaven, and many of the Hebrews also worshipped her. Over time, the Hebrew priest class felt strong enough to start the overthrow of the Goddess, even though the Goddess and the Hebrew Yahweh had been worshipped side by side for hundreds of years. Those who refused to convert to the pure patriarchal god system were slaughtered.[12]

The old myths were rewritten, as they always are, by the victors, to reflect the values of the dominant hierarchy — in this instance, a male dominant society. References to the Goddess were stricken from religious texts, or modified, save for some unaccountable exceptions that appear to have been accidentally left intact. These mistakes have added a great deal of confusion to the religious teachings of the Jewish and Christian theologies for centuries.

The gods of nature have been relegated to cartoon status because of the continued, albeit subconscious, rewriting of history and ridicule of the "Old Religion." Perhaps the most successful mind control in history has been accomplished by the large-scale organized religions that have dominated cultural development in recent centuries — mind control accentuated by torture, murder, slavery and cultural subjugation. However, you cannot keep a good idea down! The nature gods continue to rear their heads in the subtlest way. Christian churches were adorned with images of nature spirits; new mythologies grew out of the old and were added to the cultural library. These mythologies created links to the Old Religion and still survive as folklore. Contemporary fantasy writers such as Charles De Lint and Robert Holdstock continue to add to these mythologies and keep them alive — mixing ancient themes in a contemporary setting.

The Green Man image is found worldwide in contemporary jewelry and "garden décor." The Fairies can be found in every gift shop and their popularity only continues to grow. What is happening? Because the Old Religion has been part of the human world and the human spirit since the beginning, it continues to resurface and to insinuate its creeping vines of influence into human existence — to keep the message flowing: that only with the cooperation, respect and love of humans towards nature can any of us survive.

---

12. Patai, Raphael. *The Hebrew Goddess.* New York: Avon Books 1978. See Joshua 10:40: "So Joshua smote all the country of the hills, and of the south, and of the vale, and of the springs, and all their kings: he left none remaining, but utterly destroyed all that breathed...".

CHAPTER 2. NATURE: TO DOMINATE OR TO NURTURE IT?

It was only in November 1997 that a leader of a patriarchal religion, Bartho-lomew I, head of the Greek Orthodox Church, stated that the "degradation of nature is a sin." No other leader of a Christian, Jewish, or Islamic body has ever made such a statement. To do so is revolutionary, even though pagans and indig-enous people around the world have held that belief since the beginning of time.

Most if not all of the world's indigenous cultures view nature as a divine essence — the very essence of life. James G. Cowan, writing about the Australian aborigine, said "they have studied nature, drawn their conclusions from it, and found it to be the embodiment of a profound metaphysical principle pertaining to all existence. For they have seen in nature much more than its visible beauty, fraternity and practical purpose as a provider. They have seen in it a symbol of an underlying reality which needs to be understood as sacred if true wisdom is to be attained."[13]

Although the indigenous people of the non-Christian world viewed nature as the source of life and the real spiritual and sacred power of the world, early Christian missionaries condemned such thoughts and traditions, saying that to continue the rituals, healings and worship at trees, stones and waterways "con-secrate them to the devil."[14]

Stephan A. Hoeller, writing of Carl Jung and the gnostic view of the world, said that gnostics and those who practice pantheistic paganism "love[s] nature not because of its external appearance or its creator, but because of an over-whelming, mysterious, unknowable and yet ever-present Divinity that resides concealed in nature itself. While to the orthodox Christian this is God's world in the sense that it has been fashioned and is now owned by the God of the Bible, to the Gnostic, the alchemist and the magician, and of course to Jung, this is God's world, because *God lives in it*."[15]

We find then that most "civilized" and "advanced" countries and societies have lost the sense of wonder and the knowledge that nature is much more than trees to be cleared for cattle and hills to be flattened for construction or oil to be

---

13. Cowan, James G. *The Elements of the Aborigine Tradition.* Shaftsbury: Element Books Limited 1992, 2.

14. St. Eligius, 640 CE as quoted by Brian Bates in his article "Sacred Trees" in *Resur-gence Magazine* #181, March/April 1997.

15. Hoeller, Stephan A. *The Gnostic Jung and the Seven Sermons to the Dead.* Wheaton: The Theosophical Publishing House 1982, 160.

pumped for increasingly larger vehicles. How did this occur? Humankind has always altered the environment and it would not be fair, or accurate, to think otherwise. Prehistoric people were also guilty of eradicating species and whole forests. Easter Island is a prime example of misguided thought and poor planning decimating the landscape. Ronald Hutton reminds us, too, that "the Iron Age Celts...may have had their holy stands of trees, but this did not stop them from clearing virtually all the large areas of forests spared by their predecessors...[and] under the pagan Roman Empire, the remaining woods were stripped from much of the North African coast, producing an ecological catastrophe."[16] However, early on these events were normally confined to certain specific areas and had to do with military tactics during times of conquest. Since the ascendancy of Christianity, and with it "civilization" as we know it, this has become a worldwide catastrophe. For strange reasons patriarchal religions, consumerism and big business seem to go hand in hand. The rapid expansion of villages, towns and cities along with associated manufacturing have decimated, and still are decimating, huge tracts of ancient forests. Theologian Rosemary Radford Ruether wrote of the conflict in her book *Gaia & God*:

> One side of this tradition (of Christian asceticism), with its hostility to women, sexuality, and the body, and its contempt for the material world in favor of life after death, reinforces the patterns of neglect and flight from the earth. But asceticism can also be understood, not as rejection of the body and the earth, but rather as rejection of exploitation and excess, and thus as a return to egalitarian simple living in harmony with other humans and with nature.[17]

For the most part this asceticism is defined narrowly and is not eco-friendly. This is slowly changing with the works of Christian scholars such as Matthew Fox, Ruether, and others but even now; most Christian/Catholic clergy and congregations are very resistant to looking upon the natural world as something more than a hindrance to their journey to heaven or a temptation toward evil. Nature became "evil"; it was associated with witchcraft. Women were viewed as untrustworthy, evil and the essence of death and sin. "This ambivalence toward women," writes Ruether "was closely related to Christian ambivalence toward physical nature."[18] The ambivalence toward women was also a result of the fear of women on the part of the patriarchal leaders, the fear of

---

16. Hutton, Ronald. *The pagan Religions of the Ancient British Isles: Their Nature and Legacy.* Oxford: Blackwell 1993, 253.

17. Ruether, Rosemary Radford. *Gaia & God: An Ecofeminist Theology of Earth Healing.* San Francisco: HarperSanFrancisco 1992, 188.

18. Ibid., 189.

the Goddess religion and the possibility that a matriarchal society would once again become a dominant force around the world.

The negative attitudes expressed today towards women and nature in general reflect those same attitudes expressed since the advent of patriarchal religion in Biblical times. Sex and fertility are regarded as sinful, as evil temptations to be shunned, ignored and suppressed.[19] Women are at the disposal of men. One of the ignominious questions of early theologians was, "Do women have souls?" Conservative Christian attitudes regard nature and all of her plant and animal children as soulless, present on Earth purely for the exploitation and dominance of man and regarded as habitats for evil. Eleventh century theologians Peter Abelard and Hildegard of Bingen both believed that demons occupied trees and that the devil existed within nature. An example of this is found in carvings located in St. Lazare Church in Autun, France. Built in the twelfth century, the church features one notable piece showing two demons hanging a soul from stalks of flowering vines.[20]

There is no stewardship professed in most religions today as there was during the pre-historic Goddess era, although there are signs that this may be changing — hopefully, before it is too late. Those few societies that do still exist today that view nature as sacred and to be protected are regarded as "primitive." Indigenous cultures generally have "depended on being able to enter into the very psyche of the environment."[21] "Our forefathers of fifteen hundred years ago," writes Brian Branston, "lived not what we call 'close to nature' but actually *involved* with nature: they were not creatures apart, different from the birds, plants or animals, but fitted into the natural cycle of synthesis and disintegration which any kind of civilization always modifies....It is from the constant awareness of the living connection between man and the phenomenal world that the myths of our ancestors arise, that their gods are born."[22] The representatives of today's "advanced" societies are no longer able to do this wonderful thing,

19. Clyde Kluckhohn noted that the Navajo, as other indigenous cultures, believe that sex is a "part of nature, something to reckon with, but not a thing to be denied." (*The Navaho*. Garden City: Doubleday & Company Inc./The Natural History Museum 1962, 308).

20. Kostof. Spiro. *A History of Architecture: Settings and Ritual*. Oxford: Oxford University Press 1985, 300.

21. Bates, op. cit.

22. Branston, Brian. *The Lost Gods of England*. New York: Oxford University Press 1974, 52-53.

which has resulted in billions of people losing touch with their spirituality and ethical living on the earth.

To the Navajo it is wise to try to influence nature with ritual and song but foolhardy to believe that man can control and master it. White men's belief, according to Harvard anthropologist Clyde Kluckhohn, is "that nature will destroy them unless they prevent it; the Navahos' is that nature will take care of them if they behave as they should and do as she directs."[23]

The Christian religion did not fully reject nature and tree worship even though it was late in embracing it. Simon Schama noted, "It was to be expected, then, that Christian theology, notwithstanding its official nervousness about pagan tree cults, would, in the end, go beyond the barely baptized Yggdrasil of a twelfth-century Flemish illumination where the boughs of the world-tree support paradise."[24] In fact, there is a certain "timber history" of Jesus that links him to nature and trees in particular. Jesus was born in a wooden stable, his earthly father was a carpenter, Jesus became a carpenter, he was crowned with a thorn crown and was crucified on a wooden cross (often referred to as a "verdant cross") much as Odin sacrificed himself on a tree.

There are a number of symbols in Christian theology that are linked to nature and to trees in particular, from the burning bush seen by Moses, to the Tree of Knowledge and the Tree of Life, to other miraculous trees and bushes that apparently bloom only on Christmas and Easter. However, the obvious symbolism of trees and vegetation that symbolize fertility and resurrection has been overtaken by other, darker symbols, which call for the destruction of nature as an abode of evil.

The Green Man, that enigmatic image carved on both cathedral and secular building, represents the nurturing aspect of nature and the symbiotic relationship between nature and the basic characteristics of the human spirit untarnished by brutality or a destructive spirit.

"Perhaps the most fundamental difference between the medieval and modern concepts of the Green Man," write Fran and Geoff Doel, "is that for medieval man he signified personal spiritual resurrection, whilst for modern man he symbolises our attempt to save the planet from our own excesses."[25]

23. Kluckhohn, Clyde and Dorothea Leighton. *The Navaho.* Garden City: Doubleday & Company Inc./The Natural History Museum 1962, 308.
24. Schama, Simon. *Landscape and Memory.* New York: Vintage Books 1995, 218
25. Doel, Fran & Geoff. *The Green Man in Britain.* Glouchestershire: Tempus Publishing Ltd. 2001, 130.

CHAPTER 3. THE LORE OF THE OAK

Why a chapter specific to the Oak? The Oak has been recognized since ancient times for its strength, its power, its beauty, and its connection with the divine. The Oak is also closely associated with the Green Man. Many of his carvings include oak leaves sprouting from the ears, eyes and nose of the figure. In addition, oak leaves commonly compose the hair and beards of the male Green Man image. Many Green Man carvings were originally crafted from the oak and these wooden images are still found in many church misericord carvings and roof bosses.

When the Sacred Oak is mentioned, we normally visualize the hooded and mysterious Druid priest or priestess worshipping in a sacred grove. Nevertheless the symbolism of the oak, and the belief in its powers and sacred ties to the Divine, is widespread. It was a prevalent belief among European, Asian, Mediterranean and Native American peoples, to name just a few.

While the armies of the Roman Empire and the Catholic Church destroyed many oak groves to drive the Druids and the surviving pagan worshippers' underground, the oak is threatened today by new armies of "developers" striving to meet the demands of a burgeoning population, which by many measures has already exceeded the limits of the Earth's capacity to sustain it.

One of the most horrendous tenets of the religion of the Sky God, the basis of the religion of the Christian and Jewish faiths, is that the Earth exists only for the domination and consumption of man. This belief, fostered to counteract the nature-based religious beliefs of the pagans, has resulted in the destruction and exploitation of the rain forests, the degradation of our waterways, the loss of fertile soil, the extinction of thousands of birds, mammals, fish, and insects as well as a host of plants that may have been suitable for treating and curing a variety of diseases. As part of this degradation and destruction of nature, those who recognized the intimate linkage of humankind and Gaia and who spoke in opposition to the Judeo-Christian patriarchal approach of *ownership* of nature suffered torture and death — and still do. Non-indigenous entrepreneurs who take the land, burn the rainforest to make room for cattle grazing, and destroy not only a way of life but also a whole ecosystem, kill many indigenous people in the Amazon basin every year. As noted previously, it was only in the last decade that a leader of a patriarchal religion, Bartholomew I, head of the Greek Orthodox Church, stated that the "degradation of nature is a sin."

The oak tree is widely distributed throughout the world, from Europe and the British Isles to North America and even parts of the Pacific. Wherever humans have encountered this tree, they have regarded it as sacred. Trees in themselves are seen as holy. Nigel Pennick in his book *Celtic Sacred Landscapes*[26] wrote:

> The tree, like the human, is a mediator between the upper and lower worlds, linking with its serpentine watercourses the underworld of the ground, the surface of the ground, upon which we live, and the sky and air. Thus, the tree is an image of the cosmic axis, a physical manifestation of the maxim "as above, so below."

Today, far removed from the ancient days of the pagan past, the oak is still regarded as a sign of strength, longevity, abundance, and of enduring quality. In addition, its history is rich in associations with magical properties and the gods themselves.

The oak was an important part of the lives of the pre-industrial peoples of the world. The acorns provided a source of food for both wandering and settled tribes of the world. In addition the mistletoe, that parasite which is found in the upper branches of the oak in certain regions and which is valued for its romantic associations even today, was held sacred by the Druids and was used as a cure-all. In fact, the very word "Druid" may be derived from the Indo-European "*dru-wid*," which literally meant "oak-wise."

The oak is also present in Biblical passages that hint at the oak's sacredness. In Genesis (35:8), it was recorded that "Deborah Rebekah's nurse died, and she was buried beneath Bethel under an oak." Saul, too, was reportedly buried under an oak, indicative of a "sacred king" in pagan belief, and Jacob buried not only amulets but also the "strange gods" of his household under an oak (Genesis 35:4). Sir James Frazer mentioned similar practices in his work *The Golden Bough*.[27] Frazer wrote that during Mid-Lent it was the practice to "bury Death under an oak." Alexander Porteous noted, "In Croatia witches were formerly buried under old trees in the forest, and it was believed that their souls passed into these trees."[28] The Druids, as well, buried some of their dead under oak trees, although most appear to have been interred in barrows, pits or underground tombs. Celtic lore, according to Pennick, states that "when the human being enters a tree at death, it is a return to the origin: part of the soul of the

---

26. Pennick, Nigel, *Celtic Sacred Landscapes*. New York: Thames and Hudson, 1996, 21.
27. Frazer, Sir James. *The Golden Bough: A Study in Magic and Religion*. Hertfordshire: Wordsworth Editions LTD., 1993, 309.
28. Porteous, Alexander, *The Lore of The Forest*. London: Senate, 1996, 166.

deceased enters a tree planted on the grave."[29] In Germany until the late Middle Ages tree-burial (burying the corpse in the hollow of a tree) was common and it is believed that the idea of a wooden coffin is a derivative of these tree burials.

Other Biblical references to the oak include the mighty tree which caught the hair of Absalom, by which "he was taken up between heaven and the earth." Many oaks in the Middle East are regarded as "inhabited oaks," including the one venerated tree referred to as Balutat-Ibrahim, or Abraham's oak.

The Bible treats the oak in somewhat contradictory fashion. It is at once holy but also representative of evil. It would seem that in the earliest books of the Bible the oak is held to be sacred, probably due to the fact the early worshippers of the Sky God, Yahweh, still held many of the pagan Goddess beliefs close to their hearts. Abraham was said to have built an altar to God in a grove of oaks and was visited by God in the likeness of three men under the shade of the oak trees (see Genesis 12:6 and 13:18).

Early Jewish practice was to sacrifice children to "Moloch," which was simply a term meaning "king." This "king" has been identified with Yahweh and with Astarte; however, the title of "king" obviously would not be the appropriate title for a goddess. The oaks in the sacred groves were said to be smeared with the blood of the sacrificed children before they were burned. The Grove of Moloch was located just outside of the walls of Jerusalem.

Later Biblical writings indicate a shift in the beliefs of the Jews towards oaks. Hosea, Ezekiel and Isaiah, all Levite priests, condemned the sacred groves as "heathenish." However, as in most instances where attempts have been made to destroy pagan beliefs, the belief in the sacredness of the oaks at Hebron continued long into the Christian era.

Interestingly enough, many early Christian leaders made it a point to preach near sacred trees. Many times this was done to convey a subtle shifting of the tree's pagan symbolism to the new Christian theology. Statues of the Virgin Mary and crucifixes were placed on or near the sacred trees. One such pagan site, the Allonville Oak, was actually turned into a Catholic church in 1696 and was consecrated to the Virgin Mary. This huge tree, still living in France, is over a thousand years in age and its trunk measures forty-five feet in circumference.

One of the methods used by the Church to turn public opinion against the Oak was through storytelling. One such tale relates that when Jesus' crucifixion was planned, all of the trees met and agreed that they would not be part of the

---

29. Pennick, op. cit., 23.

bloody event. As the laborers attempted to construct the cross, each tree that was selected splintered into thousands of pieces, all except the ilex oak. The oak allowed itself to be used and came to be viewed as a traitor, like Judas. The ilex oak was condemned and many people would not allow any part of the tree to be brought into their homes. Woodsmen's axes were not allowed to touch this tree.

Charles Skinner, however, leaves a softer image of the ilex in his book, *Myths and Legends of Flowers, Trees, Fruits, and Plants.* [30] Skinner wrote:

> ...but though it thus became accursed, Jesus forgave it as content to die with Him, and in the shade of an ilex he reappeared to the saints.

The oak's association with the divine is an ancient one. In ancient Italy, the Romans regarded all oaks as sacred to Jupiter,[31] as they were to Zeus in Greece. Frazer wrote "Perhaps the oldest and certainly one of the most famous sanctuaries in Greece was that of Dodona, where Zeus was revered in the oracular oak".[32] Dodona was one of the most important and revered sacred places in the Greek world until 219 BCE, when Dorian invaders swept down upon the Greek frontiers. J. B. Bury wrote in his book, *A History of Greece*,[33] that the Dorians "destroyed instead of adopting the civilisation which they found." Dodona became a neglected and little used outpost, although the Sacred Oak was reported still standing in 180 CE. There are indications that the priestesses continued to serve at the site until approximately the 3rd century. It is interesting to note that the Sacred Oak at Dodona was also an ilex oak. The Sacred Oak of Dodona was, as Aeschylus reported, "a lofty and beautiful tree, an incredible wonder...regarded as the Tree of Life."[34]

Located in Epirus, Dodona contained a temple dedicated to Zeus established near the oracular oak. Epirus was thought to have more storms than anywhere else in Europe and was sacred to Zeus, the God of Thunder. Large gongs were hung from the huge oak and were used to produce sounds similar to thunder when the wind rose. People believed that Zeus was present when the leaves rustled, and his messages were transmitted through the leaves. Abraham's

---

30. Skinner, Charles M. *Myths and Legends of Flowers, Trees, Fruits, and Plants In All Ages and In All Climes.* Philadelphia: J.B. Lippincott Company, 1911, 194.

31. Frazer, op. cit.,160.

32. Ibid. 159.

33. Bury, J.B., *A History of Greece to the Death of Alexander the Great.* New York: The Modern Library, no date, 49-50.

34. Porteous, op. cit., 59.

oracular oak was used in a similar manner; the rustling of the leaves and the calls of birds were thought to hold divine messages.

To the Slavs, the oak was sacred to the god Perun — who was at once the god of harvest and rain as well as the god of thunder and war. An outdoor shrine to Perun was found in 1951 approximately two and a half miles from the Russian city of Peryn. "Archaeologists," wrote Charles Phillips, "found a central mound surrounded by a ditch filled with charcoal, which led them to speculate that an idol had once stood there surrounded by sacred fires." [35] Perun was also the Lord of the Harvest.

Prior to the patriarchal Sky Gods of the Roman, Greek and Judeo-Christian mythology, there was the Great Mother, the Goddess of all that was, that is and that is still to come. The tree is closely associated with the Great Mother as well. Eric Neuman, in his work *The Great Mother: An Analysis of the Archetype*, wrote:

> The Great Mother who brings forth all from herself is eminently the mother of all vegetation. The fertility rituals and myths of the whole world are based upon this archetypal context. The center of this vegetative symbolism is the tree....The protective character is evident in the treetop that shelters nests and birds. In addition, the tree trunk is a container, "in" which dwells its spirit, as the soul dwells in the body. The female nature of the tree is demonstrated in the fact that treetops and trunk can give birth, as in the case of Adonis and many others.[36]

However, in pagan belief the Goddess is part of the dual nature of The One. As in the rest of nature, both female and male make up the whole of the universe. In this way, the tree is also reflective of the male/female aspects of the Ancient Divine. While the tree is female, sheltering the nests and birds in Her branches and giving birth through Her fruit, it is also male. As Neumann describes the tree, it *"is also the earth phallus, the male principle jutting out of the earth."* [37]

Much of the reason for the Judeo-Christian denouncement of the sacred tree is the age-old pagan belief in the spiritual duality of the tree, the duality seen in all of nature. Patriarchal leadership must substitute pagan values with their own patriarchal values if they are to continue and flourish. The female aspect of the tree, of its existence in general, was denigrated, maligned, and made base so

---

35. Phillips, Charles & Michael Kerrigan. *Forests of the Vampire: Slavic Myth*. New York: Barnes & Noble Books 1999, 37.

36. Neumann, Eric. *The Great Mother: An Analysis of the Archetype*. Princeton: Princeton University Press, 1963, 48-49.

37. Ibid. 49.

that the male aspects could become dominant. Neumann summarized this struggle in *The Great Mother*:

> Whereas under matriarchy even the male-phallic tree retains its character of dependence on the earth, the patriarchal world...knows of a tree whose roots are "above," in the patriarchal heaven. The "anti-natural" symbolism of this spiritual tree is, of course, distinctly patriarchal in meaning.[38]

Patriarchal teachings, such as those found in Christianity, show the spiritual tree represented by its connections with heaven, not with the Earth, which has nurtured it. Mircea Eliade wrote:

> ...we find the symbols of the Cosmic Tree and of the center of the world incorporated into the symbolism of the Cross. The Cross is described as a "tree rising from earth to Heaven," as "the Tree of Life planted on Calvary," the tree that "springing from the depths of the Earth, rose to Heaven and sanctifies the uttermost bounds of the universe."[39]

Nevertheless, these intentional twists of mythology do not erase the long-held pagan beliefs concerning the Oak. The ancient Greeks referred to the oak as "The Mother Tree" and thought that the first men were created from its branches (in addition, the Ash is also given this distinction). In some parts of the world, the souls of the unborn are thought to reside in trees until birth and the souls of women who die in childbirth also reside in trees.

The "Mother Tree," the "Great World Tree," is a universal myth. As Neumann wrote:

> Mysterious in its truthfulness, the myth makes the vegetative world engender the animal world and also the world of men, which thus appears merely as a part of the World Tree of all living things.[40]

We must not assume that "myth," in the sense used, is merely a child's tale or that of a simple mind. Enduring mythology is comprised of a universal memory, perhaps using images that allow for an easier subconscious understanding, but nonetheless is a collective accounting of natural and supernatural relationships. Some phenomena that used to be considered "superstitions" are today being verified as fact, such as the healing powers of certain herbal medicines, the inter-relatedness of the organisms on the Earth with the Earth itself, and the Earth in relationship with the universe.

---

38. Ibid. 50.

39. Eliade, Mircea. *Rites and Symbols of Initiation: The Mysteries of Birth and Rebirth.* New York: Harper & Row, Publishers, 1958, 119.

40. Neumann, op. cit., 52.

The Oak, among the most sacred of trees, has long been linked to other mystical entities. Fairies were thought to live in the hollows of oak trees. These hollows were referred to as "fairy doors" and it was believed that in touching fairy doors, healing properties could be tapped into. The Celts believed that the tree could be the home of a deity, or could be a deity itself. The individual trees were believed to have their own spirits, but they also could house the spirits of humans, fairies or demons. John Aubrey wrote, "When an oake is falling, before it falles it gives a kind of shriekes or groanes that may be heard a mile off, as if it were the genius of the oake lamenting."[41] The souls of humans that resided in trees between incarnations were thought to go on into their new existences easier.

Wayland D. Hand, in his book *Magical Medicine*,[42] related that farmers used to milk their cows by passing their hands through clefts in trees when the cow's milk production had fallen off. It was thought that by doing so, the farmer would be able to tap into the supernatural powers left by the "fairy folk" that had used the cleft as their doorway between the worlds. The Oak, among many of the other hardwoods, was a favorite vehicle in which to transfer diseases. Skinner noted "even in our country we find survivals of that belief in the curability of diseases by pushing the patient no longer through the 'fairy doors,' but through the forks of an oak, or a gap made artificially, with axes, and thereafter to be repaired with loam."[43]

Folk medicine in America called for the boring of a hole in an oak and plugging the hole with a child's hair to cure asthma, or blowing into the hole and plugging it to cure chills.[44] (The Druids would not have permitted transferring diseases to the oak through such harmful methods.)

The Druids had strict laws prohibiting the harmful treatment of any tree in a sacred grove. Frazer wrote:

> for such as dared to peel the bark of a standing tree....the culprit's navel was to be cut out and nailed to the part of the tree which he had peeled, and he was to be driven round and round the tree till all his guts were wound about its trunk. The intention of the punishment clearly was to replace the dead bark by a living substi-

41. Aubrey, John. "Remaines of Genilisme and Judaisme" in *Folklore Society*, No. IV 1881, 247.

42. Hand, Wayland D. *Magical Medicine: The Folkloric Component of Medicine in the Folk Belief, Custom, and Ritual of the Peoples of Europe and America.* Berkeley: University of California Press, 1980, 134.

43. Skinner, op. cit., 196-197.

44. Hand, op. cit., 84, 99.

tute taken from the culprit; it was a life for a life, the life of a man for the life of a tree.[45]

The Sacred Tree was viewed throughout the world as an embodiment of the gods themselves and "anyone injuring it was thought to have inflicted the injury on the god himself, which act merited the severest retribution." [46]

In every locality where forests covered vast areas of land, the oak was considered sacred, and in each case, the oak was held to be dedicated to the god of thunder. The Romans considered it sacred to Jupiter, the Greeks to Zeus, the Germans to Donar, the Norsemen to Thor, the Slavs to Perun, the Lithuanians to Perkuns, and the Celts to Lugh.

Frazer wrote, "The Druids esteemed nothing more sacred than the mistletoe and the oak on which it grew; they chose groves of oaks for the scene of their solemn service, and they performed none of their rites without oak leaves."[47] The belief in the sacredness of the oak continued into relatively modern ages. Frazer noted that in Shropshire "it was believed within living memory that the oak-tree blooms on Midsummer Eve and the blossom withers before daylight."[48] Frazer thought that this mysterious "bloom" was in actuality the mistletoe.

The belief of the oak as a totem in Britain and Gaul is thought to have arrived between 1600 and 1400 BCE — some 500 years prior to the first Celtic incursions into the area. It is perhaps this belief in the oak as a totem that continued certain forms of folklore into the 21st century that would otherwise seem somewhat out of place. According to Thompson "in Westphalia, the peasantry are accustomed to announce formally to the nearest oak any death that may have occurred in the family, with the words, 'The master is dead. The master is dead.'"[49]

The designation of sacred groves likely was an attempt to keep intact the ancient psychic unity that forests have provided. In Gaul and the western portions of Europe, forests covered immense areas of land. Caesar wrote of Germans who traveled two months through one such forest, called the Hercynian,

45. Frazer, op. cit., 110.

46. Ibid., 217.

47. Ibid., 160.

48. Frazer, James G. *The Golden Bough: The Roots of Religion and Folklore, Vol. 1.* New York: Avenel Books 1981, 368 (A Reprint of the 1890 edition published by The Macmillan Company Ltd., London).

49. Thompson, C.J.S. *The Hand of Destiny: Everyday Folklore and Superstitions.* London: Senate 1995, 217 (A reprint of the 1932 edition published by Rider & Company, London).

without reaching the end. In America, a redwood forest stretched from the west coast to the Mississippi River. Today, attempts to preserve the last few hundreds or thousands of acres of old growth trees from the chain saw meet with little success. America has ironically replaced many oak groves with housing developments or shopping centers which have incorporated the "soul" of the oak into their names: *Lost Oaks, the Oaks, Oak Tree Manor, Oak Haven, Oakwood Village,* etc.

Pennick writes:

> The natural forest symbolizes the untamed, wild part of the human soul: it is an archetype of wildness. Wildness, however, is not a state of being out of control; rather it signifies innate naturalness existing in balance with natural principles. Eternal, elemental powers reside in the forest, and those who seek may come into contact with them. [50]

But the oak is still revered for its strength and majesty. The Charter Oak of Connecticut is one example. According to legend, the huge oak was 400 years old when Columbus first set sail. The Indians had regarded it as sacred for generations when the first Dutch explorers encountered it in 1614. Sometime after 1660, the English Monarchy demanded that the Connecticut Charter, which had granted the colony some of the most liberal rights of all of the colonies, be returned. In an effort to retain the charter, some of the colonist hid the charter in the oak trunk's crevices and there it remained safe. The oak continued to grow until August 21, 1856, when it finally toppled in a storm. "Then did the city of Hartford, indeed all of Connecticut," wrote David Philips, "begin a period of civic mourning. On the day the Charter Oak fell, an honor guard was placed around the remains, Colt's Band of Hartford played a funeral dirge, an American flag was attached to the shattered trunk and, at sunset, all of the bells of Hartford sounded in mourning knell."[51] Today direct descendents of the oak grow in a forest nurtured from acorns gathered from the tree.

Pennick wrote in *Celtic Sacred Landscapes:*

> The wild wood is the place in which we can restore our conscious link with our inner instincts by contacting the "wild man" within all of us. When we are supported by the elemental powers of the wood, a rediscovery of forgotten things can take place.... But this can only happen when the untouched wild wood still exists. Once it is destroyed, then the wild part of the human soul is no longer accessible. Reintegration is no longer possible, and the Wasteland comes."[52]

---

50. Pennick, op. cit., 24.

51. Philips, David E. *Legendary Connecticut: Traditional Tales from the Nutmeg State.* Willimantic: Curbstone Press 1992, 141.

52. Pennick, op. cit.

Even in the modern urban environment, humans crave the presence, the sight, the company of plants and trees. In some sense, do we *need* the Wild Wood to survive, so that we may also survive in spirit? The day we lose our link to the Sacred Groves is the day that our link to our archetypal past is also severed. Mankind has a responsibility to the Earth and to all the Earth's inhabitants, to protect them from the Wasteland. The Green Man is a symbol of the importance of the Oak, as well as the other spirits of nature, and the need to protect them.

CHAPTER 4. TREE SPIRITS, TREE DWELLERS AND THE COSMIC TREE

Trees are wondrous creatures. Certain trees have been known throughout time as the Tree of Life and the Tree of Knowledge. Trees have created a sense of awe in the minds of humankind since abstract thought was possible. To many, trees were the source of life and fertility. Trees not only were rooted in the Mother Earth but also reached into the heavens. Trees became symbols of stability and immortality. Because of this sense of awe, the tree has been worshipped and condemned, nurtured and felled. This awe and fear have also created a host of other legendary creatures that are closely associated with the tree and the forests. Most cultures have myths of tree gods and tales of strange fairy-like creatures that live deep in dark forests or in the very trees themselves. Such stories reflect an ancient animistic belief system that gives every object in nature its own spirit and power. As will be discussed later, these vegetation spirits and gods are the foundations for classic and contemporary religious thought.

Tree and Forest Spirits

The very *feel* of the forest imparts a sense of wonder and hidden power, of spirits and unseen creatures, and of a time stretching back into the dim past where anything and everything was possible. "The edge of the forest," writes Carol and Dinah Mack, "is always the boundary between the wild and domesticated, the animal and the human community. It holds its genius loci, which may appear as demonic guardian species of wilderness and wild creatures and attack trespassing hunters, mischievous fairies...and the many huge man-eating species...."[53] This statement may be applied to any forest in the world, for they all seem to be populated with these local spirits and fairies who are not often kind to human intrusion. The Cherokee, according to anthropologist James Mooney,

28

believed that "trees and plants also were alive and could talk in the old days, and had their place in council."[54] The intelligence of trees and plants, as well as other inanimate objects, were taken for granted by the Cherokee and the other indigenous people around the world.

The Lakota believed in a race of "ugly" small men and women that they referred to as "tree dwellers." Similar to tales of other fairy folk around the world, the tree dwellers, called *Can Otidan*, reportedly stayed in the woods and forests and "would lure hunters away and lose them or they would frighten them so that they would lose their senses."[55] The *Can Otidan* apparently were more than simple fairy spirits as they were classed in a group referred to as "bad gods."

Little people[56] referred to as "travel-two" were among the forest spirits in the Nehalem Tillamook (Oregon) world. Called "travel-two" because they always traveled in pairs, these fairy-like creatures were hunters and would often give a human they encountered on their travels the skills to become a good hunter — if they happened to speak to him.[57]

The Coos Indians along Oregon's southern coast believed that the forests were filled with ghosts and spirits. There were five types of spirits identified as residing in the forest:

Ghosts or spirits that "reentered a corpse and escaped into the forest to do evil things to humans, especially poor people"

A "mirror image" of oneself, a doppelganger; if you should see one of these, your life would be shortened

Giant people who live on the fish in the streams; they are neither good nor bad "and do not scare people"

A visible spirit or ghost, and

---

53. Mack, Carol K. and Dinah Mack. *A Field Guide to Demons, Fairies, Fallen Angels, and Other Subversive Spirits*. New York: Owl Books 1998, 91.

54. Mooney, James. *Myths of the Cherokee*. New York: Dover Publications Inc. 1995 (A reprint of the *Nineteenth Annual Report of the Bureau of American Ethnology 1897-98* published in 1900 by the Smithsonian Institution), 231.

55. Walker, James R. *Lakota Belief and Ritual*. Lincoln: University of Nebraska Press 1991, 107.

56. Other "little folk" in Tillamook lore are the di_kátu who lived in lakes. He is described as "like a little brownie, about one and a half feet high."

57. Jacobs, Elizabeth D. *The Nehalem Tillamook: An Ethnography*. Corvallis: Oregon State University Press 2003, 182.

The "noisy ones," the little people usually covered in long hair, who leave tracks along creek banks. These creatures are usually seen only at night and are known to throw rocks at people's homes.[58]

Other Oregon tribes such as the Alsea and Yaquina believed in longhaired female wood sprites called *osun*, who could give certain special powers to humans that would enable them to become shamans.[59]

The Russians had their own form of *Can Otidan*. Called the *Leshy*,[60] this mysterious creature inhabited the forests (mostly forests of birch trees) and would disappear and reappear with the falling leaves and the sprouting vegetation. Philpot described him as having "human form, with horns, ears, and feet of a goat, his fingers are long claws, and he is covered with rough hair, often of a green colour."[61] Some have described him as having green, bark-like skin and green hair. They could also change their stature at will, remaining as small as grass stalks or as tall as the tallest tree. Each spring the *Leshy* would awaken from hibernation and seek out travelers to cause them to become lost in the new and rich growth of vegetation. "He springs from tree to tree, and rocks himself in the branches, screeching and laughing, neighing, lowing, and barking."[62] The trees and animals of the forest, however, are under his protection. Philpot wrote, "The migrations of squirrels, field-mice, and such small deer are carried out under his guidance."[63] The animals protected the Leshy as well, as he was prone to drinking and vulnerable to attacks from other woodland spirits. "Uprooted trees, broken branches and other storm damage were a clear indication that *leshie* had been fighting among themselves," wrote Michael Kerrigan.[64] The only way to protect yourself from the Leshy while traveling through the forest was to wear your clothing inside out, shoes on the wrong feet, continuously making the sign of the cross or making peace offerings of tobacco and food.

58. Beckham, Stephen Dow. "Coos, Lower Umpqua, and Siuslaw: Traditional Religious Practices" in *Native American Religious Practices and Uses, Siuslaw National Forest*. Eugene: Heritage Research Associates Report No. 7(3), September 20, 1982, 41.

59. Ibid., 27.

60. Also spelled *Leshii*, or *Ljeschi.*.

61. Philpot, Mrs. J. H. *The Sacred Tree in Religion and Myth*. Mineola: Dover Publications Inc. 2004, 69 (A reprint of the 1897 edition published by Macmillan and Co. Ltd, New York & London).

62. Ibid.

63. Ibid.

64. Charles Phillips & Michael. *Forests of the Vampire: Slavic Myth*. New York: Barnes & Noble Books 1999, 72 .

The person who was most in danger from the wrath of the Leshy was the woodcutter. Even though this tree spirit was greatly feared, he could also be summoned — if one dared. According to Porteous, "very young Birches are cut down and placed in a circle with the points towards the center. They then enter the circle and invoke the spirit, which at once appears. Then they step on the stump of one of the cut trees with their face turned towards the east, and bend their heads so that they look between their legs. While in this position they say: 'Uncle Lieschi, ascend thou, not as a grey wolf, not as an ardent fire, but as resembling myself'. Then the leaves tremble, and the Lieschi arises under a human form, and agrees to give the service for which he has been invoked, provided they promise him their soul."[65] As in many cultures that were eventually dominated by the Christian Church, the spirits and deities of the Slavs were slowly changed. As Porteous noted above, the Lieschie bargained for the soul of the person in exchange for supernatural aid and thus are cast as acolytes of Satan.

Another Russian vegetation entity is the "polevoi." Michael Kerrigan wrote that the polevoi's body "matched the colour of the local soil, and grass grew in tussocks from his head instead of hair."[66] The polevoi could be friendly to humans but could signify disaster, as well, should one spot him in the forest.

Tree elves have been said to inhabit the elm, oak, willow, yew, fir, holly, pine, ash, cherry, laurel, nut, apple, birch and cypress trees. Because each of the tree elves is created from the specific tree, it takes on the characteristics of that tree. While all of these species of trees have a resident elf, "the elder," writes Nancy Arrowsmith, "has without doubt the highest elf population."[67] The lives of the "elder elves" are tied directly to their trees and so they are very protective of them. According to German folklore one should always ask permission (and be sure to leave an offering!) before cutting or otherwise harming an elder tree. The consequences of not doing so are usually serious and can result in blindness or ill health to the woodsman's children or cattle.

---

65. Porteous, Alexander. *The Lore of the Forest: Myths and Legends.* London: Senate 1996, 105 (A reprint of *Forest Folklore* published in 1928 by George Allen & Unwin Ltd., London).

66. Kerrigan, Michael. "The Harvester of Souls" in *Forests of the Vampire: Slavic Myth.* New York: Barnes & Noble 2003, 74.

67. Arrowsmith, Nancy and George Moorse. *A Field Guide to the Little People.* London: Macmillan Company 1977, 180.

The appearance of tree elves varies according to the tree from which they originated. The oak elf will appear as a gnarled old man and the birch elf appears as a thin white female.

In England, an Apple Tree Man was said to reside in the oldest apple tree in each orchard. According to Franklin, "He can grant a good harvest for the whole orchard, and other benefits besides. The last of the crop should be left on the ground for him...".[68]

To the Saxons, elves were to be feared. They were "hostile creatures [that] brought disease...as well as nightmare."[69]

The belief that trees are somehow supernatural beings is apparently universal. Lore from the Ozark Mountains says that agents of the Devil propagated the ironwood tree and that the sassafras tree does not grow from seeds, but rather "somehow sprout from grub worms."[70] The belief in "Devil Trees" was common in Africa and the Malay Archipelago. However, these trees are receptacles of evil and not sources of evil. Like the holy wells in England and elsewhere, where people tie strips of cloth and ribbon (known as "clooties") to nearby trees, Devil Trees are also sought out for this purpose. In both cases the purpose is the same, to tie a piece of cloth that belongs to an ill person to the tree so that the disease is transferred from the human to the tree.

In Celtic lands, the gods were worshipped in sacred groves, which removed the need to have temple structures — although a few did exist. The Romans and then the Christians destroyed these groves in their attempts to destroy the fabric of Celtic pagan traditions. However, there is significant evidence that these groves, or rather their descendants, did survive into later ages in the form of "gospel oaks" in Britain and innumerable place names across Europe. Hutton writes that these groves, after Christianization, "kept their place in the sentiments of the tribes even while apparently losing all direct religious connotations."[71]

Because tree worship and sacred groves were so ingrained in the human mind, the Church fought long and hard to eliminate all aspects of them, passing

---

68. Franklin, Anna. *The Illustrated Encyclopaedia of Fairies.* London: Paper Tiger/Chrysalis Books 2004, 15.

69. Owen, Gale R. *Rites and Religions of the Anglo-Saxons.* Dorset Press 1985, 65.

70. Randolph, Vance. *Ozark Magic and Folklore.* New York: Dover Publications 1964, 261 (A reprint of *Ozark Superstitions* published by Columbia University Press 1947).

71. Hutton, Ronald. *The pagan Religions of the Ancient British Isles: Their Nature and Legacy.* Oxford: Blackwell Publishers Ltd.1991, 293.

A "Devil Tree"

Caption: This European Olive Tree Appears to Struggle to Uproot Itself

law after law and levying heavy fines on those who continued to honor the tree. "S. Martin of Tours," wrote J.A. MacCulloch, "was allowed to destroy a temple, but the people would not permit him to attack a much venerated pine-tree which stood beside it — an excellent example of the way in which the more official paganism fell before Christianity, while the older religion of the soil from which it sprang, could not be entirely eradicated."[72]

The struggle to defeat and subjugate pagans who worshipped trees, or viewed them as sacred, or who believed that the gods live in certain trees, was not the only battle waged by the early Christians. H.R. Ellis Davidson reminds us, "a number of Christian missionaries...counted the felling of a tree sacred to a heathen god among their achievements in the cause of Christ."[73] The early Jews also waged this battle. Deuteronomy 12:2-3 depicts God instructing the Hebrew leaders to "utterly destroy all the places, wherein the nations which ye shall possess served their gods, upon the high mountains, and upon the hills, and under every green tree. "And ye shall overthrow their altars, and break their pillars, and burn their groves with fire..." Because of this, the Hebrews were forbidden to plant any tree near a sacred altar.

In many cultures (among them the Nordic peoples, Greeks, Romans, Babylonians, Persians, Indian and Native Americans as well as some African tribes) it was said that humans were created from trees. Porteous noted, "among the South American tribes of Guiana a great creator is acknowledged. They say that all created things came from a branch of a Silk-cotton tree which had been cut down by the Creator, but that the white man had sprung from the chips of a particularly useless tree."[74]

In Norse mythology three Creator Gods walked on a seashore, where, according to Davidson, "they found two trees, driftwood washed ashore, breathed vitality and spirit into them, and gave them movement, so that the first man and woman came to life."[75]

The belief that humans came from trees is also widespread in Africa. John S. Mbiti wrote, "The Herero tell that God caused the first human beings, a man and his wife, to come from the mythical 'tree of life' which is said to be situated

---

72. MacCulloch, J.A. *The Religion of the Ancient Celts.* Mineola: Dover Publications, Inc. 2003, 204 (A reprint of the 1911 publication from T. & T. Clark, Edinburgh). Another version of this story is told by W.Y. Evans-Wentz in his book *The Fairy-Faith in Celtic Countries*, page 435: "The people agreed to let it be cut down on the condition that the saint should receive its great trunk on his head as it fell: and the tree was not cut down".

73. Davidson, H.R. Ellis. *Gods and Myths of the Viking Age.* New York: Bell Publishing Company 1981, 87.

74. Porteous, op. cit., 160.

75. Davidson, H.R. Ellis. *Myths and Symbols in pagan Europe: Early Scandinavian and Celtic Religions.* Syracuse: Syracuse University Press 1988, 173.

in the underworld."[76] Similar stories were common throughout Africa from Angola to Zambezi, the Congo and Sudan.

The stories that predominate, however, are those of the nature spirits, gods and goddesses that inhabit the tree. Frequent discussions were held in the days of early Buddhism as to whether trees had souls. It was decided then that trees do not have souls but that they may be inhabited by wood spirits that, at times, may speak through the trees. Other people, however, such as the Tahitians and Greeks, did believe that each tree had a soul and an intellect of its own.

For some reason most tree-spirits are ambivalent at best and demonic at worst. Stories abound of tree-spirits that take savage revenge on those that dare to cut trees down. Indian legend says the Banyan tree is inhabited by spirits that will "wring the necks of all persons who approached their tree during the night."[77] The guardian spirit of the Brazilian rainforest is Corupira, who is not evil but will disorient those who are intent on harming the trees and the forest animals — much like Pan.

However, other tree and forest spirits exhibit traits of kindness towards humans. Some forest spirits were said to protect hunters and fishers, and in fact leading game to them. It was to these spirit-gods that the forests were dedicated and sacrifices made. In other cultures, tree spirits provided the rains and sun that made crops grow.

The Mesquakie, known as the Fox Indians of Iowa, believed that the spirits of their ancestors lived within the trees. It was said, "the murmur of the trees when the wind passes through is but the voices of our grandparents."[78] The Fox felt that all wood was sacred and that objects made from wood "were thought to contain the very essence of a tree's spiritual substance."[79]

Belief in nature spirits, frequently described as miniature people but not necessarily the same as fairies, is common throughout most third world societies, providing a sense of linkage and connection with nature that the more "developed" and "western" societies have lost. The Gururumba, a New Guinea people, believe in nature spirits, some of whom live in the forests and others in the reeds along the riverbanks. Other than the location of territory, there is little difference between the two. The Gururumba say that these spirits are seldom seen because, even though they reside in our world, in our reality, they appear as

76. Mbiti, John S. *African Religions and Philosophy*. Garden City: Anchor Books 1970, 121.
77. Porteous, op. cit 123.
78. Anon. *The Spirit World*. Alexandria: Time-Life Books 1992, 90.
79. Ibid.

mist or smoke. They are also always male. While generally ambivalent to the humans who live in the area, the spirits will attack anyone who stumbles into their territory. Ethnologist Philip L. Newman, who researched the Gururumba, writes that "each spirit has its own dwelling place — a certain clump of reeds, a particular configuration of boulders along the river, or the exposed roots of some tree. Anyone wandering into one of these sanctuaries is attacked by the spirit which may cause him illness or even death."[80]

The Gururumba have created a cooperative arrangement with many of the nature spirits by providing a small dome-shaped house (about two feet in diameter) in an enclosure in the family garden. The Gururumba provide housing, food and information to the nature spirit in exchange for the spirit's protection of the garden and care for the Gururumba's pig herds.

Tree spirits are also commonly believed in throughout Africa. The Ashanti reportedly believe that certain nature spirits are present that animate trees, stones and other "inanimate" objects as well as animals, rivers and charms. The powers of these spirits are great and respected. John Mbiti reports in his book *African Religions and Philosophy* an incident that took place in Ghana in the 1960s. During the construction of a new harbor at Tema, equipment was repeatedly stolen and a company investigator, and Englishman, was sent to look into it. After his investigation was over, one of the European supervisors mentioned to him that a lone tree was causing him a great deal of trouble. All the other trees in the area had been cleared but this one, which was relatively small; it remained in place as all the heavy equipment stalled when approaching the tree. One of the African foremen said that the tree was magic and could not be removed unless the tree spirit could be persuaded to move on to another tree. A shaman was called in, who sacrificed three sheep and poured three bottled of gin onto the roots of the tree as an offering. Evidently, the ritual worked; soon, the machinery could be started. In fact, a few of the workers simply walked up to the tree and were able to pull it up out of the earth by hand.[81]

The gods of vegetation, discussed in another chapter, were all originally tree spirits who are credited with giving the gift of agriculture to humankind as well as the arts and other learning that create civilization. They were also closely connected with death and the underworld.

---

80. Newman, Philip L. *Knowing the Gururumba*. New York: Holt, Rinehart and Winston Case Studies in Cultural Anthropology 1965, 63.
81. Mbiti op. cit 255.

The sycamore fig tree located in many desert areas of Egypt is said to be inhabited by goddesses. "These goddesses or spirits," Porteous noted, "sometimes manifest themselves, and...the head, or even the whole body, would emerge from the trunk of the tree, after a time re-entering it, being reabsorbed, or, as the Egyptian expression has it, the trunk *ate* it again."[82] The goddesses said to reside in the sycamore are Hathor (given the epithet "Lady of the Sycamore"), Nut, Selkit, and Isis. While certain male gods were also associated with trees (such as Osiris with the willow, Horus with the acacia and Wepwawet with the tamarisk), only these few goddesses were so closely associated with sacred trees. Like the carvings of females rising from vegetation found in contemporary architecture, these goddesses were most often shown as a "composite of the upper body of the goddess rising from the trunk at the center of a tree."[83] In the Egyptian world, the maternal deities were the tree goddesses, offering food to the deceased or, in the case of a mural in the tomb of Tuthmosis III, nursed by Isis in the form of a sycamore tree.

Dryads, or tree goddesses in India, are often depicted giving the trunk of a tree a little kick. The reason for this, according to Heinrich Zimmer, is found in a formula derived "from a ritual of fecundation. According to an ageless belief, nature requires to be stimulated by man; the procreative forces have to be aroused, by magic means, from semi-dormancy."[84] This ritual formula continues to be used in contemporary Indian culture. Zimmer adds, "There is in India a certain tree (*aśoka*) which is supposed not to put forth blossoms unless touched and kicked by a girl or young woman. Girls and young women," Zimmer wrote, "are regarded as human embodiments of the maternal energy of nature. They are diminutive doubles of the Great Mother of all life, vessels of fertility, life in full sap, potential sources of new offspring. By touching and kicking the tree they transfer into it their potency, and enable it to bring forth blossom and fruit."[85]

The Persians as well, according to J.H. Philpot, "venerated trees as the dwelling-place of the deity, as the haunts of good and evil spirits, and as the habitations in which the souls of heroes and the virtuous dead continued their existence."[86]

---

82. Porteous, op. cit 164.

83. Wilkinson, Richard H. *The Complete Gods and Goddesses of Ancient Egypt.* London: Thames & Hudson Ltd. 2003, 169.

84. Zimmer, Heinrich. *Myths and Symbols in Indian Art and Civilization.* Edited by Joseph Campbell. Princeton: Princeton University Press 1946, 69.

85. Ibid.

In ancient Crete, the Great Mother goddess was also known as the Lady of Trees and Doves — representing birth and fertility. In her early form the Great Mother of Crete, the Earth Mother, was rather vague — she was an ancient Neolithic goddess. In time, she became Demeter, goddess of animals, crops and forests.[87]

The gods and goddesses also lived within the trees of old Hawaii. The goddess of the ohia-lehua forest is one of these. The flower of the ohia tree is considered sacred and to pick it is forbidden unless proper invocations are said. One of the sacred ohia trees located in a cave of the god Ku-ka-ohia-laka is regarded as the body of this forefather-god.[88] The Hawaiian wind god, Makani-keoe, is another tree deity. Also known as a "love god," he is able to transform himself into a tree at will. An amulet made from such a tree is a powerful love charm but causes visions and voices to be heard by the one who obtains it.

Sacred groves in Germany were the homes of the gods as well. At Romove, the chief sacred grove, a holy oak figured in religious ceremonies and images of the gods were placed in its trunk. The Prussians who remained pagan long after the rest of Germany had converted to Christianity used these groves into the 16th century. Davidson notes "writers who visited them described sacred woods in which they made sacrifices and sacred springs which Christians were not allowed to approach."[89] The god worshipped in the Prussian groves was Perkuno — the thunder god. Sacred groves dedicated to Perkuno were still utilized in Lithuania and Estonia into the 18th century. As Frazer wote, Perkuno "presents a close resemblance to Zeus and Jupiter, since he was the god of the oak, the thunder, and the rain."[90] Every Dying God, such as Osiris, Adonis, Attis, Dionysus and Jesus, died on a tree. Medieval Christian carvings of the Tree of the Living and the Dead (fruit of good and evil on opposite sides) depict Jesus as the trunk of the tree.[91]

---

86. Philpot, Mrs. J.H. *The Sacred Tree in Religion and Myth*. Mineola: Dover Publications, Inc. 2004, 13 (A reprint of the 1897 edition published by Macmillan and Co. Ltd, London and New York).

87. Mackenzie, Donald A. *Crete & Pre-Hellenic Myths and Legends*. London: Senate 1995, 175 (A reprint of the 1917 publication by the Gresham Publishing Company, London).

88. Beckwith, Martha. *Hawaiian Mythology*. Honolulu: University of Hawaii Press1970, 16-17 (A reprint of the 1940 edition published by Yale University Press).

89. Davidson, op. cit.

90. Frazer, Sir James. *The Golden Bough: A study in magic and religion*. Hertfordshire: Wordsworth Editions Ltd. 1993, 161.

Gautama Buddha is said to have been a tree spirit "no less than forty-three times" in past incarnations.[92]

Cosmic Trees

The "cosmic tree" is a universal symbol. Legends of its existence appear in Native American, Scandinavian, Mesoamerican, and Siberian, Asian, African, Middle Eastern and Indian lore. It is perhaps one of the oldest universal tales of humankind.

Estonian folklorist Aado Lintrop describes the universal concept of the World Tree:

> The World Tree is usually depicted as a huge, often opulent thick tree with a certain number of branches. The size and colour of the leaves are specifically mentioned. The tree's bark is exceptional and its fruits, if mentioned at all, are very large. The tree is often located in a specific mythical spot, the centre of a continent, for example, and is commonly associated to celestial bodies, which either rest on its branches or revolve around its top. The great World Tree is often equated with the Tree of Life — in some regions it yielded fruit giving everlasting life, in others the tree grows near a well or source containing the Water of Life. The fate of humankind may be inscribed on the leaves of the world tree. The world tree is often the abode of a winged mythical creature. As the snake that lives near the world tree or under its roots is the symbol of the underworld, so the winged being that lives on top of the tree is the symbol of the heavenly kingdom.[93]

Siberian Yakut shamans speak of the Tree Yjyk-Mas — a type of cosmic tree — that has no branches but grows from its mountain peak to the Ninth Heaven — at the top of this sacred tree resides the Lord of the World. In its knots are the souls of deceased shamans.[94] This cosmic tree is also the source of creation of Yakut shamans. A giant bird "hatches" shamans in the Tree Yjyk-Mas, the tree becoming at once the life-giver and the soul-receiver of the shaman.

A somewhat similar tale of the Great Tree comes from the Flathead Indians of eastern Oregon. According to ethnologist James A. Teit, the Flathead believed "that there are three worlds, one above the other, the middle one being the earth on which we live. A great and good chief, who is the source of life, lives in the

91. Cooper, J.C. *An Illustrated Encyclopaedia of Traditional Symbols.* London: Thames & Hudson Ltd. 1978, 178.

92. Philpot, op. cit 14.

93. Lintrop, Aado. "The Great Oak and Brother-Sister" in *Folklore*, Vol. 16 Published by the Folk Belief and Media Group of ELM, Tartu, Estonia 2001, 38.

94. Eliade, Mircea. *Shamanism: Archaic Techniques of Ecstasy.* Princeton; Princeton University Press 1964, 37.

upper world and rules it, while the chief in the underworld is of an evil disposition.

"Another...belief was that there is a great tree, the roots of which sink far into the earth, and the top of which reaches the sky. The great good chief *Amo'tken* sits on top of the tree, while the bad chief *Amte'p* sits at the root within the earth. The Flathead prayed to *Amo'tken*, but not to *Amte'p*. The former makes rain and snow, makes everything go right on earth and in the sky, makes food plentiful, and tries to benefit people..."[95] *Amo'tken*, the "great chief" of the Flathead, so closely associated with the Cosmic Tree, was also believed to have brought the knowledge of arts and crafts to the people and salmon to the river. He is, like many other "green gods," a teacher.[96]

In Hindu lore, the sacred tree is called the Tree of Skambha, which is actually an elementary form of the god Brahma. Each branch of the Tree of Skambha, like the Siberian Yakut Tree Yjyk-Mas, represents each of the other Hindu gods and goddesses. There are several other names for the sacred tree in the Vedas including Parig?ta, the World Tree, which is one of the five trees in the Hindu paradise. Another, called the Cloud Tree, fulfills all desire, gives knowledge, wisdom, and "inconceivable bliss," and Soma, from which flows the sacred essence of immortality.

The World Tree, as the Cosmic Tree, is the Center of the World — the World Axis. People recognized a central part of their world — it could be a Cosmic Mountain or Tree — and that part was sacred. In Norse mythology, that central point was the sacred ash tree Yggdrasil. "This tree," wrote Tamra Andrews "was the reason the world existed. It miraculously renewed itself with the dew from the heavens and with magic waters from the wells and springs that flowed beneath the roots."[97] Yggdrasil held up the heavens with its lofty branches, its roots descended into the Underworld, and its trunk supported the nine worlds in between. Davidson theorizes that the ash was chosen for the Norse World Tree because of its "keys" "which hang from the branches like

---

95. Teit, James A. "The Salishan Tribes of the Western Plateaus," edited by Franz Boas. In *45th Annual Report, 1927-28*, Bureau of American Ethnology. Washington: Smithsonian Institution, 383.

96. Clark, Ella E. "Indian Thanksgiving in the Pacific Northwest," in *Oregon Historical Quarterly* Vol. LXI, Number 4, December 1960, 444.

97. Andrews, Tamra. *A Dictionary of Nature Myths: Legends of the Earth, Sea, and Sky*. Oxford: Oxford University Press 1998, 227.

bodies of tiny men, recalling the practice of hanging sacrificial victims from trees."[98]

Russian lore speaks of a cosmological tree in the form of an oak located on Bujan, an island in the sea. It is here that "the sun retires to rest every evening and from which it rises every morning; watched by a dragon, it is inhabited by the Virgin of the Dawn."[99] An ancient piece of lore, with a decidedly Christian perspective, is given by Count D'Alviella: "a legend...relates that the Tree of Adam reaches to hell by its roots and to heaven by its branches; in its top lives the infant Jesus."[100]

The Plains Indians, the Lakota, Cheyenne and Crow, regard the cottonwood tree as the cosmic tree. It figures importantly in the Sun Dance ceremony and is representative of the center of the sacred universe during the Sun Dance. Like all of the other cosmic trees, its branches seek the clouds, "its spiritual roots spreading deep into Mother Earth and to the four directions."[101] The center post of the Delaware Indian's Big House represented the World Tree and it was subject to a rite of thanksgiving that lasted 12 days.

The World Tree in the Ngadju Dyak cosmology, on the island of Borneo, represents the universe in its totality. However, it also represents the dualism of nature and that two conflicting forces (a feminine and a masculine divinity) acted to create the world. In the great conflict, the World Tree is destroyed. Nevertheless, as the World Tree is the "archetype of all creative human activity, the World Tree is destroyed only that it may be reborn."[102] The continued importance of the World Tree to the Dyaks on Borneo is that a representative tree is found in each Dyak village and home and is also placed in the Indonesian "ships of the dead" used to transport the soul to the land of the dead. Eliade notes that the Indonesian shamans also utilize a tree as a ladder to climb to the world of the spirits to seek the souls of ill patients.[103]

---

98. Davidson, op. cit. 1988, 170.

99. D'Alviella, The Count Goblet. *The Migration of Symbols.* New York: University Books 1956, 168 (A reprint of the1894 edition).

100. Ibid.

101. St. Pierre, Mark and Tilda Long Soldier. *Walking in the Sacred Manner.* New York: Touchstone Books 1995, 19.

102. Eliade, op. cit 284-285.

103. Ibid. 285.

Similarly, the people in Central and North Asia believe that the souls of children are perched on the Cosmic Tree and wait until shamans come to take them to their earthly mothers.

The World Tree is often depicted with a serpent. Unlike the serpent in the tale of Adam and Eve, it does not reflect evil or temptation but the "cycles of manifestation."[104] The serpent is also the guardian of the tree, representing the obstacles and difficulty of obtaining wisdom and eternal life. African and Indonesian images depict the World Tree with a bird (usually an eagle) perched on the top and a serpent at its roots. Eliade states that this image is "typical of Central Asia and the ancient Germans" but probably has an "Oriental" origin.[105]

A serpent did not accompany the World Tree in Mesoamerican art, but the Tree was associated with a reptile, a caiman. This alligator-like creature was depicted in Mesoamerican art from the Formative Olmec period on a representative of the trunk of the World Tree — presumably due to the bark-like appearance of its skin. To the Maya, the sacred ceiba tree was, according to Miller and Taube, "frequently recognized as a living axis mundi that penetrated the naval of the earth, reaching from the underworld to the heavens."[106] Called by the Maya *yaxché*, meaning first tree or green tree, one of these was placed in the center of most Mayan cities and villages and it may have been used to mark the four cardinal directions. In Mayan tradition, the ceiba arises from a caiman. The ceiba was said to shade "the divine paradise, offering refuge to those fortunate enough to ascend there."[107]

In ancient Babylon, the temple of Enki had a holy tree called *kiškanū* that served as the focal point for rituals. Some scholars suggest that each temple "had a holy grove or garden with a 'tree of life' under the supervision of the king. He functioned as a 'master-gardener,' who watered the tree of life, and so had power over life."[108]

Why are stories about the World Tree so prevalent around the world? Folklorist H.R. Ellis Davidson surmised that "the cosmology of a people must be based to some extent on the features of the natural world around them, and the

---

104. Cooper, op. cit 177.

105. Eliade, op. cit 273.

106. Miller, Mary and Karl Taube. *An Illustrated Dictionary of the Gods and Symbols of Ancient Mexico and the Maya.* New York: Thames and Hudson 1993, 57.

107. Ibid.

108. Ringgren, Helmer. *Religions of the Ancient Near East.* Philadelphia: The Westminster Press 1973, 78.

World Tree in northern mythology may have come from memories of forest sanctuaries."[109] A world covered in such sanctuaries would certainly be the sort of thing one could expect to linger in humankind's collective memory.

Do we still believe in Tree Spirits, in our contemporary society? While many may object to the claim, there is plenty of evidence that the answer is "yes." The angel that graces the top of our Christmas trees is symbolic of the Spirit of the Tree, and of course the decorated tree itself represents a mixture of the new and old religions.

CHAPTER 5. THE FOLKLORE OF TREES

Forests and trees in particular have a great deal of folklore and mythology associated with them. Folk medicine is one component of this lore that continues to thrive. Some of the medicinal folk practices associated with trees call for treatments, such as transference, that are also common at other sacred sites around the world, such as at holy wells and megalithic complexes. "Spirit-caused" diseases were diagnosed by taking the clothes of the victim to certain trees associated with spirits, such as willows, blackthorns, or roses. The clothing would be left at the tree, along with offerings, and a prayer would be said. The next morning the clothes would be checked and if they were found to have been disturbed, it is understood that the victim was enchanted.

A rather elaborate ritual to "diagnose" disease comes from Ontario, Canada. An immigrant "conjure doctor" living there was reported to perform the following: "First she went into the orchard and cut off nine small rods from the ends of the twigs of nine different apple trees. These she put into a basin filled with water, and if they all sank to the bottom the disease would be fatal, but if a few remained on the surface, it was not so serious and could be cured."[110]

Apple trees have long been associated with magic and the Tree of Life. Apples were at once symbols of fertility and, at least for the denizens of the Other World, everlasting food. Davidson notes that the Síd would carry a branch of an apple tree with them when venturing into the world of humans, and the leaves "made tinkling music which could lull men to sleep or banish pain." It was common in England, through the end of the 19th century, for people (children in

---

109. Davidson, op. cit. 1988, 168.

110.   Wintemberg, W. J. *Folk-Lore of Waterloo County, Ontario.* Ontario: National Museum of Canada, Bulletin No. 116, Anthropological Series No. 28, 1950, 22.

particular) to be "passed through" holes in stones and trees to effect a cure for certain diseases. A news article appearing in an 1876 issue of *Report Transactions of the Devonshire Association* (vol. viii, p. 54) said: "Passing lately through a wood at Spitchwich, near Ashburton, a remark on some peculiarity in an ash sapling led to the explanation from the game keeper that the tree had been instrumental in the cure of a ruptured infant, and he afterwards pointed out four or five others that had served the same good purpose." The disease was "transferred" to the tree by squeezing the person through the opening and "wiping" the illness off.

Other forms of transference included hammering nails into trees to transfer the pain of toothache and tying pieces of cloth worn by an ill person to a tree to transfer the illness. The custom of hammering nails into trees to treat illnesses or pains dates back at least to the Roman era. Czech writer Josef Cizmár noted, "the custom was practiced in Slovakia up to the most recent times."[111]

In England, it was custom to place coins, needles and pins in the bark of certain trees as offerings to the local spirit or fairy. This occurred most often when a holy well was nearby. Reportedly, in 1877 Queen Victoria placed silver coins in the bark of a tree growing beside a holy well dedicated to St. Mourie on Loch Maree. The leaving of offerings on sacred trees in exchange for healing is a practice spoken of in the *Odyssey* as well as by Ovid in *Metamorphoses*.

These rituals are not confined to the Old World. The Salish Indians in the Bitterroot Valley, Montana, have similar traditions associated with the Medicine Tree, a giant Ponderosa pine. According to tribal lore, Coyote tempted an evil bighorn ram that had killed everything in sight to knock over a little tree. When the ram smashed into the tree, one of its horns penetrated the trunk and stuck out the other side — trapping the ram. Coyote then cut the ram's head off and threw it high up on a rocky hillside where, according to custom, it left the profile of a human face. Coyote said that the face "will be a sign of my doings here" and "this tree will be a place for human beings to leave offerings of their prized possessions, and to give thanks, and to pray for their well-being, for good fortune and good health."[112] Today the tree is over 350 years old and Native Americans still leave offerings of tobacco, clothing, photographs and other items hanging from the tree's limbs or affixed to the bark.

---

111. Cizmár, Josef. *Lidové lékarství v Ceskoslovensku. Vol. 1.* Czechoslovakia: Melantrich, A.S. 1946, 158.

112. "Medicine Tree Needs Powerful RX" in *Montana Magazine*, Sept-Oct 1999.

Novelist Craig Lesley writes of a different version of this tale in his fictional account of a modern Nez Perce community, *River Song*. In his version Coyote planned to eat the ram while it was stuck in the tree, however, "while he worked up his appetite traveling around the country, some Indian people freed the sheep. One of its horns remained embedded in the tree, and the sheep promised the people good luck and freedom from evil spirits if they hung bright strips of cloth, wampum beads, or other adornments from the horn."[113] After the tree had grown around the horn, the people continued to hang offerings. Lesley wrote that the Medicine Tree was adorned with brightly colored ribbons, beads, and strips of cloth, and in addition coins had been left in the bark and cracks as offerings.

Mackenzie[114] tells us that in England and Scotland it was believed that each person had a "double soul" that existed within a tree. Traditionally, a tree was planted at the time a child was born, and the child's soul was considered to be intimately linked to that tree. A person might die if his tree were cut down or, likewise, the tree might shrivel up and die when the individual died. Similar stories come from the United States where "birth trees" of oak were planted after a child was born. The belief was that as oak grows to be strong, so would the child; and the child would be protected throughout its life. An associated bit of folklore recorded in Cleveland, Ohio in 1958 indicated that the clothes of a "weakly child" should be hung on "strong" trees, such as the oak, to give some of the tree's strength to the child.

Some people enjoy following these customs even today. An anthropologist friend of mine buried the placenta and umbilical cord from the birth of his child and planted a tree over it to ensure that his child would grow strong and live long.

A Japanese tale speaks of a young man who admired a willow tree that grew in the center of his village. One day the man met a beautiful girl under the willow tree and fell in love with her. In time, they married and were very happy. However, one day the Emperor ordered the willow tree to be cut down to make room for a new temple. The young man attempted to save the tree but was unsuccessful. As the tree was felled, according to the story, "his wife told him

---

113. Lesley, Craig. *River Song*. New York: Picador USA 1989, 127.
114. Mackenzie, Donald A. *Ancient Man in Britain*. London: Senate 1996, 190 (A reprint of the 1922 edition by Blackie & Son Limited, London).

that it housed her spirit. He held her tightly, but neither physical nor spiritual love could keep her with him, and she died as the tree crashed to the ground."[115]

There are many stories of Old Europe that tell of particular trees linked to particular royal families. In each case when the tree died, the head of the royal family or the royal house itself suddenly died as well.

In German lore, babies came from hollow trees — the hollowed areas possibly representing a pathway to the underworld that allowed the spirit from this mysterious realm to grow as a baby in the tree situated in the upper world. In many cultures, human beings were said to have originated as trees, or trees as human beings. Nineteenth-century folklorist J.H. Philpot noted that "an Italian traveler of the fourteenth century was assured by the natives of Malabar that they knew of trees, which instead of fruit bore pigmy men and women. So long as the wind blew they remained fresh and healthy, but when it dropped they became withered and dry."[116] In India, it is still customary today for childless men and women to worship in sacred groves and to pray for children.[117]

Ancient Akkadian literature indicates that the belief in the powers of certain trees and plants to produce human offspring is a long one. The incomplete myth of Etana, one of the first kings of the Sumer city of Kish, tells of his search for "the plant of birth" to help him obtain offspring. According to the myth, this mystical plant grew only within the bounds of heaven.[118]

In the South Pacific, an abundance of oral lore tells of sacred trees that become the "roadway" of the souls of the dead to traverse from the physical world to the underworld. Usually the tree stretches from a cleft of rock on a high bluff, which is regarded as the "leaping off" or "casting off" place where the soul takes its first leap from the land of the living. By climbing onto, and carefully following the tree branches, the soul is finally able to reach heaven and one's ancestors. By grasping the wrong branch, the soul may fall into the world of the dead.

---

115. Piggott, Juliet. *Japanese Mythology*. New York: Peter Bedrick Books 1982, 71.

116. Philpot, Mrs. J.H. *The Sacred Tree in Religion and Myth*. Mineola: Dover Publications, Inc. 2004, 74-75 (A reprint of the 1897 edition published by Macmillan and Co., Ltd. London and New York).

117. Sahi, Jyoti. *The Child and the Serpent: Reflections on Popular Indian Symbols*. London: Arkana 1980, 151.

118. Ringgren, Helmer. *Religions of the Ancient Near East*. Philadelphia: The Westminster Press 1973, 75.

Lore from around the world speaks of trees that were either the abodes of spirits or souls waiting to enter the bodies of lone females walking by. The Semang of the Philippines say that the dead journey to a miraculous island where the Tree of Life, the Mapic Tree, is located. Here, "the newly deceased become real spirits and may eat the fruits of the tree. This, of course, is a miraculous tree and the source of life; for at its roots are breasts heavy with milk, and there too are the spirits of infants — presumable the souls of the yet unborn."[119] It is assumed the new spirits wait here to be born again. The Yupa Indians of Vene- zuela tell of a time when "most trees were human beings. However, these soon split into two groups which quarreled — for the one did not wish to let the other live in the plains. After a long struggle both groups gave up and the mountain trees let those in the plains live in peace."[120]

It is a custom in present day Scotland, as it was in years past, to nail branches of rowan over the doorways of homes and barns to protect the inhab- itants from evil witches, and travelers from fairies who had evil intent. Rowan was considered so effective that it was, and still is, carried by travelers to keep them safe on their journey. Another wood protective against witches, ghosts and evil is the elder. The Druids made their wands from rowan and yew wood. Row- anberries were said to contain magical properties to "abolish sickness and renew youth."[121] Mackenzie wrote that the red rowanberries "contain in concentrated form the animating influence of the deity" that cured disease and restored youth or protected one who possessed them as charms against evil.[122] The rowan- berries were "luck-berries."

Another tree with magical fruit is the hazel. Hazelnuts eaten from the tree growing next to the Well of Segais, near the source of the Boyne River, gave the gift of poetry or prophecy. The wood of the hazel tree has been the preferred source for divining rods. Druidic Bards carved their poems onto hazel wood.

Hunting "superstitions" recall ancient taboos and practices. One hunting custom from Kansas recorded in 1965 says that each animal species hunted has its own type of tree. "When a hunter shoots an animal, he is to break off a twig from that tree, dip it in the animal's blood, and put it in his hat."[123] This practice

---

119. Eliade, Mircea. *Shamanism: Archaic Techniques of Ecstasy.* Princeton: Princeton University Press 1964, 281.

120. Wilbert, Johannes. *Yupa Folktales.* Los Angeles: Latin American Studies Volume 24, Latin American Center, UCLA 1974, 143-144.

121. Rutherford, Ward. *Celtic Lore.* London: Aquarian/Thorsons 1993, 73.

122. Mackenzie, op. cit 180.

is similar to the Native American tradition of offering a prayer of thanks to the animal before taking its life, although in this case the ritual is completed after the fact.

While the withering of trees may signal the death of an individual, it was also believed that one could see the soul of a deceased person appearing as a small, clear flame near large, holy trees.

As has been mentioned earlier, the Druids exacted a particularly gruesome punishment for anyone who peeled the bark from the holy oak trees. In later years, the death sentence also applied for any who should cut down a tree — any tree. Such an act "was held to offend the Tree Spirits, which were worshipped (and of which, incidentally, the May Day revels are a survival). A man who cut off a branch of a tree," wrote the Radfords "would lose a limb of his body."[124]

The Karok Indians of California would cut limbs from the fir or pine tree to use as "sacred fuel" in "assembly chambers." This act was not completed, however, without ritual or caution. Nineteenth-century anthropologist Stephen Powers wrote:

> The Karok selects a tall and sightly fir or pine, climbs up within about twenty feet of the top, then commences and trims of all the limbs until he reaches the top where he leaves two and a top-knot, resembling a man's head and arms outstretched.
>
> All this time he is weeping and sobbing piteously, shedding real tears...[125]

The intentional arrangement of the limbs into a "man's head and arms outstretched" is an obvious attempt to recognize the spirit of the tree and the tears were offered in sorrow for the desecration.

Fourteenth-century knight Sir John Mandeville wrote of the Trees of the Sun and the Moon in his famous travel-log, *The Travels of Sir John Mandeville*. Located in the Middle East, possibly around the present day islands of Bahrain in the Persian Gulf, these trees were said to have spoken to Alexander and warned him of his death. "Some say," wrote Mandeville, "that the people who look after

123. Koch, William E. "Hunting Beliefs and Customs from Kansas" in *Western Folklore*, Vol. XXIV, July 1965, Number 3. Published by the California Folklore Society, UCLA. pg. 173.

124. Radford, Edwin and Mona A. *Encyclopaedia of Superstitions*. New York: Philosophical Library 1949, 244.

125. Powers, Stephen. *Tribes of California*. Berkeley: University of California Press 1976, 25. A reprint of the 1877 publication *Contributions to North American Ethnology, Vol. III* published by the Department of Interior, Government Printing Office, Washington, D.C.

those trees eat the fruit of them and the balm that grows there, and live four or five hundred years...."[126]

Other intelligent, speaking trees appear in folklore around the world. The Cherokee, according to 19th-century ethnologist James Mooney, believed "trees and plants were also alive and could talk in the old days."[127] The belief that trees possessed souls resulted in an extension of that concept to include speech. "Naturally, when a soul was given to a tree," Porteous wrote, "it was likewise endowed with the power of speech. This speech is often in a mysterious, emblematical, or silent language, which, however, often makes itself heard...Many trees have even taken human speech..."[128] The Indians of British Columbia had similar beliefs. Porteous noted, "among some of the Indian tribes...the belief prevails that men are transformed into trees, and that the creaking of the branches in the wind is their voice."[129]

In Yaqui mythology, a story is told of a talking tree that appeared to the original race of Little People that inhabited the earth. According to John Bierhorst, "One day a tree began talking in a strange language. None of the *surem* [dwarves] knew what it was saying except one little girl. She explained that the tree foretold the coming of the whites, who would bring new weapons, railroads, and bloodshed....dismayed at the prospect of so much violence, the *surem* went underground to live, and they remain there to this day."[130]

At times, the spirits of humans and trees evidently are able to interact and communicate with one another. In *The Spirit World*, by the editors of Time-Life Books, a Lenape (Delaware Indian) herbalist called Touching Leaves Woman experienced such a connection when she was a young girl. "She was riding a horse with her aunt through deep woods, when the older woman fell unconscious on the ground. It was evening, and the little girl was terrified by the deepening forest shadows. Suddenly, she saw the trees become almost human. As a

126. Mandeville, Sir John. *The Travels of Sir John Mandeville.* Trans. by C.W.R.D. Moseley. London: Penguin Books 1983, 181 (A translation of the 1356 publication).

127. Mooney, James. *Myths of the Cherokee.* New York: Dover Publications Inc. 1995, 231 (A reprint of the *Nineteenth Annual Report of the Bureau of American Ethnology* 1897-98 published in 1900 by the Smithsonian Institution, Washington).

128. Porteous, Alexander. *The Lore of the Forest: Myths and Legends.* London: Senate 1996, 152 (A reprint of the 1928 publication, *Forest Folklore* published by George Allen & Unwin Ltd. London).

129. Ibid., 180.

130. Bierhorst, John. *The Mythology of Mexico and Central America.* New York: William Morrow and Company, Inc. 1990, 9.

breeze gently stirred their leaves, they smiled and spoke kindly to her, promising no harm would befall her. They kept their pledge. The girl and her aunt were soon found, and the older woman recovered completely."[131]

Philpot tells us "the spirits inhabiting the three trees of the Hesperides gave advice to the wandering Argonauts. Philostratus[132] relates that at the command of Apollonius a tree addressed him in a distinct female voice. When Rome was invaded by the Gauls, a voice from out of the grove of Vesta warned the Romans to repair their walls or their city would fall."[133] In addition, of course, we have the oracular trees at Delphi and Dodona, which the gods spoke through to humankind.

In many traditional cultures, it was believed that heaven is reached by climbing certain sacred trees. This is true of Indian tribes in South America, Polynesians and certain groups in India. D'Alviella wrote in 1894, "the Khasias of India take the stars to be men who scaled heaven by climbing up a Tree, and were obliged to remain in the branches, their companions, who had stopped on earth, having cut down the trunk."[134] In the Samoan Otherworld, the Tree of Life stood which provided all of the needs for the residents of the underworld. A tree also stood on the shores of the Water of Life in the Melanesian Land of the Dead. From the tree, the soul was able to dive into the subterranean sea of life.[135]

The Trees of the Ogham

There are fifteen different species of trees that figure in European folklore and which also make up part of the Celtic tree-alphabet known as "ogham" or "ogam." Ogham is the earliest known form of Irish writing and was probably inspired by Latin script, sometime between the 1st century BCE and the 3rd century CE. There is no evidence that this form of writing survived past the 8th century CE. Celtic mythology says that the ogham was the creation of the god of eloquence and literacy, Ogma. Each of the ogham "letters" is named after a tree and each was created in a series of lines at different angles to a vertical line.

---

131. Anon. *The Spirit World. Op. cit.* 105.

132. Flavius Philostratus, who in 216 CE by request of the Empress Julia Domna wrote a biography of the 1st century Greek philosopher/mystic Apollonius of Tyana.

133. Philpot, op. cit. 101-102.

134. D'Alviella, The Count Goblet. *The Migration of Symbols.* New York: University Books 1956, 171.

135. Anderson, Johannes C. *Myths and Legends of the Polynesians.* Rutland: Charles E. Tuttle Company: Publishers 1969, 420.

Ogham script is mentioned in many of the Celtic myths and was probably used for divination, record keeping and magic by the Druid class. R.J. Stewart, however, notes that Ogham "seems to have been reserved for important funerary inscriptions or for god names, and occasional permanent statements."[136] While most ogham letters are found carved into stone, it may be that they were also used on wood tablets that no longer exist. Peter Berresford Ellis, perhaps the foremost expert on the Celts, noted, "we hear that in earlier times Ogam was used to write ancient stories and sagas; it was incised on bark or wands of hazel and aspen. These 'rods of the Fili' (poets) were kept in libraries or Tech Screptra."[137] Unfortunately, the libraries and the "rods of the Fili" have long since returned to nature. Evidence exists, from a book written around 1400 CE (The *Yellow Book of Lecan*), that Patrick had 180 of these ancient books burned in his effort to eradicate the Druid influence. While ogham marks are found on stones in Wales and Scotland, the vast majority are located in Ireland and a full one-third are found in County Kerry alone.[138]

The trees which are reflected in the ogham alphabet are the birch, rowan, ash, alder, willow, hawthorn, oak, holly, hazel, elder, dwarf elder, silver fir, heather, white poplar and the yew. The vine, furze (a cereal grain), and ivy, while certainly not trees, are part of the group. The ogham alphabet consists of thirteen consonants and five vowels. The vowels are the silver fir, furze, heather, white poplar, and yew.

The folklore associated with each tree is rich. Each one (other than the oak, which is covered in detail in Chapter 3), and the three non-tree species, are discussed below.

The Alder

The alder is associated with death, the power of evaporation (and the smith's fire) in Celtic lore; alder is closely tied to the fairy, to divination and to resurrection. For the ancient Greeks, the alder was associated with spring and fire festivals and was an emblem of Pan.[139] Porteous states that in the Tyrol area

---

136. Stewart, R. J. *Celtic Gods Celtic Goddesses.* London: Blandford 1990, 34.

137. Ellis, Peter Berresford. *The Ancient World of the Celts.* New York: Barnes & Noble Books 1998, 32.

138. Anon. *Celtic Mythology.* New Lanark: Geddes & Grosset 1999, 439.

139. Cooper, J. C. *An Illustrated Encyclopaedia of Traditional Symbols.* London: Thames & Hudson Ltd. 1978, 10.

of Austria, the alder was a favorite tree of sorcerers who could use the wood to make the dead come back to life.[140]

The alder has long been prized for resisting the "corruptive power of water," and was used in the foundations of many cathedrals; the Romans, famous for road building, relied on it when driving causeway piles in marshes. In Ireland, alder wood was the material to use for milk pails and whistles. Alder appears in the *Odyssey* as one of the three trees of resurrection that guarded the cave of Calypso. In ancient times, the alder was highly valued for the three dye colors it would produce: red from the bark, green from the flowers, and brown from its twigs. These colors represent fire, water and the earth.

An alder branch at one time was tied to the cradle of newborn boys to protect them from being kidnapped by fairies. This is rather surprising, since the alder was "under the protection" of water fairies — another example of the many dual aspects of nature and the folklore of nature.

The Ash

Like the oak, the ash is regarded as a "progenitor of mankind."[141] In ancient Greece, it was said that the first of humankind originated from a vast cloud-ash created by the Nymphs of the Ash. These Nymphs were cloud-goddesses. The ash was also the sacred tree of Poseidon. Three of the Five Magic Trees of Ireland, the Tree of Tortu, the Tree of Dathi, and the Branching Tree of Usnech, all ash trees and all sacred to the Druids, were cut down in 665 CE by the Christians. The felling of these trees symbolized the conquest of Christianity over paganism. Writer and folklorist Robert Graves noted that "a descendent of the Sacred Tree of Creevna, also an ash, was still standing at Killura in the nineteenth century; its wood was a charm against drowning...."[142] Irish emigrants to America brought pieces of the tree with them for its protection.

The power of the ash is represented in a ritual Druidic wand made of ash, with a spiral decoration, found in Anglesey and dating back to the 1st century CE. The negativity of the ash, as perceived by the Christians, resulted in various legends. Scandinavian lore says that the ash was the favorite tree of witches and that they were ogres or became the habitation of ogres.[143] Porteous notes that

---

140. Porteous, op. cit., 276.
141. Ibid. 157.
142. Graves, Robert. *The White Goddess.* New York: The Noonday Press 1948, 168.
143. Porteous op. cit 86.

the Askafroa, "wife of the Ash," was an evil spirit and very destructive. "To propitiate her," Porteous wrote, "it was necessary to make a sacrifice on Ash Wednesday."[144] Evidently, as time passed, Ash Wednesday was utilized as a Christian holy day to nullify the evil powers of these pagan demons. It is interesting to note that Ash Wednesday was originally a Roman pagan festival, derived from Vedic India. During this festival people would bathe in ashes as they had the power to absolve all sins through the power of the fire god Agni. These ashes were said to be the "purifying blood of Shiva" and, by bathing in them, one could wash away sins.[145]

Other traditional festivals around the world indicate that Ash Wednesday has far more to do with ancient pagan traditions than with Christian ones. Frazer wrote of the Ash Wednesday ritual held at Braller, Transylvania:

...two white and two chestnut horses draw a sledge on which is placed a straw-man swathed in a white cloth; beside him is a cart-wheel which is kept turning round. Two lads disguised as old men follow the sledge lamenting. The rest of the village lads, mounted on horseback and decked with ribbons, accompany the procession, which is headed by two girls crowned with evergreen and drawn in a waggon [sic] or sledge. A trial is held under a tree, at which lads disguised as soldiers pronounce sentence of death. ...he is...handed over to the executioner, who hangs him on a tree."[146] The death sentence was given to the straw man "because he had done them harm, by wearing out their shoes and making them tired and sleepy.[147]

We must also recall that the World Tree Yggdrasill, sacred to Odin, was an ash.

The leafing of the ash has figured in weather lore over the years. "When the oak comes out before the ash," a 19th-century saying in the English Midland Counties went, "there will be fine weather in harvest; but when the ash comes out before the oak, the harvest will be wet."[148]

---

144. Ibid. 93.

145. Walker, Barbara G. *The Women's Encyclopedia of Myths and Secrets.* Edison: Castle Books 1996, 67.

146. Frazer, James G. *The Golden Bough: The Roots of Religion and Folklore, Vol. 1.* New York: Avenel Books 1981, 255 (A reprint of the 1890 edition published by Macmillan, London).

147. Ibid.

148. Inwards, Richard. *Weather Lore.* London: Senate 1994, 151 (A reprint of the 1893 edition published by Elliot Stock, London).

The ash, according to J. C. Cooper, "also typifies adaptability, prudence, modesty."[149] In Welsh folklore, the ash leaf provides for prophetic dreams (such as dreaming of a future husband) and if worn as a garter will provide protection against witches and the devil.[150] In the Scottish Highlands the sap from the ash tree was believed to protect newborns from witches, fairies "and other imps of darkness."[151] Anna Franklin notes that "ash buds placed in the cradle prevent fairies exchanging a changeling for the child."[152]

The ash was also used in an ancient "passing through" cure. Children in particular were passed through an ash, which had been split down the middle or had natural openings in the trunks, as a treatment for "rupture." They were "passed through" at least three times, at sunrise. The tree was then bound up, with clay and mud plastered over the split. If the tree healed, so would the child. In another version the child was passed through the split "three times three" (nine times) each day for nine successive days, attended by nine persons who took turns passing the child. As noted earlier about "birth trees," these "passing trees" were intimately connected with the children that had been passed through them — "that should the tree die, the child, also, would die." [153] The danger lasted throughout the individual's life.

Natural holes in the trunks of trees were also believed to be the doorways to the spirit world and were often used to cure certain diseases because of the tree's link to the spirit world. As Thompson noted, "...the pine and pollard ashes were regarded with special veneration when a hole was found in them, and in Somersetshire and Cornwall it is still believed...that a rickety child passed through the aperture would be made strong and healthy."[154]

Similar beliefs and rituals have been observed as well in Latin American traditions, according to folklorist Wayland D. Hand.[155] Such a widespread practice, from Britain to Latin America, would indicate that this is an ancient and universal bit of folk medicine.

---

149. Cooper, op. cit 16.

150. Radford, op. cit 22.

151. Ibid. 23.

152. Franklin, Anna. *The Illustrated Encyclopaedia of Fairies.* London: Paper Tiger/Chrysalis Books 2004, 17.

153. Ibid.

154. Thompson, C.J.S. *The Hand of Destiny: Everyday Folklore and Superstitions.* London: Senate 1995, 218.

155. Hand, Wayland D. editor, *American Folk Medicine: A Symposium.* Berkeley: University of California Press 1976, 5.

A 'Passing Through' Tree. Like sacred stones, certain trees with natural holes in them were used to heal both children and adults.

The ash was also used as a cure for diseased livestock. An ash rod was passed over the animal to affect a cure for whatever ailed them. The ash was especially regarded as a "neutralizer" of snake venom. John Fiske, in a "Lecture on Philosophy" at Harvard University in the 19th century, wrote of the powers of the ash against the serpent:

> The other day I was told, not by an old granny, but by a man fairly educated and endowed with a very unusual amount of good common sense, that a rattlesnake will sooner go through fire than creep over ash leaves or into the shadow of an ash-tree. Exactly the same statement is made by Pliny, who adds that if you draw a circle with an ash rod around the spot on the ground on which a snake is lying, the animal must die of starvation, being effectively imprisoned as Ugolino in the dungeons of Pisa. In Cornwall it is believed that a blow from an ash stick will instantly kill any serpent.[156]

---

156. Fiske, John. *Myths and Myth-Makers: Old Tales and Superstitions.* Boston: Houghton, Mifflin and Company 1881, 61.

The Birch

Sacred to Thor, Donar and Frigga, the birch is associated with fertility and light, protecting against witches and evil spirits. In Teutonic myth, the last battle in the world will be fought around a birch tree.[157]

Birch twigs and rods were used in the "Beating of the Bounds" — a possibly pagan survival into early 20th century Britain. During this ritualized festival, a group of men would rove from boundary to boundary and "capture" any newly appointed parish officer, who was turned upside down and placed head first into a newly dug hole. His "latter end" was "saluted with the shovel." Reportedly, "it was also usual to flog a boy at certain points of the parish boundary."[158] The reasons for these actions were entirely vague but it is suspected that they were remnants of ancient sacrificial rites.

To the Siberian Yakuts, the birch was the Cosmic Tree. On the eight branches of this tree nested the children of the creator, Ai Toyon, the "Creator of Light."[159] Each Yakut shaman is connected spiritually with a sacred birch and his life is dependent on that tree. Living at the top of this cosmic tree is a sacred eagle that is a representation of the Lord of the World, and on its branches lives the souls of future shamans.

It was not shamans but Forest Devils that lived in the tops of birch trees in the Russian forests. We have already discussed the Leshy and the power they wield in the birch forests of Russia.

Through the nineteenth century, "ritual towels" were hung on the branches of birch trees by Russian peasants — left as offerings to the Mother Goddess who was closely associated with the birch. Another Russian tale speaks of the Mother of God, seated at the top of a birch tree, and another birch, which together saved a young girl from a witch.

Obviously, the sacredness of the birch has a complex and contradictory meaning to many people. Its symbolism is not one of contradiction for the people of Estonia, however. The birch tree is the emblem of the nation.

---

157. Cooper, op. cit 20.
158. Bilson, Charles. *Vestiges of paganism in Leicestershire.* Loughborough: Heart of Albion Press 1994, 17 (A reprint of the 1911 article appearing in *Memorials of old Leicestershire* published by George Allen, London).
159. Eliade, op. cit 70.

The Dwarf Elder

The Dwarf Elder represents the 12th letter of the ogham alphabet. It is an important tree, not because it has magical properties or because it is inhabited by spirits, but because it was this tree that the reed scepters were made for the pharaohs of Egypt. It was also a reed of the dwarf elder that was reportedly placed in Jesus' hand when he was draped in scarlet and the crown of thorns was placed on his head.[160]

The Elder

The elder, long associated with magic and witchcraft, was the 13th letter of the ogham script. The elder has been linked to witchcraft[161] and the powers of ghosts, and some legends say that this (not the ilex oak) was the wood from which the cross was made, and the tree from which Judas hanged himself. Because of these traditions, Christian lore regards the elder as the "ultimate in evil." Because of the elder's association with supernatural powers, in Scotland the leaves of the elder were scattered about doorways and windows to protect against witches and evil.[162] This is contradictory to another bit of folklore. According to Richard Inwards, "witches were thought to produce bad weather by stirring water with branches of elder."[163] And some folklore indicates that an elder could actually be a witch in disguise. However, in Germany, hair and nail clippings were buried under an elder to keep witches from obtaining them and using them for evil purposes. In the Baltic countries, those who honored Puskaitis placed offerings to him at elder trees; he was a god of the underworld and fairies.[164]

---

160. Graves, op. cit 185.

161. Elder has been traditionally worn on Walpurgis Night in Germany. Walpurga (also spelled "Walburga") was originally a pagan May Queen, the female half of the sacred marriage rite held every Spring. The cult surrounding Walpurga was so popular in Germany that the Church had no option but to canonize the May Queen and change the traditionally orgiastic festival to a Church sponsored event with the processionals, dances and song twisted to fit the fictional St. Walpurga. The Church changed the date of the festival from the pagan May Day to February; however, the local populations continued to observe May Day as the effective date. The Church then claimed May Eve as the commemorative date of the transference of the relics of St. Walpurga to the town of Eichstätt.

162. Radford, op. cit 113.

163. Inwards, op. cit 153.

164. Jones, Prudence & Nigel Pennick. *A History of pagan Europe.* New York: Barnes & Noble Books 1995, 176.

A charm, Lady Wilde tells us, made from nine twigs of elder and worn around the neck of a patient, was a safeguard against epilepsy and convulsions.[165]

Seventeenth-century English superstition held that if boys were beaten with elder sticks their growth would be checked.[166] In addition, it was believed that elder leaves gathered on the last day of April and applied to a wound would ensure that the wound would heal. However, as already indicated, elder had a dual nature — one of protection and one of evil. Another bit of folklore said that elder wood burned in a fireplace would cause a death in the family.[167]

The elder, in folklore from the Scandinavian peninsula — where the sun stays low in the sky for long parts of the year — had the "unpleasant habit of taking a walk in the twilight and peeping in through the window at the children when they were alone."[168] In other parts of Scandinavia, such as Copenhagen, this bit of lore was evidently unheard of, as each house had its own elder tree, called a Guardian Tree, for protection. According to tradition "any baptized person whose eyes were anointed with the green juice of [the elder's] inner bark, was able to see witches in any part of the world."[169]

In Denmark the Elder Queen, Hulda, lived at the roots of the elder — she was the mother of all elves. Hulda is also the guardian of the elder and her permission had to be obtained before any berries were taken or any branch cut from the tree.

The Hawthorn

Unlike most of the trees in the ogham script, the hawthorn was known for being unlucky and potentially harmful. This may be because the hawthorn was also associated with the fairy. Both spirits and fairies met at the hawthorn in Europe. However, as is typical with sacred symbols, the hawthorn also symbolized positive values such as virginity, chastity, and the "miraculous virgin conception." It also reportedly protected against sorcery and was sacred to Hecate (which is particularly interesting, in that she is the goddess of witches

165. Wilde, Lady. *Irish Cures, Mystic Charms & Superstitions*. New York: Sterling Publishing Company, Inc. 1991, 15.

166. Radford, op cit 112.

167. Ibid.

168. Porteous, op. cit 279.

169. Thompson, C.J.S. *The Hand of Destiny: Everyday Folklore and Superstitions*. London: Senate 1995, 224. (A reprint of the 1932 edition published by Rider & Company, London).

and the underworld), Flora, Hymen and Maia.[170] One of the traditions associated with Walpurgis Night was to place branches of hawthorn and other thorny plants on the thresholds of barns to keep witches out.[171]

Many taboos were traditionally associated with the hawthorn. An Irish saying, "to cut down a hawthorn tree is to risk great peril" evidently was backed by suitable anecdotal examples. The Radfords tell of two brothers named Bergin who cut down an entire grove of hawthorn trees on their property; one of the brothers became "fairy stricken," and he was untreatable.[172] Another farmer at Garrglass cut down one hawthorn with dreadful results. He lost all of his cattle, his children died, and he was evicted from his farm for non-payment. "Two generations of successors at the farm," the Radfords wrote, "are said never to have prospered."[173]

The hawthorn symbolized chastity; it was prohibited to marry in the month of May, which was the hawthorn month in the ancient world. It was also the month of purification, when all of the temples of Vesta were swept clean. Yet, with the passage of time, the hawthorn and the month of May became associated with the goddess Flora, Maypole dancing and sensuality.

The Glastonbury thorn, or hawthorn, with its Christian tale of Joseph of Arimathea striking his hawthorn staff in the earth and the staff turning into a grown tree, was probably the result of the Church canonizing the tree "as a means of discouraging the orgiastic use of hawthorn blossoms."[174]

Certain folk medicinal lore has come down through time in association with hawthorn, as well. In the 1920s, some people in Utah believed that to bring a flowering hawthorn into a home would also bring death to the family. However, to those in Arkansas, the wearing of hawthorn around the neck was believed to be a certain cure for rheumatism.

An almost universal piece of folklore throughout the west and southwest of the United States in the 1920s and 1930s said, "If you want to be beautiful, you must wash your face in the dew of the hawthorn on the first of May."[175] Such links with Mayday are significant.

---

170. Cooper, op. cit 80.
171. Porteous, op. cit 257.
172. Radford, op. cit 145.
173. Ibid.
174. Graves, op. cit 176.
175. UCLA Folklore Archives, Record # 5_6336.

Another ritual was reported in Canada, also in the 1920s. For "rosy cheeks,"[176] it was prescribed to sit next to a hawthorn with a red silk ribbon at dusk, to touch the painful cheek with the ribbon, and then walk three times around the hawthorn reciting a certain "formula."[177]

Hawthorns growing on hills or near certain holy wells were said to mark the boundaries to the fairy world.

The Hazel

Hazel was the sacred tree in the Druid grove, representing wisdom, magic, divination, inspiration and chthonic powers. In England, the hazel was associated with fertility and divination. It was the Celtic Tree of Life and was associated with the Mother Goddess. Hazel nuts would bestow wisdom to those who ate them — but only the sacred salmon were allowed to eat them. "All the knowledge of the arts and sciences," wrote Graves, "was bound up with the eating of these nuts."[178] The "nine hazels of poetic arts" that grew next to the Connla's Well, near Tipperary, were said to produce both fruit and flowers at the same time.

In Scandinavia, the hazel was sacred to Thor. Sacred hazel groves at one time existed near Edinburgh and Glasgow.[179] Hazel was valued for forming powerful wands as well. Called the Wishing, or Divining, Rod, it was used in magic and for locating hidden springs and treasure. The hazel was also regarded as a "lightning shrub." Thought to serve as a lightning rod, it was often attached to door or window frames for a bit of added protection during storms.[180] "Wishing Caps" were once made of hazel twigs and, if worn, "it is possible to obtain any wish." [181] Ship captains would wear them, as they believed that by doing so their ship could weather any storm.

---

176. "Rosy cheeks" was evidently a painful skin condition.

177. Cantero, Antonio. "Occult Healing Practices in French Canada" in *Canadian Medical Association Journal*, New Series 20, (1929), 305.

178. Graves, op. cit 182.

179. Ibid. 49.

180. Thompson, C.J.S. *The Hand of Destiny: Everyday Folklore and Superstitions.* London: Senate, 219 (A reprint of the 1932 edition published by Rider & Company, London).

181. Radford, op. cit 145.

The Holly

The holly was sacred to the Roman god Saturn and was a symbol of health and happiness. It is also an attribute of the sun gods, and in Christianity it has been the symbol of the tree used to build the cross, "its spiked leaves signifying the crown of thorns and the passion and its red berries being the blood of Christ."[182]

To the Druids holly was the plant of death and regeneration and sacred to the goddess of the Underworld, Hel. The practice of decorating the home with boughs of holly and ivy dates back to the Dionysian solstice festivals and was condemned by the early Church when the Christians continued the practice. The Council of Bracara, in 563 CE, also condemned it, saying that no Christian should bring holly into his or her house, as it was a custom of "heathen people."[183]

Walker writes that the "holy" holly "was linguistically linked with Hel's yonic 'hole' (Germanic *Höhle*, a cave or grave)."[184] The red berries, contrary to Christian tradition, represented the female blood-of-life color. Holly, like many other sacred trees and plants, has a dual nature. It is said that German witches often favored holly wood for ritual wands, but other folklore suggests that holly was used to protect property and animals from the doings of witches. "No witch or fairy," according to Franklin, "can cross a threshold made from holly wood, and a holly hedge keeps them off the property."[185]

"That witches hate it," wrote Ronald Millar "is a strong indication that it is a Druidical charm far older than its Christian association."[186]

The Rowan

The very name "Rowan" is related to the old Norse word "runa" — meaning a "charm." Like the hawthorn and several other sacred trees, rowan placed at the entryways of homes and barns was believed to keep witches away. In Germany, for the boughs to be effective against witches, the rowan must be cut on Ascension Day. In Scotland, it was gathered on May Day (Beltane).

---

182. Cooper, op. cit 84.
183. Walker, op. cit 407.
184. Ibid. 406.
185. Franklin, op. cit., 129.
186. Millar, Ronald. *The Green Man Companion and Gazetteer.* East Sussex: S.B. Publications 1997, 68.

There are a variety of folklore traditions associated with the rowan — as there are for all of the other sacred trees and plants. In Nordic traditions, the red berries had magic powers to prolong life. The berries, according to lore, contained the "animating influence of the deity."[187] American folklore from the Midwest said that if a woman shook a rowan branch over her bed three times and then tossed it under the bed, she would not conceive. However, Finnish lore states if the rowan berries are prolific in the fall, many illegitimate children will be born the following year. The rowan also healed wounds and was used to transfer illnesses. This bit of transference was not innocuous, however, for the illness was not transferred to the tree but to rowan berries, which were then hung on bushes along a walkway where passersby might touch them — thus receiving the disease and freeing the original individual who had been ill.[188]

The Druids utilized the rowan as a way to compel demons to answer questions and it was widely used throughout Britain for protection against lightning and the charms of witches.[189] In Ireland, its uses were many; it could even be hammered through a corpse to pin the ghost in the grave. In Scotland, rowan wood was the most potent and general charm carried throughout the land and used to keep the Evil Eye from cattle, people and homes and to keep diseases, witches and fairies away from the livestock. Rowan wood was also made into shepherds' crooks in Estonia and Sweden.[190]

"Flying rowan," rowan found growing on a wall, high mountain or between limbs of other trees — produced from a seed dropped by birds — was considered especially effective against witchcraft. The thinking was that, because it does not grow on the ground, witches would be powerless against it.[191]

The rowan was sacred in many Slavic countries and the sun-goddess Saule was said to perch on top of a birch or rowan tree.[192] Millar notes, "That rowan is frequently found growing near standing stones is considered significant, but that rowan gave protection against witchcraft might be a factor here."[193]

187. Mackenzie, op. cit 180.

188. Black, William George. *Folk-Medicine: A Chapter in the History of Culture.* London: Publications of the Folk-Lore Society #12, 1883, 39.

189. Graves, op. cit 167.

190. Radford, op. cit 206.

191. Frazer, op. cit 361.

192. Jones & Pennick, op. cit 174.

193. Millar, Ronald. *The Green Man Companion and Gazetteer.* East Sussex: S.B. Publications 1997, 68.

The Silver Fir

The fir was sacred to Pan and Odin, and the Moon Goddess Artemis. It is important to know that the fir was a sacred tree to Artemis as she was the goddess of childbirth; the fir was regarded as the prime birth-tree throughout Northern Europe.

Like many of the other trees described in this chapter, the fir was believed to have certain healing properties. Part of the rituals utilized the ancient technique of transference. In Germany, those who suffered from gout would go to a young fir tree, tie a knot in one of the twigs, and say: "God guard thee, noble fir tree, I bring thee my gout."[194]

A more nefarious tradition observed by poachers was to swallow seeds from a fir cone found growing upwards before sunrise on St. John's Day, thus rendering the poacher invisible.[195]

The White Poplar

The poplar is "a tree of the waters."[196] In Greco-Roman mythology, the white poplar (also known as the aspen) represents the Elysian Fields, while the black, according to some, represents Hades, the underworld land of the dead. To be more generous to the black poplar, we may add that it was sacred to Mother Earth and was the funereal tree of pre-Hellenic Greece. Robert Graves writes that the white poplar is "the tree of the autumn equinox and old age."[197] Philpot also reminds us that the goddess Rhea gave birth to Zeus beneath a poplar in Crete.[198]

The aspen has been assigned certain roles in Christian lore due to its "trembling leaf" characteristics. Porteous noted that the most popular legend "is that which says that the Aspen was one of the trees chosen to furnish wood for the Cross, and that its leaves have trembled ever since."[199] Obviously, in the early attempts of the Christian Church to throw mud on the sacred symbols of paganism, many of the trees sacred to pagan traditions were listed as having pro-

---

194. Radford, op. cit 120.
195. Ibid.
196. Cooper, op. cit 134.
197. Graves, op. cit 193.
198. Philpot, op. cit 76.
199. Porteous, op. cit., 276.

vided wood for the Cross. Not only the aspen, but the oak, mistletoe, fig, ash and the elder have similar legends attached to them.

The Willow

The willow was one of the symbols of the goddess Hecate in her virgin form. It is an enchanted tree sacred to the Moon Goddess, Europa, Kwan-yin, Artemis, Hera, Tammuz, and Esus. A willow was the Cosmic Tree of Accadia. Willow wands figured prominently in the rituals of several Middle Eastern religions, including that of Dionysus, and were incorporated in the Day of Willows feast, later known as the Feast of the Tabernacle.[200] Willow was also favored as a source wood for the construction of divining rods due to the magical properties it supposedly contained. These rods not only led one to hidden treasures but could also drive away the "powers of darkness, serpents, and other evils."[201] Cooper notes that it is especially sacred to the Ainu, "since the spine of the first man was made of willow."[202] In Britain, the village hedge witch used willow bark to treat fevers and arthritis, which was effective due to its aspirin qualities. However, according to lore, animals struck with a willow rod "will be seized with internal pains"[203] and, like the elder, children struck with it were said to stop growing.[204]

The willow's association with magic in some cases reflects the fact that it naturally grows near water; it is believed to mark the entrance to the underworld. "Willow" may be related to the Old Norse word *vigger* of which "wicker" is another derivative.

The Yew

The last tree of the ogham script is the yew. The yew is sacred to Hecate in Greece and Italy and has been known as the "death tree" in all European countries. The yew may also figure in the creation of the Green Man. "In Brittany," Graves writes, "it is said that church-yard yews will spread a root to the mouth of each corpse."[205] The yew was also one of the Five Magical Trees of Ireland.

200. Walker, op. cit 1076.
201. Porteous, op. cit 262.
202. Cooper, op. cit 192.
203. Burns, Charlotte Sophia. *The Handbook of Folklore*. London: Senate 1996, 32 (A reprint of the 1914 edition published by Sidgwick & Jackson Ltd., London).
204. Simpson, Jacquelin and Steve Roud. *Oxford Dictionary of English Folklore*. Oxford: Oxford University Press 2000, 392

The yew is not a death tree in that it causes death (although some lore does suggest that death will soon follow if certain yews are irreverently plucked), rather, it is regarded as a "gentle guardian of the dead." The yew has been a common churchyard tree for this reason. In Wales, it was sacrilegious to burn or cut down a yew.[206] The yew's association with death made it an unlucky tree that was not to be taken into the home.

The yew is another of those trees with a dual symbolism. While it represented mourning and sadness, it also symbolized, for Christians and Celts, immortality. As researcher Gale Owen writes, "The yew-tree can be either an optimistic or a pessimistic symbol; as an evergreen its branches might be used in winter fertility ceremonies as a reminder of rebirth. Yet its leaves are very dark...to the Romans the yew was associated with poison and death."[207] The yew was also one of two trees that the Druids utilized for their wands — the other being the rowan. The use of yew in the making of power wands was common around the world. The "power sticks" of the Tillamook shamans along the Oregon coast were also made of yew.

The yew, as with the other sacred trees and plants, was utilized in treating illnesses and injuries as well. Seventeenth-century treatments for heart palpitations included the use of yew berries. Czech folklorist Josef Cizmár noted in "some regions, blessed twigs of yew-tree are used in smoking cures of eye ailments,"[208] and the sawdust of yew was used as a cure for rabies. Another remedy for rabies involved a rather complex ceremony involving cooking and ritual:

One has to boil savory and yew, to mix in the extract rye flour (after cooling), and cut in the dough a little bit of window lead. Then three cakes should be baked of the mixture, and the ill one should eat them on an empty stomach. After prayers (Lord Prayer and Ave Maria said five times; Credo, one time), he should offer everything to the Five Wounds of Jesus Christ.[209]

I have not determined if yew was regarded as a cure for lead poisoning!

Other Sacred Trees

The Cedar

205. Graves, op. cit 194.
206. Radford, op. cit 264.
207. Owen, Gale R. *Rites and Religions of the Anglo-Saxons.* Dorset Press 1985, 56.
208. Cizmár, Josef. *Lidové lékarství v Československu. Vol. 2.* Czechoslovakia: Melantrich, A.S. 1946, 200.
209. Ibid. 44.

The cedar, while not part of the Celtic ogham script, was sacred in many lands and many cultures. The cedar was closely associated with the Accadian-Chaldean god Ea, whose name, tradition says, was inscribed on the core, or heart, of the tree. To the Chaldeans, the cedar not only represented the god Ea, "the god of wisdom," but also reflected the divine power actually inherent in the tree;[210] the cedar of Ea was a divine oracle. In India, the cedar was believed to be a great aid in the fertility for cattle and women alike.

To the Sumerians, the cedar was the Cosmic Tree and the Tree of Life. It was also sacred to the Green God Tammuz and, of course, had magical properties. The cedar represents strength, nobility, and incorruptibility.[211]

Native Americans universally regarded the cedar as sacred. It was an important part of the Ghost Dance religion of the Sioux in the late 1800s, standing tall as the sacrificial pole in the rituals of that religion. The Ghost Dance, a Native American revivalist-messianic movement, was performed around a small cedar tree planted in the ground specifically for that reason. "The selection of the cedar," wrote ethnologist James Mooney in 1896, "...is in agreement with the general Indian idea, which has always ascribed a mystic sacredness to that tree, from its never-dying green, which renders it so conspicuous a feature of the desert landscape; from the aromatic fragrance of its twigs, which are burned as incense in sacred ceremonies...and from the dark-red color of its heart, which seems as though dyed in blood."[212]

According to Mooney, the cedar incense was so potent that malevolent ghosts are unable to endure it and are driven away by its fragrance, even though "the wood itself is considered too sacred to be used as fuel."[213]

In Cherokee mythology, the red color of the cedar comes from the blood of a wizard who was slain and decapitated by a Cherokee warrior. The wizard's head, according to the myth, was hung from several trees but continued to live. A shaman told the people to hang the head from the topmost branches of a cedar, where it finally died.[214] In this way, the cedar became a "medicine tree."

---

210. Philpot, op. cit 95.

211. Cooper, op. cit, 31.

212. Moony, James. *The Ghost-Dance Religion and the Sioux Outbreak of 1890*. Chicago: The University of Chicago Press 1965, 53 (A reprint of Part 2 of the *Fourteenth Annual Report of the Bureau of Ethnology to the Secretary of the Smithsonian Institution, 1892-93*. Washington: Government Printing Office 1896).

213. Mooney, James. *Myths of the Cherokee*. New York: Dover Publications Inc. 1995, 421 (A reprint of the *Nineteenth Annual Report of the Bureau of American Ethnology 1897-98* published in 1900 by the Smithsonian Institution, Washington).

The cedar is sacred to the Lakota as it was a special tree of *Wakinyan*, the Flying God, or Thunderbird. In Lakota lore, "the cedar tree is the favorite of *Wakinyan*, and he never strikes it with lightning. The smell of the cedar is pleasing to him."[215] The Lakota lit the cedar incense to propitiate Wakinyan and to keep thunderstorms from causing damage.

The Egyptians also considered the cedar a holy tree. On the Obelisk of Thutmose III, hieroglyphs speak of the creation of the sacred barge of Amun-Ra made from cedar cut down by the pharaoh himself. The barge was ceremoniously sailed down the Nile for the annual river festival.[216]

The cedar tree, like most other sacred trees, has a dual nature. It is at once healing and deadly. Native Americans used cedar to treat asthma and arthritis and even to relieve persons in coma. Other American folk-cures used cedar to stop night sweats (accomplished by placing cedar bark or leaves under the pillow), and if one carried a "double cedar knot" in his or her pocket, rheumatism was "certain" to be cured.[217]

On the other side, cedar was often regarded as a source of evil and danger. It was commonly believed in the Midwest and southern parts of the United States that if a planted cedar tree died, so did the owner. Canadian Indian shamans used cedar as a "soul trap." A piece of netting, made of cedar, was constructed three feet square with a quarter-inch mesh to trap a "wandering soul."[218]

Frazer notes that a girl was sacrificed each year to an old cedar in the Kangra Mountains of India, "the families of the village taking it in turn to supply the victim." [219] The sacrifice was to appease the spirit of the tree.

It is, however the evergreen nature of the cedar that invokes its greatest value — it symbolizes eternal life, and victory over the bindings of death.

---

214. Ibid., 228.

215. Walker, James R. *Lakota Belief and Ritual.* Lincoln: University of Nebraska Press 1991, 77.

216. Budge, E.A. Wallis. *Cleopatra's Needles and Other Egyptian Obelisks.* New York: Dover Publications, Inc. 1990, 156 (A reprint of the 1926 edition published by the Religious Tract Society, London).

217. Sackett, S.J. "More Folk Medicine from Western Kansas" in *Western Folklore #23* 1964. Published by the California Folklore Society, UCLA, 76.

218. Darby, George E. "Indian Medicine in British Columbia" in *The Canadian Medical Association Journal #28* 1933, 437.

219. Frazer, Sir James. *The Golden Bough: A Study in Magic and Religion.* Hertfordshire: Wordsworth Editions Ltd. 1993, 112.

The Laurel

The laurel, the last tree that we will examine, is another of those trees regarded around the world as sacred. The laurel was Apollo's tree and the original Temple of Apollo at Delphi was constructed of laurel branches. Philpot wrote of Apollo's laurel:

> No sanctuary of his was complete without it....No worshipper could share in his rites who had not a crown of laurel on his head or a branch in his hand. As endowed with the power of the god...the laurel assumed an important and many-sided role in ceremonial symbolism.[220]

There is considerable agreement that the laurel was sacred at Delphi long before Apollo's temple was constructed there. A sacred laurel grew at the site when the earth goddess Gaia was the dominant deity there and the laurel was regarded as an oracular tree.

The laurel was also sacred to Dionysus, Juno, Diana and Silvanus, its leaves crowned Dionysus' head and, in Christianity; it represents the crown of martyrdom. The laurel continued to be regarded as "the surest way to the gods' protection and favour"[221] into the 3rd century CE when it was used to gain the protection and favor of the Christian god as well.

Native Americans valued laurel for the valuable tools that were made from the wood. The leaves were important medicinally as well. However, it was never burned, "as it is believed that this would bring on cold weather, and would furthermore destroy the medicinal virtues of the whole species."[222] Evidently, the leaves, when burned, make a hissing noise similar to the sound of snow falling.

However, burning laurel leaves was one way to treat rickets in Spain. According to Spanish medical folklore, apparently modified with the advent of Christianity, if a child comes down with rickets due to a young girl's "spell," the child should be "fumigated" nine times with the smoke from burning laurel branches which have been blessed. For this cure to work, the ritual must be performed on Saturday, with a specific charm recited at the time of the fumigation. Another Spanish cure, this one for fever, called for the placement of a cross of laurel on the stricken person's chest while a priest reads the Gospel. This

220. Philpot, op. cit. 36.
221. Ibid.
222. Mooney, James. *Myths of the Cherokee.* New York: Dover Publications Inc. 1995, 422 (A reprint of the *Nineteenth Annual Report of the Bureau of American Ethnology 1897-98* published in1900 by the Smithsonian Institution, Washington).

treatment required a Sunday application in order to receive the promised "instant cure."[223]

Other illnesses treated with laurel leaves include headache, arthritis, eye ailments, kidney stones, stings, herpes and lameness. In 19th-century California, insanity (the "sudden fit" kind) was treated with a poultice made of laurel leaves, nutmeg, cinnamon and olive oil. The poultice was placed on the person's head, which immediately created perspiration. After several applications, the person should awaken from a deep sleep, cured.

A bit of 1950s folklore from Utah called for the rubbing of laurel leaves on the legs of any newborn child who happens to be born feet first. It was believed that the child would meet with an accident later in life that would make it lame unless the legs were rubbed with laurel leaves within four hours of birth.[224]

CHAPTER 6. SACRED GROVES

Sacred groves were perhaps the first temples of worship in the world. They still exist today, and are used in many parts of the world as they always have been. We only have to experience a short time in one of the remaining old growth groves to understand the reason for this. These huge trees exude a sense of power, of wisdom, of timeless existence. They provide a habitat for thousands of species of other known plants and animals as well as creating a scene worthy of habitation by those creatures and beings that we would so like to see — fairies, elves, nature spirits, wild men and women, and even the darker forces of nature such as Herne the Hunter. They also have vast powers to heal both the body and the spirit and they are direct conduits to whatever each of us perceives to be God.

Over the centuries, however, these sacred groves have been the target of both political and religious warfare. Caesar destroyed many Druidic groves as a way to combat the Celtic resistance. Later, Christian leaders destroyed any grove held sacred by the local pagan people in an effort to uproot their rival traditions, religions and ideologies. Today, many of the old growth forests in the world are also under attack by developers and farmers.

---

223. Sébillot, Paul. "Additions aux Coutoumes, Traditions et Superstitions de la Haute-Bretagne" in *Revista des Traditions Populaires #7, 1892, 156.*
224. UCLA Folklore Archives Record # 15-6683, collected 1950-1959.

Holy Groves of the Ancient World

No one can determine when the first grove of trees was designated as "sacred" — to be used only for religious ceremony and ritual, to be protected at any cost. However, there is abundant information that indicates that such groves existed throughout Europe and the Near East thousands of years before Christianity.

"The Votiaks of Eastern Russia," states early 20th century folklorist Charlotte Burne, "have sacred woods, where not a single tree may be cut down, or the god of the place will avenge the injury. In the midst of such a wood there is often a hut, or simply an altar, on which animals are offered in sacrifice."[225]

Similar traditions existed throughout the world. Every tree in Swedish sacred groves was regarded as being divine, and in Lithuania, such groves were often located around homes and entire villages. To break even a twig off one of these trees was a sinful act. Anyone who intentionally cut a bough off a sacred tree was expected to "either die suddenly or was crippled in one of his limbs."[226]

A certain "species" of Swedish elf were called Grove Damsels or Grove Folk. It was their responsibility to live in the sacred grove and protect the trees and animals living there.[227]

Cleared areas in the midst of groves were often used for worship in Finland and Estonia. Frazer tells us that "such a grove often consisted merely of a glade or clearing with a few trees dotted about, upon which in former times the skins of the sacrificial victims were hung. The central point of the grove... was the sacred tree, beside which everything else sank into insignificance."[228] Altars were set up in the middle of the glade under the sacred tree and animal sacrifices were offered up to the spirits and gods of the trees.

In most areas, only the priest classes were allowed inside these groves, but in some areas the sacred grove promised protection to any who entered. A particular cypress grove located on the Acropolis was haven to any fugitive who reached it, and they would hang their discarded chains from the limbs of the holy trees.[229]

---

225. Burne, Charlotte Sophia. *The Handbook of Folklore*. London: Senate 1996, 35 (A reprint of the 1914 edition published by Sidgewick & Jackson Ltd., London).

226. Frazer, Sir James. *The Golden Bough: A Study in Magic and Religion*. Hertfordshire: Wordsworth Editions Ltd. 1993, 111.

227. Porteous, Alexander. *The Lore of the Forest*. London: Senate 1996, 101 (A reprint of the 1928 edition *Forest Folklore* published by George Allen & Unwin Ltd., London).

228. Ibid.

Early Roman visitors described the groves of the Druids as dark and terri-fying places. Wooden figures of the gods were placed in these groves, with the effect of the "ghastly pallor" of the figures effectively terrifying the wor-shippers.[230]

One of the great Druidic groves in southern Gaul was cleared by Caesar's troops in an effort to remove the spiritual power inherent in the grove. Another sacred grove on Anglesey was destroyed in 59 CE and yet another, located in what is now Bath, England, was cleared a few years earlier, around 43 CE. The Romans constructed a military road through the sanctuary within thirty meters of the sacred spring,[231] thus removing the sanctuary from local control. However, twenty years later, after Rome had taken firm control, the road was removed. The sanctuary was rededicated to the Roman goddess Minerva, and the grove replanted.[232] Davidson notes that even the Irish King Brian Boru, during the Viking Age, "spent a month wreaking destruction on the sacred wood of Thor near Dublin."[233]

There is some evidence that the Celts actually created sacred groves in certain areas where natural ones did not exist. The Oxfordshire Lowbury Hill site is one such example. First excavated between 1913 and 1914, and again in the 1990s, Lowbury was a sanctuary with a boundary of planted trees that marked the sacred enclosure area. Constructed during the 1st and 2nd century CE, the artificial grove enclosed a temple building which has yielded a large amount of votive offerings, such as spears and coins and at least one burial.[234]

Contemporary Sacred Groves

Sacred groves remain an important part of religious traditions around the world. Perhaps the most interesting are those intentionally created where none existed before. In India, pure water is scarce and obviously valued. For centuries

229. Philpot, Mrs. J.H. *The Sacred Tree in Religion and Myth.* Mineola: Dover Publications, Inc. 2004, 51 (A reprint of the 1897 edition published by Macmillan and Co., Ltd., London).

230. Green, Miranda J. *The World of the Druids.* London: Thames and Hudson 1997, 55.

231. A sacred well or spring was often an important feature in a sacred grove. The trees reflected the powers of the vegetative spirits and of the heavens and the wells and springs represented the Underworld.

232. Cunliffe, Barry. *The Ancient Celts.* Oxford: Oxford University Press 1997, 198.

233. Davidson, H.R. Ellis. *Myths and Symbols in pagan Europe: Early Scandinavian and Celtic Religions.* Syracuse: Syracuse University Press 1988, 25.

234. Green, op. cit 108.

ponds, or "tanks" of water, have been constructed and managed by villagers throughout the sub-continent. These ponds are not simply excavated basins filled with runoff. They are intricate creations which incorporate sacred teachings and include the planting of sacred trees to create a grove and pool system.

Specific trees are the Deodora (*Cedrus deodora*), which is considered to be the "abode of the gods," Sal (*Shorea robusta*), Rudraksha (*Elaeocarpus* sp.), Bel (*Aegle marmelos*), Ashok (*Saraca asoka*), Kadam (*Anthrocephalus chinensis*), and Pipal (*Ficus religiosa*). These individual species are regarded as sacred in specific locales in India. However, many of them are also associated specifically to individual deities. For instance, Pipal is associated with Vishnu; Bel with Shiva; and Rudraksha with an incarnation of Shiva, Lord Rudra.[235]

Small temples are also constructed at these pool-grove areas. The sacred trees and groves are planted on the constructed embankments of the pools, which protects the soil from erosion. However, what is perhaps more important, the created sacred space, according to Deep Narayan Pandey, associate professor and coordinator of the International Network on Ethnoforestry, is that they "provide a meeting place on various occasions including social gatherings, marriage, after-death rituals, etc. Groves are also used as a place for village fairs during festivals. The groves are the favorite places for *goth* ('picnic in rains') in Rajasthan."[236]

In India, then, we see an intentional creation of sacred places comprising sacred groves and pools. After their creation, they become an integral part of village life, being important additions to the fairs, rituals and social gatherings that are features of Indian life. In addition, these areas are important for the collection of drinking water, wildlife habitat, worship and protection of important species of plants. The creation of the small temples also acts to sanctify the vegetation that has been planted. As Penday notes, an "embankment without trees is perceived as temple without deity."[237]

Sacred groves are not important only for their spiritual value but "they are priceless treasures of great ecological, biological, cultural and historical

235. Pandey, Deep Narayan. "Sacred Water and Sanctified Vegetation: Tanks and Trees in India," a paper presented at the conference of the International Association for the Study of Common Property (IASCP), May 31-June 4, 2000, Bloomington, Indiana, 10.
236. Ibid. 12.
237. Ibid.

value."[238] Sacred groves in India can still be found near the Himalayas, central India and the deserts of Rajasthan.

According to Gadgil, the holy groves of India, still so important to Indian life, originated in the time that followed the introduction of agriculture some 3500 years ago. As the expanding savannas and agricultural areas pushed back the natural and expansive forests, "safety forests" were established that continued to provide fire-resistant plant life as well as wood products necessary for basketry, construction and food.[239] "The safety forests," notes Gadgil, "would naturally turn into sacred places as well. Each grove has at least two deities, a male and female. Each is sacrificed to (usually goats and fowl are offered) to obtain the gods' blessings. Tree cutting here would be taboo, which is true to this day in many parts of the country."[240] Only trees that have naturally fallen are cut up for utilitarian purposes. This not only preserves the groves but the springs and ponds and delicate habitats that are so necessary for other plants and animals to survive.

These groves, called *kans*, continue to exist as temples and, although the indigenous religions of the area have been modified through successive "Brahmanization," they provide for the survival of the earliest form of religion in the area. Many of the groves were seriously damaged under British rule when forestry "management" cleared some of them or changed the makeup of the trees — converting some groves from their native and sacred trees to eucalyptus groves.[241] In many groves, wooden images or rock carvings are situated that represent the gods and spirits. The creation of these images appears to be a common practice around the world where sacred groves have been an established and important part of religion. The Celts also left such images.

Sacred groves are also a part of the ancient history of Belarus. One of the pagan beliefs, dating back to the Paleolithic, is the cult of Volas. Volas was the pagan god of prosperity and cattle. Reportedly, Volas was revered into the 20th century and may still be in the many rural areas of the country. The Volas Stones are a direct link to this ancient religion. These are large recumbent stones nor-

---

238. Gadgill, M.D. Subash Chandran. "Sacred Groves and Sacred Trees of Uttara Kannada" in *Lifestyle and Ecology*, edited by Baidyanath Saraswati. New Delhi: Indira Gandhi National Centre for the Arts 1998. For an on-line version see www.ignca.nic.in/ed_08.htm (July 25, 2004).
239. Ibid.
240. Ibid.
241. Ibid.

mally found in small forest clearings. Cattle skulls were placed in trees around the stone where a priest would seek insights into the future, and cure diseases. Pilgrims would visit these groves and stones to offer sacrifices before and after certain ventures.

Other stones, found in what must have been sacred groves, were dedicated to the god of agriculture Dazhdbog who, like other gods of agriculture, was also the god of the sun and rain. Dazhdbog Stones are recumbent stones that served as altars. These stones are characterized by cup depressions used to mill sacral grain for the sacrificial bread made to ensure the continuation of the crops. Many of the forest clearings used in these rituals were strewn with rock alignments, cairns and standing stones.[242]

These are just a few of the accounts of contemporary sacred groves located around the world. There are many more scattered in isolated pockets from Britain to Europe and from Asia to Africa that continue to provide a natural spiritual place to commune with the spirits and the gods. Are there any in the United States? While the United States has many magnificent forests, and some small areas where the old growth forests are still allowed to live, enchanting visitors with their ancient atmosphere, for the most part forests are seen as camping sites, rock climbing challenges, and fishing/hunting opportunities — not to mention locations for money making ventures in the timber industry. To some degree, this is slowly changing. Alexander Porteous wrote, "The ancients were wont to bury their dead in the shades of the sacred grove."[243] Today, there is a growing movement to bury our own dead in special forested areas. Without expensive permanent caskets or embalming, individuals are being buried in paper caskets, or with no casket at all, with simple engraved stones marking the burial site. Forests are providing a spiritual, living location for our bodies to be disposed of inexpensively and reverently.

"Green burials," a popular practice in Britain, are becoming more acceptable in the United States. The practice, according to a website titled "Probate & Estate Trouble," is based on the premise of returning our bodies to the earth to form a vital link in the cycle of life.[244] The body may be "wrapped in a shroud or natural fabric, lying on a wicker burial stretcher or contained in a biodegradable casket" [245] with the plot marked by trees or flowers planted for

242. "Belarusian Sacred and Historical Stones". http://www.belarusguide.com/historyl/stones.html. January 9, 2004.

243. Porteous, op. cit 51.

244. www.gottrouble.com/lagal/estate_planning/funerals_green_burials.html.

that purpose or by natural rocks carved with the individual's name. Currently, there are natural burial sites at the Ramsey Creek Preserve in South Carolina,[246] the Ethician Family Cemetery[247] at Waterwood in San Jacinto County, Texas, and others in Marin County, California and on the East Coast. Eventually, these groves will take on a spiritual characteristic that is part of those sacred groves already in use around the world. There are already one hundred thirty forested burial grounds in Britain in use and the feeling is that humans, as a part of nature, must honor that connection by returning our bodies to the earth so that they may contribute to the fertilization of the earth and the continued renewal of life. Most US National Parks will allow the ashes of cremated individuals to be scattered in certain areas of the parks with permission.

CHAPTER 7. MAY DAY: THE FESTIVAL OF THE TREES

A few decades ago, those of us over a certain age will recall, May Day festivals were held in either our hometowns or schools. Sometimes dancing around a Maypole was involved but always these events celebrated the arrival of spring. Sadly, these festivals came to an end except in those few "alternative" schools or communities or as a show in the popular "Renaissance Faires" held around the country. It still survives in Britain and Europe but the festival has become so watered down over the centuries that it is difficult to get a taste of what it once was.

How did May Day become so important? What did May Day really signify?

May Day celebrations may have originated with the Roman festival of Flora, goddess of flowers. This festival marked the beginning of summer. Houses were decorated with flowers and fresh cut foliage "in the belief," notes Maggie O'Hanlon, "that the vegetation spirits thus brought into the community would bring good fortune."[248] The marking of the end of winter and the rebirth of life in the spring was such an important and universal event that May Day celebrations might not have their origins in the festival of Flora. The day that was considered

---

245. Ibid.

246. *Memorial Ecosystems, 113 Retreat Street, Westminster, SC 29693* www.memorialecosystems.com.

247. An 81 acre, woodland with ancient oaks, hickories, and pines where "earthly remains are naturally returned to nurture the earth". www.dusttodustcemetary.org.

248. O'Hanlon, Maggie. *Customs & Traditions in Britain.* Hampshire: Pitkin Unichrome Ltd. 2000, 2.

to mark the beginning of spring was an important date throughout Europe and even into the Indian sub-continent, and was greeted with practically identical rituals and customs. It would appear that this date is one that has been observed since time immemorial. And, as the Radfords point out, "observances were found in places where the Romans never settled."[249]

May is the month of the Virgin Goddess of spring, Maia, also known as the Maiden. Barbara Walker wrote that May "was the traditional month of 'wearing of the green' in honor of the Earth Mother's new garment, and of fornicating in plowed fields to encourage the crops."[250] May Day festivals "were a survival of the ancient belief, held in all countries, of the power of the Tree Spirits..."[251] During the Middle Ages it was the custom of reigning monarchs to "give out mantles and other garments to their courtiers...sometimes bearing emblems of the spring."[252] Of course green was the color of garment most often given. As part of the festival both Ladies and Knights were "crowned or garlanded with leaves."[253] May Eve is also one of the four cross-quarter days on which witches were said to celebrate their Sabbaths. Because of this, there are wide varieties of fears and prohibitions set for May Eve and May Day — along with the joyous celebration of life.

Various superstitions involved cattle and the farm. In Ireland, according to Evans, "it was the custom...in the Glens of Antrim, to stick a sprig of rowan tree upright in the midden on May Eve to protect the farm from mischievous fairies."[254] The "midden," or "muck," represented the fertility of the farm. Another ritual involved driving a pig around the farmhouse on the morning of May Day, for luck.[255] In Germany, whole herds of cattle were driven around the village Maypole to ensure that the cattle remained healthy and to bring luck to the farmers. In Scotland, it was customary to place rowan boughs on cow enclosures to keep witches away — witches who would steal the milk if one were not careful. The various rituals involved to counter witchcraft were, at times, com-

---

249. Radford, Edwin and Mona A. *Encyclopaedia of Superstitions*. New York: The Philosophical Library 1949, 171.

250. Walker, Barbara G. *The Women's Encyclopedia of Myths and Secrets*. Edison: Castle Books 1983, 624.

251. Radford, op. cit.

252. Sitwell, Sacheverell. *Gothic Europe*. New York: Holt, Rinehart and Winston 1969, 64.

253. Ibid.

254. Evans, E. Estyn. *Irish Folk Ways*. Mineola: Dover Publications Inc. 2000, 101 (A reprint of the 1957 edition published by Routledge & Kegan Paul Ltd., London).

255. Ibid., 117.

plicated. The Radfords record one Irish remedy: "To ensure good butter and freedom from witches, herbs gathered on May Day should be boiled with some hairs from the cow's tail and preserved in a covered vessel."[256]

Trees were an important aspect of May Day festivals and rituals. In India tribal leaders would, with other villagers, cut a large tree down and carry it back to the village center, where it was raised up and then danced around. Similar events occurred throughout Europe, Britain and Eurasia. In England, this ritual was known as "fetching the May," and the tree became the Maypole. Originally, a new tree was cut each year for this purpose, as Philpot notes, "in order that the newly-awakened energy of the forest might be communicated to the village..."[257] The intent, according to Pennick, was to "re-create for a short time the forest within the town" and all of the spiritual energy that forests provide.[258] Maypoles, commonly of birch, were decorated with streamers of ribbon and flowers. In Wales, even pocket watches, tankards and dishes were added to the decorations. Even though the reasoning behind placing these decorations has been lost, they obviously had been important offerings to the spirit of the tree in times past. May Day festivals also included Jack-in-the-Green and a May Queen, also known as the May Lady, and King. The May Queen and King were chosen for their beauty and youth and their coronation was followed by feasting, dancing, "rustic sports" and processions. The May Queen and King normally held their titles for a year until the next couple was chosen for the role. The May Queen and King (who is the Green Man) personified the spirits of the trees and vegetation, denoting the fertility of nature and, as Frazer wrote, "imply[ing] that the spirit incorporate in vegetation is a ruler, whose creative powers extends far and wide."[259] The symbolic "marriage" of the May Queen and King was viewed as a magical aid to the growth and fertility of vegetation.

The Maypole represented the *axis mundi*, the center of the universe, the Cosmic Tree. J.C. Cooper states, "Originally it was the sacred pine of Attis which was taken in procession, or on a chariot, to the temple of Cybele and set up for

---

256. Radford, op. cit 170.
257. Philpot, Mrs. J.H. *The Sacred Tree in Religion and Myth.* Mineola: Dover Publications Inc. 2004, 155 (A reprint of the 1897 edition published by Macmillan and Company, Ltd. London).
258. Pennick, Nigel. *Celtic Sacred Landscapes.* London: Thames & Hudson 1996, 37.
259. Frazer, James G. *The Golden Bough: The Roots of Religion and Folklore.* New York: Avenal Books 1981, 90 (A reprint of the two-volume 1890 edition published by Macmillan, London).

veneration; it was followed by men, women and children and dances were performed round it."[260] Later, the Romans "borrowed" the ritual and incorporated it into their Spring Festival. The celebration then became part of the May Day celebrations throughout the world with the May Queen and the Green Man so prominently figuring. Cooper continues in her summary by stating, "the entire ceremony is symbolic of renewed life, sexual union, resurrection and Spring."[261]

Over time, permanent Maypoles were erected in most English villages and cities and the fresh trees were substituted with decorations of flowers and garlands. May Day festivities were often in conflict with the wishes of both Church and State, in Britain, with Henry VIII actually banning them in the 16th century. Riots soon occurred, and fourteen of the men who were arrested were hanged. Another four hundred were a tad luckier, and were pardoned by the king. After the English Civil War and the overthrow of the monarchy, the Puritan government attempted to abolish all forms of "heathen" practices — including the May Day and Maypole festivals. Calling these ancient festivals "heathenish vanity generally abused to superstition and wickedness,"[262] various laws were passed to suppress the events and punish any who would continue them. The permanent Maypoles were destroyed throughout England and Wales. When Charles II regained the throne, the popular May Day festivals and dances once again took place. A 130-foot tall Maypole was placed in the Strand of London, where it proudly remained for another fifty years.[263]

In Sweden and Bohemia, the Maypole was known as the Midsummer-tree and was burned in a great bonfire.[264] The association of fire with May Day is an important one. Frazer notes that in Russian festivals a straw figure known as Kupalo, representative of vegetation, was placed next to the Maypole and passed back and forth over a bonfire.[265] Bonfires were also common throughout Britain, France and Germany. The fires banished evil and illnesses and announced the arrival of life-bringing spring. Fires were lit to "encourage the sun...to shine on through the harvest."[266] Evans recalls a time in the 1950s when over a hundred

260. Cooper, J.C. *An Illustrated Encyclopaedia of Traditional Symbols.* London: Thames and Hudson Ltd. 1978, 104.

261. Ibid.

262. Alexander, Marc. *A Companion to the Folklore, Myth & Customs of Britain.* Gloucestershire: Sutton Publishing Limited 2002, 191.

263. Ibid.

264. Frazer, Sir J.G. *Adonis: A Study in the History of Oriental Religion.* London: Watts & Co 1932, 210.

265. Ibid., 211.

bonfires were blazing on a May Eve in the hills around Donegal.[267] It was common in these festivals for boys and girls to leap over the flames to help ensure the crops would grow and they themselves would be fertile. "It is remembered," wrote Evans, "that 'the oldest woman in the town' would go round the fire three times on her knees, reciting prayers."[268] In doing so, she would ensure a year without illness for the village. This circumambulation around the fire is perhaps one of the oldest rituals in the world. Similar rituals are still performed in this fashion at certain holy wells. Sahi notes, "Circumambulation around the tree in a clockwise fashion was a basic rite of tree worship,"[269] as is the "offering of fire."

May Day was one of four festivals wherein a "holy fire" was kindled each year. The fire was shared with all of the households to light the cooking and heating fires for the next year. Mackenzie tells us "the house fires were extinguished once a year and relit from the sacred flames"[270] that would protect livestock and human beings from injury and evil. The other three festivals are New Year's Day, Midsummer, and Halloween.

In Great Britain, at least, the Maypole and related events have seen a revival, especially after being "recharged" by John Ruskin in the 1890s. In some locations, the Maypole lost its significant role in the celebrations and has been replaced by a human representation garbed in leaves and flowers. Green George and Jack-in-the-Green figures replaced the Maypole and acted out an ancient sacrificial rite, the sacrifice of the spirit of vegetation.

Similar May Day celebrations were also held in the United States, although they disappeared to a great degree in the late 1950s. American folklore though does have several May Day observances — mostly featuring foretelling the future in regard to husbands-to-be. One such piece of lore from Arkansas said that a young girl who looks into a spring before breakfast on May Day "will see, not only her future husband, but also the children she is to have by him."[271] Another

---

266. Evans, op. cit 274.

267. Ibid.

268. Ibid., 275.

269. Sahi, Jyoti. *The Child and the Serpent: Reflections on Popular Indian Symbols*. London: Arkana 1980, 157.

270. Mackenzie, Donald A. *Ancient Man in Britain*. London: Senate 1996, 181 (A reprint of the 1922 edition published by Blackie &Son Ltd., London).

271. Randolph, Vance. *Ozark Magic and Folklore*. New York: Dover Publications Inc. 1964, 186 (A reprint of the 1947 publication, *Ozark Superstitions* published by Columbia University Press).

method was for the girl to skip a flat stone across the spring, the number of skips indicating the number of her future children.

A fairly common beauty treatment in days gone by was to rise early on May Day morning and wash one's face with the dew. Such a practice ensured a perfect complexion throughout the next year. Peasants and royalty alike were eager for this treatment. According to the Radfords, "in 1515...Catherine of Aragon, with twenty-five of her ladies-in-waiting, went into the fields to gather May dew for the preserving of the Queen's complexion."[272] However, the peasants of Slovenia neglected their own complexions and gathered the dew "to wash their cows...to preserve the beasts from 'the charm of witches.'"[273]

May Day festivals then were not just an innocent day of games and bonfires. They were celebrations marking the end of winter, the renewal of life and the efforts of everyone to ensure a prosperous and healthy year to follow. They also recognized the importance of the forests and trees and the spirits that protected and lived within those trees. The Green Man was present in each festival as the May King or Jack-in-the-Green and figuratively laid his life down so that the life of nature would continue.

272. Radford, op. cit 171.
273. Ibid.

PART TWO

THE GREEN MAN

CHAPTER 8. THE ARCHETYPE[274]

Who, what is the Green Man? William Anderson wrote:

> The Green Man signifies irrepressible life....He is an image from the depths of prehistory; he appears and seems to die and then comes again after long forgettings at many periods in the past two thousand years. In his origins, he is much older than our Christian era. In all his appearances he is an image of renewal and rebirth.[275]

The image of the Green Man is that of a foliated head, a face with vines and leaves sprouting from the mouth, eyes and nose, the hair and beard formed, as well, from leaves and twigs. The image may be stern and almost frightening, or a beguiling face peering out of a wealth of vegetation. The Green Man represents the creation of all plant life and its continued renewal. The Green Man is also associated with the ability to make rain and create lush meadows.

Dale Pendell characterized the Green Man as "the projection of the Tree of Life, the life force. He is sap, fertility, semen....He is the Natural Prophet, the Primal Word. He is creative but oddly passive."[276]

Many of the images of the Green Man found throughout the world are not just of leafy heads but are hybrid figures half human and half plant. Human

---

274. This chapter appeared in a modified version in *Essays in Contemporary paganism* by Gary R. Varner. San Jose: Writers Club Press Inc. 2000 & 2002, 105-115.

275. Anderson, William. *The Green Man: The Archetype of Our Oneness With the Earth.* London: Harper Collins 1990, 14.

276. Pendell, Dale. *Pharmako/Poeia: Plant Powers, Poisons and Herbcraft.* San Francisco: Mercury House 1995, 212.

torsos seemingly sprout out of vegetation. Some readers may be surprised to learn that these images are found in cultures from around the world and throughout time. From England and Ireland to Iraq, Bolivia and Thailand, Germany and Colombia, to San Francisco and Manhattan, these ancient pagan symbols can be found on structures ranging from cathedrals and government buildings to apartment rows and the sculptures in lush gardens.

One of the earliest known carvings of the Green Man in Europe is that known as the "Pillar of St. Goar." This 5th century BCE stone carving, found near Pfalzfield, Germany, is not a true "Green Man" foliate head but is more a pro-totype image. While the pillar is ornately decorated with vines and greenery, the head is carved to show the eyebrows "sprouting" into two large flat, broad leaves, with smaller leaves sprouting from the mouth. Artistically speaking, the pillar seems to be a mixture of Celtic and Etruscan influences. Barry Cunliffe, Oxford Professor of European Archaeology, notes that the Pillar of St. Goar is "a four sided pillar....Each of the sides, framed by cabling, bears a stylized human head carving in high relief. The heads wear the so-called 'leaf crowns' — a common motif presumable of religious significance — and appear to be sprouting three-pointed beards. Between the heads and the frames the space is filled with running scrolls and lyre patterns composed of S-shaped motifs."[277] Similar leaf-crowned carved heads have been found near Heidelberg and Holzgerlingen, Germany, also from the 6th to 4th centuries BCE. Cunliffe comments that these German carvings are "a common motif presumably of religious significance"[278] to the ancient Celts. This style was also imported to America in the 1800s, with fine examples still in existence in New York on East 85th Street. A pair of limestone heads resembling a Janus figure (one face looking forward and one backward) with a leaf crown was found in a sanctuary at Roquepertuse, Bouches-du-Rhône, France, that dates to the third or second century BCE. There were many carvings found in this sanctuary, which was probably important to the Celtic "head cult"; several columns with niches for severed human heads were recovered there as well.

However, exquisite Green Man images, many very similar to those of later British origin, have been found around the ancient world and date to a time a few hundred years later. Basford shows many dating from the 1st and 2nd century CE, found in what are now Lebanon, Iraq and other countries, in her landmark book

277. Cunliff, Barry. *The Ancient Celts.* New York: Oxford University Press 1997, 126.
278. Ibid.

The Green Man.[279] Some of the most beautifully carved examples date from 6th century Istanbul. Foliate masks almost identical to those referred to as Green Men in Britain are found on the Temple of the Sun and the triumphal arch of Septimus Severus in Rome and the temple of Bacchus in present-day Iraq.

Nicholas Mann believes that the vegetation spurting from the foliated head represents language and the dark, primitive, and mysterious wisdom of ancient power. Mann wrote, "The abundance of the natural life force made directly available by the archetype, when focused and channeled in the appropriate manner, gushes from the head of the Green Man in inspired, oracular, and poetic outpourings."[280]

Why are so many "pagan" images found on Christian monuments? An interesting theory put forth by Mann is that when ancient forces and knowledge are repressed they will emerge, at times in disguised forms, in places most ironic. In Europe, the Green Man, among the many other ancient pagan images, emerged in Church architecture as decorations on the symbols of religious repression. Mann noted, "It is in the ecclesiastical architecture that the foliate head disgorging vegetation becomes a ubiquitous and finally triumphant motif."[281] Ronald Millar echoes Mann's observation in his book *The Green Man: Companion and Gazetteer*, Millar wrote the Green Man "occurs all over Western Europe, wherever Christianity pertains. Like old enemies, they seem to be mutually attracted, inseparable."[282]

Kathleen Basford notes that the early Green Man images were found on ancient Roman temples dedicated to pagan gods, many of them taken as decorative additions by later Christian monks and priests and incorporated into Christian church architecture. However, the meanings behind many of these images apparently changes over time. The images may have began as representatives of the pagan Bacchic cult and changed to a more demonic appearance in Christian churches. However, some Christian tombs dating to the 5th and 6th centuries were also decorated with these images and other pagan themes (showing a slow progression of the Christian ideology), which indicates that they were not intended to frighten but to reassure. Indeed, many of the older

---

279. Basford, Kathleen. *The Green Man.* Cambridge: D.S. Brewer 1978.

280. Mann, Nicholas R. *His Story: Masculinity in the Post Patriarchal World.* St. Paul: Llewellyn Publications 1995, 152.

281. Ibid. , 143.

282. Millar, Ronald. *The Green Man: Companion and Gazetteer.* East Sussex: S.B. Publications 1997, 44.

images incorporate the horn of plenty as part of the carving, clearly associating these specific images with fertility and prosperity. Basford offers an alternative view of these tomb Green Men images. "A foliate head," she notes, "carved on a font or a tomb could allude to man's fallen and concupiscent nature, or to his brief life on earth — a reminder that 'All greenness comes to a withering.'"[283]

During the sixth century, Bishop Nicetius of Trier took the foliate-mask carvings from nearby ruined Roman temples dedicated to Bacchus and used them in his new cathedral. These Green Man masks were walled up during the 12th century by church authorities evidently embarrassed by the use of pagan symbolism in Christian cathedrals. However, at Chartres Cathedral, according to Schama, "the foliate heads seem to have been chosen by Abbot Thierry with an eye to their suitability for Christian conversion. Thus the Bacchic vine, with bunches of grapes hanging from his mischievous whiskers, served as the pious sign of the eucharist; another head, disgorging acorn-laden oak twigs, alluded to the Druid temple over which the church was said to have been built."[284]

Anderson believed that there are two forms of Green Man, representing two distinct phases. "The Green Man of the oak," he wrote "is the Green Man of the forest while the Green Man of the vine is the Green Man of agriculture."[285] It is this artistic rendering of humankind's development from pastoral nomads into settled farmers that the Green Man symbolizes.

The Green Man has appeared in many guises over the centuries. As George Bridwood wrote, in his introduction to *Symbolism of the East and West*, "even the worship of the tree still survives throughout Christendom in a variety of popular customs, prehistorically established in celebration of the annual revival of vegetation...among them are dancing around the Maypole, and the May mummery of 'Jack in the Green'...the festival of 'Green George,' or 'St. George in the Green.'"[286]

In Ruhla, Holland, it was a tradition every spring, as soon as trees began to bud, to hold the Little Leaf Man festival. Frazer wrote, "The children assemble on a Sunday and go out into the woods, where they would choose one of their playmates to be the Little Leaf Man. They break branches from the trees and twine them about the child till only his shoes peep out from the leafy mantle....Singing and dancing they take him from house to house, asking for gifts

---

283. Basford, op. cit., 21.
284. Schama, Simon. *Landscape and Memory*. New York: Vintage Books 1995, 218.
285. Anderson, op. cit., 86.
286. Bridwood, George. *Symbolism of the East and West*. London: George Redway 1900, xix-xx.

of food...Lastly they sprinkle the Leaf Man with water and feast on the food they have collected."[287]

Vegetation deities were not restricted to the male gender. Myths and legends concerning "Green Women" and female spirits of the Green abound. Swiss folklore contains tales of "green ladies" who, beneath an oak, "are wont to light a fire, and may be heard singing and dancing around it."[288] "Their special proclivity," wrote J. H. Philpot, "being to entice men away, to drag them through brake and brier, and to leave them stripped of their possessions."[289]

The Queen of the May and the Little May Rose are two of the celebrated personages of renewal. Regardless if they are identified as male or female, all of these archetypes are spirits of vegetation, rebirth and renewal. Some of these celebrations of life were carried to America and became known as Arbor Day and May Day. It was common in rural America, up through the 1940s, to dance around the Maypole in a festive marking the coming of spring.

Since 1980, the Beltane Fire Society in Edinburgh holds its annual festival on April 30th to recreate the celebration of summer through the Green Man's courtship with the May Queen and his death as a sacrificial king. The Green Man's union with the May Queen, his death and rebirth are observed to ensure a fertile harvest, new life, and the continuance of the nurturing sun.

Why does the Green Man reappear across the ages and in different parts of the world? Millar wrote, "his rebirth seems to coincide with some major human disaster...."[290] This may be true in the sense that the Green Man seems to reappear in times of stress to the Earth — often caused by humankind. The destruction of entire species of plant and animals and their habitats, the destruction of the rain forests and the ozone layer all have resurrected the need for the Green Man to enter our lives and to re-awaken our ties to Mother Earth. During the Middle Ages, the Green Man seems to have reappeared as the Wild Man and Herne the Hunter — both aggressive forms of the Nature Spirit. These images instilled a sense of fear in people and a recognition that humans were

---

287. Frazer, James G. *The Golden Bough: The Roots of Religion and Folklore, Vol. 1.* New York: Avenel Books 1981, 88 (A reprint of the 1890 two volume edition of *The Golden Bough: A Study in Comparative Religion by Macmillan Company Ltd., London*).

288. Philpot, Mrs. J.H. *The Sacred Tree in Religion and Myth.* Mineola: Dover Publications Inc. 2004, 68 (A reprint of the 1897 edition published by Macmillan and Co. Ltd, New York & London).

289. Ibid.

290. Millar, op. cit., 44.

responsible for the destruction of the wild — and would be held accountable for it. Today, the Green Man is back in more subtle forms. Contemporary images of the Green Man depict him as benign, sometimes smiling — more "friendly" than the terrifying images of the Wild Man and Herne the Hunter. His new images remind us that humans are still part of nature, and that our life depends on our maintaining a life-sustaining environment.

Some people see the Green Man's return to popularity in our age as being part of the interest in "green living" and the popular fantasy writings of Charles de Lint and Robert Holdstock, who incorporate ancient archetypes into contemporary stories.[291] All of these are helpful in reviving our collective consciousness and we regain a link to our past and find meaning in our interactions with the world, both the aspects we can see and explain, and the forces that are beyond our comprehension. The Green Man is the idea of the Lord of the Wild as he continues to watch over the plants and animals of his kingdom. He may be said to be nudging us a bit, appearing in unexpected places at unexpected times to refresh our desire for a healthy green planet. The popularity of contemporarily crafted images of the Green Man is a sign of hope. The "industrial revolution" caused the archetypes to reawaken in people's minds so that we listen more to the primordial wisdom of the Green Man. According to Millar, the voice of the Green Man "is the roar of beech in a gale, the hiss of ash in a high wind, the breathless hush of a winter forest, and the tumult of woodland in spring."[292]

Kathleen Basford, one of the first to research the Green Man image, wrote, "It is tempting to wonder whether the leaf mask also refers to some aspect of the Bacchic cult. In ancient revels held in honor of Dionysos the participants stained their faces with new wine and put on great beards made out of leaves."[293]

Comparisons with Dionysus and Bacchus are commonly made, as they should be — they are the same god. Both are gods of vegetation, but also gods of ecstasy, sensuality and emotion. Today's interpretation of pagan concepts posits the Green Man as representing the true male self, aspects of man that have been repressed since the establishment of Christianity as the "true" religion. This view invites men to see their masculine properties as being a triad of a son, lover and guardian of the Great Mother: a balanced self-image that was lost centuries ago. The Green Man is also an aspect of the Lord of the Wild and, as such, urges us to

291. Matthews, John. *The Quest for the Green Man.* Wheaton: Quest Books 2001, 39.
292. Millar, op. cit., 45.
293. Basford, Kathleen. "Quest for The Green Man," in *Symbols of Power.* H.R. Ellis Davidson, editor. Cambridge: D.S. Brewer Ltd. 1977, 110.

have a deeper connection and understanding with Nature. The symbolism of the Green Man can be part of an awakening of humankind to the innate sense of responsibility that we have to protect ad take care of the Earth.

The Green Man image has changed periodically over time. The medieval ages when the Green Man became a common architectural motif in Britain were a time of dense population when practically all the forest had been destroyed. In a very short span of time, the Green Man image changed from one of pagan fertility and renewal themes to a Christian demon-goblin concept. Basford wrote that the change in the character of the images seems to have occurred in a short, two or three year period during the 10th century:

> The change of character is clearly illustrated in two manuscripts produced either at Reichenau or Trier about the year 980. The first of these was presented to Egbert, Archbishop of Trier in 983. The dedicatory miniature is framed by a border of human masks linked together by an acanthus scroll. The idea is obviously derived from the leaf masks in the Hellenistic "peopled scroll" motif, but the faces are rather goblin like and the foliage sprouts from the mouth and not the cheeks. In the border of the corresponding dedication page of the second manuscript, presented to Egbert two years later, the human masks are replaced by horrific hollow demon masks with snakes and birds coming out of their ears. The scroll is a complex of foliage, birds and beasts, one form growing out of another — even the leaves have become demonic.[294]

Here is one point in time and space when the images underwent an important change to equate nature in the forms of its birds, animals and plants, as evil and adversarial to man.

It is probable, states C.J.P. Cave, that the artisans who created the foliate heads and fantastic animals found in many of Europe's cathedrals copied them from the many illustrated manuscripts extant during the 12th to 15th centuries.[295]

Interestingly enough "Green" animals also appear in many of these images. Basford notes that the cat is "the most common variant of the human mask"[296] although, as will be discussed elsewhere, dragons and other mythical animals also figure into this motif. The cat, in Christian mythology, represents Satan, lust, darkness and laziness, which evidently was the message being imparted in the "Green Cat" carvings. While this image is uncommon outside of religious architecture, I have seen it incorporated in the carved decorations of an 18th-century desk in the United States, which indicates that this motif did survive its

---

294. Basford (1978), op. cit. 12.
295. Cave, C.J.P. *Medieval Carvings in Exeter Cathedral.* London: Penguin Books 1953, 19.
296. Ibid., 13.

origins in Christian churches and its evil characterization. Cat-faced foliate heads are found in St. Mary's Church in Shropshire, dating to the 12th century, as well as in Much Wenlock Priory dating to the 1180s. Lion-faced creatures disgorging vines and leaves appear in Russian and Bulgarian churches dating to that same era. A serpent-like animal disgorging vegetation was also carved on Exeter Cathedral around 1250 CE.

Not all images of the vegetation archetype are male — nor are they all just foliated heads. Human figures, both male and female, are commonly shown rising out of vegetation as if being disgorged by the stalks and leaves themselves, as if being created from their very roots. Anderson compares these half-human, half-plant beings as images of "the observer and guide who appears out of vegetation and who will be a transformation of the message of the Green Man."[297]

The half-human, half-vegetation motif is found universally throughout the world. While most are found in Great Britain and other Celtic countries such as Ireland, France and the Alps region, they are also found in the Southern Hemisphere, Asia, the Mediterranean and the United States. According to William Anderson, the 2nd century CE Romanesque carvings of these hybrid figures "arise from a desire to anthropomorphize vegetation — to draw out the hidden intelligence in plant forms and to give them human forms and faces."[298] This particular motif became very popular during the Renaissance, although it certainly existed long before then, as Anderson noted above.

Philpot notes that ancient Greek legends speak of a race of vine-creatures that grew on one side of a river of wine: "These vines below had a very thick stem, but above bore maidens' bodies of perfect form. Bunches of grapes grew from their finger-tips, and vines leaves and grapes formed their hair....They shrieked aloud with pain when one attempted to pluck their grapes. Two...travellers who surrendered themselves to their embraces could not get free again, but took root and budded forth vine leaves."[299]

The images have also been used in the extreme to illustrate a warning against lust and sin. With the Black Death plague that decimated the European population, artistic depictions changed, and that included changes to the nature of many foliate masks. Researcher Jeremy Harte noted that during the Late Middle Ages "we rarely find a Green Man as wise and venerable as we would like

---

297. Anderson, op. cit., 74.
298. Ibid., 45.
299. Philpot, op. cit., 61.

him. Instead new, horrific visions gain currency, such as tendrils spouting out of eyes."[300]

What was the underlying reason for incorporating such pagan images into church architecture? There are several explanations for this, including using the ancient images as a way to entice those remaining pagans into a more comfortable environment with relevant symbols.

There are other explanations as well. Many of the churches were constructed upon sacred pagan sites, and some churches incorporated many of the reliefs taken from the destroyed and plundered pagan temples into new Christian structures. Additionally, it is likely that most of the stone cutters during the Middle Ages still embraced the folk-beliefs of the past, including pagan traditions, and inevitably incorporated them into their work. Other researchers such as Mercia MacDermott believe that the Green Man image was used simply for its decorative value, with no regard for its underlying meaning. She writes: "There is no evidence of any appreciable survival of paganism in Western Europe at the time when the first known Green Men were created...."[301] I am unsure what "appreciable survival" means, or how one would measure it — especially if carved images are singled out for exclusion from the body of evidence; however, there are many documented instances of pagan ritual and tradition that had been absorbed within the Catholic Church. Paganism certainly was alive during the first few centuries of Christianity's push for dominance when the Green Man carvings were first created.

M.D. Anderson wrote in his study *History and Imagery in British Churches*, "the personification of the spirit of the tree may have lost its pagan associations in the minds of the people at an early stage, or else the origin of the decorative motive to which it probably gave rise was forgotten. So, far from banning it, the Church allowed the foliate mask to become one of the few recurrent themes in the inexhaustible variety of designs...."[302] While many of the leaves that decorate the foliate heads are wild apple and acanthus, Anderson notes, "in the majority of cases it is the oak, the holy tree of the Druids and of many pagan faiths."[303]

---

300. Harte, Jeremy. *The Green Man.* Andover: Pitkin Unichrome Ltd. 2001, 10.
301. MacDermott, Mercia. *Explore Green Men.* Loughborough: Explore Books/Heart of Albion Press 2003, 163.
302. Anderson, M.D. *History and Imagery in British Churches.* London: John Murray Ltd. 1971, 18.
303. Ibid.

The Green Man archetype is obviously alive throughout the world. It is even blossoming in the United States. While not nearly as old or as numerous as the carvings and other depictions of the Green Man found in Europe, his representation in American architecture appears to have flourished from the mid 1800s through the late 1920s. This book will focus on many of the older Green Man images that can still be found in America, in addition to many of the new images of the archetype that are being created today. Most importantly, we will examine the many ties that exist with the ancient myths and carvings that were born in ancient Europe and those that grace the New World.

Janet and Colin Bord wrote in their book *Earth Rites* that the foliated head "is so widespread a theme that no complete list of British carvings has been, or could be, compiled. They are likely to be seen in any church with pre-1500 features." The Bords also wrote that the Green Men images "suggest strongly to us that the vital force responsible for the continuance of all life was being depicted....To look at them is to be reminded of the earth's never-failing energy which year after year ensures that life continues to flourish."[304] The representations of the Green Man are, as Basford noted, both "beautiful and sinister simultaneously. This indeed is what makes him so fascinating."[305] Harte agrees, writing, "There is no single, archetypal meaning to which the Green Men have to conform."[306]

Andrew Rothery advances an interesting theory concerning the classic image of the Green Man as the "disgorger of vegetation." The "most significant aspect of the Green Man," he writes, "is his regular appearance as a disgorger of vegetation from his mouth and sometimes his ears and eyes too. This process can be likened to a masculine form of the birthing process i.e. from the brain instead of the womb."[307] Rothery believes that the Green Man's link with re-birth and renewal is founded in "his ability to communicate and share information" originating in nature as unique images and ideas that are processed through the brain — and expressed later in words. According to Rothery, the Green Man "points to a relationship between our mind or consciousness and the green world of plants and trees — a kind of 'green intelligence' or 'green consciousness.' "[308] As

---

304. Bord, Janet and Colin. *Earth Rites: Fertility Practices in Pre-Industrial Britain*. London: Granada Publishing Ltd. 1982, 87, 90.
305. Basford, op. cit., 116.
306. Harte, op. cit.
307. Rothery, Andrew. "The Science of the Green Man". http://www.ecopsychology.org/ezine/green man.html. August 9, 2004.

Ronald Millar noted, "when we hear him no more, he — and life — will be at an end."[309]

CHAPTER 9. THE GREEN GODS

Over time, the Green Man has become associated with a variety of gods, most all of them also gods of vegetation, the woodlands and renewal-resurrection. Some of these are Osiris, Attis, Adonis, Pan and Dionysus — and, for our present work — the goddess Asherah.

All savior gods, including Jesus, have a common theme. The story of Jesus, states David Leeming, "is a full blossoming...of the dying god myth...The 'pagan' sexual elements are gone, the planted seed and the resurrection of the savior king-god results for his followers not so much in the vegetation of spring (though this is a constant Easter theme in ritual if not in myth) as in a spiritual renewal."[310] The common theme expressed is not only of the renewal of life, but also the renewal of the spirit. Many Christian writers try to show a major difference between the "pagan" gods and Jesus, saying, "although imbued with special powers, they were nevertheless subject to fate. They did, in fact, die."[311] Nevertheless, like Jesus, they were also resurrected, promising a life after death to those who lived their lives in balance. Leeming points out that in the story of Jesus, "ultimately, immortality is celebrated in this story and in its ritual as it is in the other dying-god tales and ceremonies."[312]

Was Jesus another savior-god, a dying king, in a long string of gods promising renewal and resurrection linked intimately with the earth and vegetation? According to Sufi writer Shawkat M. Toorawa, the answer is "yes." Khidr, the Green One (see Chapter Twelve), and Jesus, according to Toorawa, "have a profound connection with vegetation."[313] We may speculate that Paul and the other founders of Christianity manipulated the image of Jesus and the many religions

308. Ibid.

309. Millar, op. cit., 45.

310. Leeming, David Adams. *The World of Myth.* New York: Oxford University Press 1990, 157.

311. Carmichael, Joel. *The Birth of Christianity: Reality and Myth.* New York: Dorset Press 1989, 89.

312. Leeming, op. cit.

313. Toorawa, Shawkat M. "Khidr: The History of a Ubiquitous Master" in *Sufi Selected Article,* Issue Number 30, Published by Khaniqahi Mimatullahi Publications 2000.

of the day to incorporate all of the vital parts into one form that survived the first three centuries, ultimately dominating the Mediterranean world. Christianity, writes Carmichael, "had absorbed and digested all the essential rites, the fertile ideas, metaphors, and symbols with which pagan religions were themselves pullulating."[314]

The most important savior-gods, Adonis, Attis, Osiris, Dionysus, and Jesus met violent and untimely deaths, were "mourned by a loving goddess and annually celebrated by...worshippers."[315]

Osiris: Egyptian God of Vegetation, Death & Rebirth

When we think of the religious beliefs of the ancient Egyptians we normally see in our minds eye a plethora of gods and goddesses in a variety of shapes — both human and human-animal composites, and beasts of strange and frightening demeanor. In reality, there were only two gods that were important to the Egyptian people: Ra, the Sun god, and Osiris, the god of vegetation, death and resurrection. The Egyptians believed that Osiris was, according to Sir Wallis Budge, "of divine origin, that he suffered death and mutilation at the hands of the powers of evil, that after a great struggle with these powers he rose again, that he became henceforth the king of the underworld and the judge of the dead, and that because he had conquered death the righteous also might conquer death."[316] At the birth of Osiris, the Greek writer Plutarch wrote, in the 1st century CE, "a voice was heard, saying, 'The lord of all the earth is born.'"[317] While it is not my intent here to focus on the similarities between the Christian views of God or Jesus to Ra and Osiris, it is very interesting that the ancient Egyptians had similar views of their gods. As Budge noted, "He who was the son of Ra became the equal of his father, and he took his place side by side with him in heaven."[318]

The Egyptians regarded Osiris as a tree spirit — a true god of nature, as the Tree Spirit watched over the crops, made them fertile, and guarded them from all forces of evil and blight until they were able to grow to maturity. In Egyptian myth, the dead Osiris was enclosed in a tree — much as Merlin, thousands of years later in the Arthurian mythos, was encased in one. It was not a coffin,

314. Carmichael op. cit 14.
315. Spence. Lewis. *Ancient Egyptian Myths and Legends.* New York: Dover Publications, Inc. 1990, 71.
316. Budge, Sir Wallis. *Egyptian Religion.* New York: Bell Publishing Company 1959, 61.
317. Ibid., 63.
318. Ibid., 83.

however, as the tree is self-renewing, it survives the death of winter and blossoms once again in greenery in the spring. The tree became an important aspect of Osiris' worship, as it did to the followers of Baldar, Attis and Jesus. Each town and fishing village celebrated Osiris and erected a pillar, representative of the tree, in his honor. Originally, the pillar was simply a tree stripped of its branches but later this pillar became one of the hallmarks of Egyptian architecture. Egyptian inscriptions frequently refer to Osiris as residing in trees and Nut, his mother, is often depicted as a sycamore tree.

Osiris was perhaps the most widely worshipped god of Egypt and was the ultimate nature god. According to Tamra Andrews, Osiris was "a sky god because he maintained cosmic order, an earth god because he guaranteed fecundity of the soil, and a god of waters because his physical resurrection coincided with the annual resurrection of the Nile."[319] Burkert wrote in his book *Ancient Mystery Cults*, "authentic Egyptian tradition has linked Osiris to the Nile, the life-giving water that dwindles away and yet comes back with the flood in summer."[320]

The origin of Osiris is lost in history. Mythology states that Osiris was a human king who became a god. His Egyptian name, as depicted in hieroglyphics, was the "Eye of Ra," but even ancient Egyptian texts were vague at best as to his perceived origin. Osiris is perhaps one of the oldest surviving nature gods of the world. Osiris, in Egyptian art, was colored either black to represent death, or green, like the Green Man, to represent his ties to vegetation.

Osiris, Isis and Horus, their son, were perhaps the first holy family — the first triad of religion. The holy family was significant in their influence on the Greco-Roman mystery religions and may have been significant in Christian mythology.

Even though Osiris was resurrected from the dead, he never really left the land of the dead; instead, he became its ruler. Some scholars believe that this does not constitute true resurrection, as he did not rejoin the land of the living. One may ask, however, if Jesus is said to have risen up to heaven, did he not stay with the dead? Osiris judged the dead, like Jesus. They are more alike than different, in this regard.

---

319.   Andrews, Tamra. *A Dictionary of Nature Myths: Legends of the Earth, Sea, and Sky.* Oxford: Oxford University Press 1998, 146.

320.   Burkert, Walter. *Ancient Mystery Cults.* Cambridge: Harvard University Press 1987, 82.

Osiris was much more than the ruler of the dead, however. He was said to have given humankind the knowledge of agriculture and civilization, symbolizing the creative and fertile forces of nature and the renewing force of life.

Serapis

Serapis is another Egyptian god of fertility, renewal and rebirth. He is actually a composite god, a hybrid of several Greek and Egyptian deities. The Cult of Serapis had existed prior to the Ptolemaic Period but it was during this time that the influences of the Hellenistic deities affected this minor Egyptian cult. Originally a hybrid of Osiris and Apis,[321] Serapis was further transformed by the addition of characteristics of Zeus, Dionysus, Asklepius, Helios and Hades. He was the god of the sun, healing, fertility and the afterlife.

According to Wilkinson, Serapis "was portrayed in anthropomorphic form as a man wearing a Greek-style robe with Greek hairstyle and full beard and usually bearing a tall corn modius or measure on his head."[322] He is also depicted at times wearing ram's horns, as many of the Green Man images do up to the present day.

His main center of worship was in the Serapeum Temple in Alexandria, however evidence of smaller shrines and temples have been found as far away as York, England. A carved head of Serapis has also been found in London. Obviously, like the Green Man, Roman soldiers, traders and pilgrims were responsible for spreading the cult of Serapis throughout the Roman Empire.

Dionysus

Dionysus was a god of the vine, drink and revelry. Rather innocuous items, until you realize how important he was at one time in history. Dionysus, however, also was known for the healing powers obtained by his devotees through their ecstatic rituals. Plato, writing in his *Phaedrus*, noted that these rituals were performed as a cure "for diseases and the greatest sufferings which manifest themselves in certain families, on account of some ancient cause or wrath."[323]

---

321. Apis was the most important of the Egyptian bull deities, born of a virgin cow and the god Ptah. Apis was said to thresh the grain in the afterlife. He was an ancient god, worshipped at least in the 1st Dynasty (2920-2770 BCE).

322. Wilkinson, Richard H. *The Complete Gods and Goddesses of Ancient Egypt*. London: Thames and Hudson 2003, 128.

Dionysus, according to Ely, "was perhaps worshipped in Greece before men had learnt the art of cultivating the vine," not as a vegetation god but as "the powerful creator of the spring."[324] Like Osiris, Dionysus was associated with the life giving water, water that provides renewal and regeneration. It was reported by Euripides that the followers of Dionysus were able to strike the earth with their wands and "at once" draw forth water.[325] Originally, Dionysus was regarded as the curator of nature, the powerful force of the fertility of the earth. In mythology, the Dryads, nymphs who lived in oak trees, were companions of Dionysus. As other gods became more important, he was relegated to being only the god of the vine. "The Dionysian myth, personifying nature's cycle of death and renewed life," wrote O'Grady, "...became a cult with wild and terrifying rites."[326] These rites became so well known that they "became the pattern for later conceptions of witches' Sabbaths."[327]

Many scholars believe that Dionysus and Pan were one and the same, but as people changed and began to view nature differently, Dionysus reflected those changes.

Is Dionysus reflected in those foliate masks that came to be known as Green Men? Most assuredly. Nineteenth-century folklorist J. H. Philpot wrote of an ancient symbol incorporating a tree "dressed as Dionysus." According to Philpot, "...a mask is fastened at the top of the trunk in such a way that the branches appear to grow from the head of the god, and the trunk is clothed with a long garment; a table, or altar, loaded with gifts stands beside it."[328]

Green Man researcher Ronald Millar noted as well that Dionysus was "always depicted with leafy beard and branches growing out of his head, symbolic of his role of god of trees in general."[329] Dionysus' popularity in Britain was probably more pronounced among the Roman occupiers than among the

---

323. Ibid. 19.

324. Ely, Talfourd. *The Gods of Greece and Rome*. Mineola: Dover Publications Inc. 2003, 212. (A reprint of the 1891 edition published by G.P. Putnam's Sons).

325. Ibid., 213.

326. O'Grady, Joan. *The Prince of Darkness: The Devil in History, Religion and the Human Psyche*. New York: Barnes and Noble Books 1989, 45.

327. Ibid.

328. Philpot, Mrs. J. H. *The Sacred Tree in Religion and Myth*. Mineola: Dover Publications Inc. 2004, 31 (A reprint of the 1897 edition published by Macmillan and Co. Ltd, New York & London).

329. Millar, Ronald. *The Green Man Companion and Gazetteer*. East Sussex: S.B. Publications 1997, 11.

common folk. Near Glastonbury, a temple of Dionysus once existed but for the most part the horned god Cernunnos was already too well-established among the Celts to be replaced by this foreign deity. However, the pervasive influence of Dionysus in Celtic-Romano culture cannot be underestimated. The spread of the Green Man motif can be directly tied to the march of the Roman army and, as odd as it may seem, with the spread of the Catholic Church which had included so many of the pagan relics, myths and symbols of the religious traditions that the Church tried to suppress. Pagan survivals were well documented during the 14th century when a priory of monks in Devonshire was discovered to have been worshipping at a statue of Diana in a sacred grove.[330]

The Great God Pan: God of the Pasture and Country Life

Pan, the goat-footed, horned player of the pipes, is much more than the Disney cartoon figure romping through the daisy-covered fields of Greece. To the herdsmen of ancient Greece he was the guardian of the flocks and to the Greek soldiers he was the "All-god." He caused such terror in the hearts of the Persians, enemies of Athens, that his actions are still common in today's languages as causing "panic." It is undoubtedly the image of Pan that the Christians took as their model for their personification of evil — Satan.[331] "It was not surprising that Pan," wrote Joan O'Grady, "the most earthy of all gods, should seem to be the nearest personification of the Prince of Darkness."[332] "As a god of nature," O'Grady continues, "he possessed powers of inspiration and prophecy. But especially he represented sexual desire, the force of destruction and creation. In Christian eyes, he became connected with everything that was evil."[333] When the early Christian Church was struggling to define the image of the force of evil (Satan), Pan's image fit their requirements perfectly. Regardless how future generations viewed Pan, he was, according to Servius, "formed in the likeness of Nature, inasmuch as he had horns to resemble the rays of the sun and the horns of the moon; that his face was ruddy in imitation of the ether; that he wore a spotted fawn-skin resembling the stars in the sky; that his lower limbs were hairy because of trees and wild beasts; that he had feet resembling those of the

---

330. Ash, Steve. "Bacchus and Isis in Britain: Romano-British Mysteries and their descendants. A cultural, social, spiritual, political and psychological multiple perspective." www.angelfire.com/aka/Forum/Bl ONE.htm July 11, 2004
331. Ely, op. cit.
332. O'Grady, op. cit 45.
333. Ibid.

goat to show the stability of the earth; that his pipe had seven reeds in accordance with the harmony of Heaven...that his pastoral staff bore a crook in reference to the year which curves back on itself; and, finally, that he was the God of all Nature."[334]

Caption: *Pan with other satyrs. A detail from an illustration by 19th-century artist, Edward Corbould. From a 19th-century edition of* The Faerie Queen *by Edmund Spenser, published in London by George Routledge and Sons.*

Pan was the God and protector of the wild creatures; he was also, under a different name, one of the eight ancient and original gods of Egypt — the earliest gods of the myriad to come. "Herodotus," writes Lewis Spence, "states that the god Pan and another goat-like deity were worshipped with a wealth of symbolic display and gorgeous rite as gods of generation and fecundity."[335]

---

334. Porteous, Alexander. *The Lore of the Forest: Myths and Legends*. London: Senate 1996, 117-118.

335. Spence, op. cit, 288.

As noted, the god Pan had origins in ancient history and was almost a universal deity. Perhaps the oldest god of the Greeks, Pan, king of the Arcadian satyrs, was also a consort to the Great Goddess, like the other young male sacrificial nature gods. To the Greeks the supreme Egyptian god, Amon-Ra, was the Egyptian representation of Pan. The Greeks even referred to Amon-Ra's Egyptian holy city as "Panopolis" — the City of Pan. Barbara Walker theorizes, "Pan's legend began with the Hindu fertility god Pancika, consort of one of the primal Mother-goddesses, many-breasted Hariti..."[336] While the god's origins are uncertain, he was perhaps the most important male deity in the ancient world. Pan was so important that his image became the Christian representation of Satan from the earliest days of the church. This image of the devil still survives into contemporary culture. This technique of "demonizing" the gods of a people so that another religion may be substituted has been used for thousands of years.

Pan had begun as a god of the wood; in fact, one of his titles was "Lord of the Woods." Over time, his attributes grew to such an extent that he became the supreme god representing the entire universe. His sanctuaries have been found from Asia to Israel, from Egypt to Greece, and from Italy, where he was known as "Faunus," into Russia. If Walker is correct his influence, if not his origin, was also felt in the Indian subcontinent.

It may be that the Christians created Satan out of the image of Pan because Pan also gave freedom, freedom of choice and sexual freedom. Many patriarchal religions condemn these freedoms even today. His love of dance and music was well known. It was said that you did not approach his altars or temples quietly but with song and dance.

Pan was also closely associated with water. Many of his temples have been found in grottos with natural springs or along rivers. One such place is known as the Golden Spring. Located along the Hyllikos River near Argolis, the Golden Spring "gushes down onto a ledge in the hillside shaded by plane trees, about forty or fifty feet above the level of the river, into which it then steeply pours. There is a stone bridge," writes Harry Brewster, "in one single piece leading over the stream a few yards away from the spring, known as the Devil's Bridge....A few paces from the spring and forming part of the site are several small niches carved in the porous face of the overhanging rock, which must have contained figurines and offerings."[337]

---

336. Walker, Barbara G. *The Women's Encyclopedia of Myths and Secrets.* Edison: Castle Books 1996, 765.

The bridge was named after the Devil due to an imprint in the stone of a cloven hoof. Brewster noted, "I cannot help feeling that if a live cloven foot ever left this imprint, it was Pan's rather than the Devil's, for the place is saturated with an atmosphere of Pan far removed from the world of the Christian Devil."[338]

The belief in the divinity of Pan cannot be doubted. An early tradition of the Christian faith states that Pan died at the same exact moment that Jesus was crucified. While this may have heralded the end of paganism as an ancient religion, it also implies that Pan and Jesus were on the same level and that the world mourned for both. When it was announced that the great god Pan was dead, "there arose...a great cry of grief not from one person but of many, mingled with exclamations of dismay."[339]

That Pan was the god of nature is obvious, but he was also much more. Pan was known as the god of healing and would come to those in need through dreams, advising the ill and the tormented on how to be cured.

Over time, other horned gods came to be recognized, especially in Europe. To the Celts, Cernunnos was champion of the wild while Herne the Hunter became much feared during the Middle Age. While Pan was a half-man, half-goat figure, Cernunnos was usually depicted as a man with long hair and beard and with the horns of a stag. Herne is similarly described, but Herne was said to have a darker purpose, riding at night with baying dogs in search of souls. Cernunnos was undoubtedly the Celtic Pan and Herne was Pan evolving into a devilish figure as a response to Church teachings during the Middle Ages.

Many of the gods of nature, however, have been depicted in story and image as hunters of the souls of men. Gwynn ap Nudd is one. As Lord of the Dead and the Underworld, he is also lord of the wild. Such tales undoubtedly date back to a pre-agricultural age when hunting, shamanism and animal totems were important aspects of religious beliefs. As agriculture became more widespread, these tales changed and while the gods of vegetation became more pronounced, they did not completely replace the older gods. "As the shaman's proto-myth is that of the hunt and its magic quarry," writes Ward Rutherford, "the agriculturalist's tells of the young god, personification of both the sun and

337. Brewster, Harry. *The River Gods of Greece: Myths and Mountain Waters in the Hellenic World.* London: I.B. Tauris Publishers 1997, 65.

338. Ibid.

339. Plutarch. De defectu oraculorum, 419b-e.

dormant seed, who dies, descends to the Underworld, to be found and brought back to life..." [340]

The image of Cernunnos on the famous 2nd century BCE Gundestrup Cauldron (Denmark) is almost identical to that of the Lord of Animals, Pashupati, from Mohenjo Daro in India, raising questions of a common source or a commonality of culture, of the stages of human civilization, giving expression to the same consciousness.

The Green Man is another variation of the Great God Pan. Dione Fortune, the founder of the Western Esoteric Tradition wrote in her novel, *The Goat Foot God:* "I suppose you know who the Green Man is? He's Pan...He's Jack-In-The-Green, the wood-spirit — the fairy man who runs after the maidens on midsummer eve — What's that but Pan?...Pan is the same everywhere. He's elemental force." [341]

The worship of Pan, according to writer Charles G. Leland, continued at least into the 19th century in Italy among the peasant populations. "Whoever would beg a favour of him," wrote Leland, "must go in the evening, and kneel to him in a field by the light of the moon...." [342]

Adonis, Attis and Tammuz: Gods of Vegetation

Adonis, the beautiful young god of Greek mythology, is rarely recognized today as a far older god whose origin perhaps rests with the Sumerians. Simply put, his name means "lord" or "my lord." Adonis is one of the young sacrificed gods of vegetation. He died on or near the date of the Spring Equinox, close to the date that Christians have chosen for Easter. He was born of the Divine Father and the virgin Myrrha, who had turned into a tree. Like Jesus, Adonis was born in Bethlehem. Frazer, citing Jerome, wrote, "he tells us that Bethlehem, the traditional birthplace of the Lord, was shaded by a grove of that still older Syrian Lord, Adonis, and that where the infant Jesus had wept, the lover of Venus was bewailed....If Adonis was indeed...the spirit of the corn, [343] a more suitable name for his dwelling-place could hardly be found than Bethlehem, 'the house of Bread.'" [344] After his death, Adonis was buried in a cave — much like Jesus and

---

340. Rutherford, Ward. *Celtic Lore: The history of the Druids and their timeless traditions.* London: Thorsons/Aquarian 1993, 47.

341. Fortune, Dione. *The Goat Foot God.* York Beach: Samuel Wiser, Inc. 1980, 165. A reprint of the 1936 edition.

342. Leland, Charles G. *Etruscan Roman Remains.* Blaine: Phoenix Publishing Inc., n/d , 46. A reprint of the 1892 edition.

other savior gods. His birth and death are symbolic of the spring growth of vegetation and the decay of vegetation in the winter — but the promise of his death is the rebirth, the renewal of that very same vegetation.

Adonis has been known by other names as well; and he was remembered well into the early 20th century. Frazer wrote in 1932, "we are able to show that the gardens of Adonis...are still planted, first, by a primitive race at their sowing season, and, second, by European peasants at midsummer. Amongst the Oraons and Mundas of Begnal, when the time comes for planting...a party of young people of both sexes go to the forest and cut a young Karma-tree...Bearing it in triumph they return, dancing, singing, and beating drums, and plant it in the middle of the village dancing-ground. A sacrifice is offered to the tree: the next morning the youth of both sexes, linked arm-in-arm, dance in a great circle round the Karma-tree, which is decked with strips of coloured cloth...bracelets and necklets of plaited straw."[345] The Greeks knew him as Adonis but his older form was Tammuz, as the Babylonians knew him. Tammuz was the consort of Ishtar (also known as Inanna in Summeria) — the Great Goddess, the Earth Mother. Ishtar was the embodiment of the fertile powers of nature.

"Every year," wrote Frazer, "Tammuz was believed to die, passing away from the cheerful earth to the gloomy subterranean world."[346] Inanna/Ishtar journeyed to the world of the dead to bring Tammuz back, for in his absence "love ceased to operate: men and beast alike forgot to reproduce their kinds: all life was threatened with extinction."[347] The queen of the underworld allowed Inanna to sprinkle Tammuz with the Water of Life so that the two could return to the upper world to revive nature. He was able to spend half the year above the land of the dead in the sunlight and the world rejoiced. The other half he resided in the land of the dead and the world mourned and died as well in the cold, dark months. Among the Babylonians, Tammuz was called "Healer," "Savior," "Heavenly" and "Good Shepherd"; among the Sumerians he was known as "my Christ."[348] He was also known as the corn-spirit.

---

343. It should be noted that "corn" in reference to European tradition refers to any cereal crop, such as wheat, barley, oats, etc. True corn is a crop originating in the Americas and is more properly called "maize".

344. Frazer, Sir. J. G. *Adonis: A Study in the History of Oriental Religion.* London: Watts & Co. 1932, 217.

345. Ibid., 200.

346. Ibid., 6.

347. Frazer, Sir James. *The Golden Bough: A Study in Magic and Religion.* Hertfordshire: Wordsworth Editions Ltd., 1993, 326.

The popularity of Adonis/Tammuz was such that the entire Mediterranean world mourned his death on an annual basis. In fact, his wide spread popularity is inferred in the one reference of Tammuz in the Old Testament. In Ezekiel 8:14, Ezekiel states: "then he brought me to the door of the gate of the Lord's house which was toward the north; and, behold, there sat women weeping for Tammuz." This passage indicates that even Hebrew women held Tammuz/Adonis as a divine being and his death was mourned at the gate of the temple of Jerusalem. Frazier indicates that the Jewish priesthood, at one time, continued the far older rites of the Canaanites and actually portrayed the living Adonis in ritual — thus the weeping women were participants of the cultural and religious traditions.[349] Women observed the death of Tammuz and his resurrection each year at harvest; identifying with Inanna and her loss they would lament with cries of "Tammuz, Tammuz, Tammuz the all-great is dead." They would then plant "gardens, pots of flowers and herbs that — like the god and the vegetation he represented — swiftly bloom, wither, and die."[350]

Mackenzie believed that the myth of Tammuz "was fully developed at the dawn of history."[351] This is probably correct, as gods such as Attis, Dionysus and Osiris are simply other personifications of Tammuz and, while they are ancient deities, their stories come well after those of Tammuz.

Attis dies beneath a pine tree or, in other myths, he is crucified on such a tree. Bandages used in the attempt to stop his bleeding were hung from the branches. This has probably continued in the present day tradition of Christmas tree decorations as well as the hanging of "clooties" (strips of cloth) from trees near holy wells. Historian Franz Cumont wrote of the annual rituals surrounding Attis:

> The ceremonies proper began with the equinox. A pine was felled and transferred to the temple of the Palatine by a brotherhood that owed to this function its name of "tree-bearers." Wrapped like a corpse in woolen bands and garlands of violets, this pine represented Attis dead. This god was originally only the spirit of the plants, and the honors given to the "March-tree" in front of the imperial palace perpetuated a very ancient agrarian rite of the Phrygian peasants.[352]

---

348. Ibid., 971.
349. Ibid., 12.
350. Hallam, Elizabeth. *Gods and Goddesses.* New York: Macmillan 1996, 77.
351. Mackenzie, Donald A. *Crete & Pre-Hellenic Myths and Legends.* London: Senate 1995, 164 (A reprint of the 1917 publication published by The Gresham Publishing Company, London).
352. Cumont, Franz. *Oriental Religions in Roman paganism.* New York: Dover Publications 1956, 56 (A reprint of the 1911 edition published by C. Routledge & Sons, Ltd.).

Wherever traditions existed of the young male sacrificial god, they are always linked to the Great Goddess. As Cumont noted concerning the annual rituals mourning the death of Attis, "then followed a mysterious vigil during which the mystic was supposed to be united as a new Attis with the great goddess."[353] These traditions existed at least in 3000 BCE Egypt, ancient Sumer, Babylon, Canaan and Anatolia. As noted, the annual lamentations and mourning for Tammuz were practiced even outside the gates of the Temple of Jerusalem and in pre-Christian Rome where, Merlin Stone notes, the rituals performed there "possibly...influencing the symbolism and rituals of early Christianity."[354]

John Barleycorn and Jack-In-The-Green

Barley is perhaps the oldest cereal product grown on earth. Because of its lengthy history and usage, it also figured as an important religious symbol, depicted as an agricultural deity. As the oldest cultivated vegetation in the world, it was responsible for the settlement of humans in the first villages, cities and kingdoms. The importance of both cannot be overestimated.

The Jack-in-the-Green figure reportedly dates back at least to medieval days. A village youth, on May Day, parades through town dressed in a costume that totally encases him in a wicker framework entwined in ribbons, flowers and ivy. Jack-in-the-Green is, according to Frazer, "the spirit of vegetation."[355] The figure of Jack is closely associated with the chimney sweep. First described in print in 1801, the Jack/sweep connection would seem to be rather vague. Matthews writes that the sweeps are associated with good luck and the otherworld as well as with ancient sacrificial burnings.[356] Like the Green Man, Jack-in-the-Green also has his detractors. Trubshaw states that he was purely 18th century entertainment, devised to pry the halfpence from the hands of the revelers.[357]

Trubshaw's argument is that the need for sweeps did not arise until the early 18th century, so the Jack-in-the-Green figure most likely did not predate that age. Trubshaw bases his conclusion on a small work called *The Jack-in-the-Green: A May Day Custom*, written by Roy Judge and published in 1979. However, a

---

353. Ibid., 57.
354. Stone, Merlin. *When God Was A Woman*. New York: Barnes & Noble Books 1993, 20.
355. Frazer, Sir James. *The Golden Bough: A Study in Magic and Religion*. Hertfordshire: Wordsworth Editions LTD. 1993, 129.
356. Matthews, John. *The Quest for the Green Man*. Wheaton: Quest Books 2001, 74.
357. Trubshaw, Bob. "Paganism in British Folk Customs" in *At the Edge*, No. 3 1996.

large amount of historical references document long-established traditions around the world featuring similar Jack figures and festivals. It is unlikely that a regional bit of entertainment would have been so widely dispersed at that time in the world without some ancient causation. Early 20th-century writers attribute Jack-in-the-Green to an ancient pagan survival. W.Y. Evans-Wentz wrote in 1911: "...in many parts of modern England, the Jack-in-the-Green, a man entirely hidden in a covering of green foliage who dances through the streets on May Day, may be another example of a very ancient tree (or else agriculture) cult of Celtic origin."[358]

John Barleycorn is often mentioned as another name for Jack-in-the-Green; however, there appear to be enough differences to discuss him separately. John Barleycorn is the personification of barley, a true vegetation god. Unlike the Green Man, there are many examples of female corn spirits such as the Corn Queen, Corn Mother, and the Corn-maiden. All of theses spirits die at the hands of man, only to be reborn once again. John Barleycorn is another sacrificed king who returns in the following year to bring abundance and fertility to the crops. An 18th-century English folksong, written by Robert Burns (1759-1796), sums up the story of John Barleycorn:

> There was three kings into the east,
> Three kings both great and high,
> And they hae sworn a solemn oath
> John Barleycorn should die.
>
> They took a plough and plough'd him down,
> Put clods upon his head,
> And they hae sworn a solemn oath
> John Barleycorn was dead.
>
> But the cheerful Spring came kindly on,
> And show'rs began to fall;
> John Barleycorn got up again,
> And sore surpris'd them all.

---

358. Evans-Wentz, W.Y. *The Fairy-Faith in Celtic Countries.* Mineola: Dover Publications, Inc. 2002, 435. A reprint of the 1911 edition published by Henry Frowde, London.

Festivals which are still held year after year indicate that the survival of these ancient figures is deeply rooted in our collective minds and souls. It was common in the United States until the middle of the 20th century to find Maypole festivals held, at least in schools, on Arbor Day. This event has recently been revived in some areas of the United States, including the small town of Toledo, Oregon. Other festivals include The Burry Man festival. This custom, which used to occur annually on August 3, is now held the second Friday in August in South Queensferry, Scotland. An individual, who must have been born in the town, is elected annually by the Ferry Fair Committee to be the Burry Man.

The chosen man is covered in a layer of flannel, which is then covered in burrs from the burdock. Today the Burry Man walks seven miles from one boundary of Queensferry to the other and it is a time of strange celebration. People dress is disguises, perambulate around and collect money. While he resembles the Green Man he is, like Green Jack (Jack-in-the-Green) acting as a scapegoat. During his walk, he is absorbing the sins of the population that stick to him like the burrs. "Another theory," according to Brian Day, "connects him with an old ceremony to ensure good herring catches, as a similar figure existed in the north-eastern Scottish ports of Buckie and Fraserburgh. As the burrs stick to the netting, so may fish, and he may have been called upon to remove the ill luck following poor catches."[359] Similar rituals have also been identified in France and Germany.

All of these mythic figures may represent the collective memory of a time when individuals were selected as sacrificial kings to be, after being treated as royalty for a year, decapitated to ensure the survival and prosperity of the group. One festival still held annually is that of the Garland King, who was a central figure in the springtime celebrations throughout Britain and Northern and Central Europe. Held in Castleton, the festival appears to be a mixture of older May Day celebrations, which had been banned by the Puritans during the Reformation, and to mark the return of Charles II after his defeat at the Battle of Worcester in 1651. The date of the original Garland festival is unknown but the first printed reference to it was in 1749.

Held on May 29 as "Oak-apple Day," the event has only survived into modern days in Cornwall. Many believe that the Garland festival contains ancient survivals of tree worship and of the sacrificial king.[360] The Garland King,

---

359. Day, Brian. *Chronicle of Celtic Folk Customs*. London: Hamlyn 2000, 136.

dressed head to foot in garlands of flowers and greenery, is symbolically decapitated at the end of a long day of parades, dancing, and visits to the pubs. "The remainder of the garland," writes Fran and Geoff Doel, "is hoisted up the church tower and displayed for a week on one of the pinnacles of the tower, all the other pinnacles being decorated with sycamore."[361] The day ends with young girls dancing around the maypole.

Hun Hunahpu and the Gods of Mesoamerica

Thus far, we have only examined the vegetation gods of Europe but there are far more. Indigenous peoples in both North and South America worshipped maize gods and many of the images carved of deities in Mesoamerica depict them with maize, vines and other plant life sprouting from their heads, just like the Green Man in the northern latitudes. "Representations of the maize plant," wrote archaeologist Robert Rands, "are commonly depicted as growing from the head of the Maize God, while with equal certainty water lilies emerge from the heads of other beings."[362] Mayan carvings actually depict three types of Maize God. One from the Early Classic Period is of a young man with maize leaves sprouting from the top of his head, the "Tonsured Maize God" is associated with one of the Hero Twins and the other, referred to as the "Foliated Maize God has a solitary ear of maize springing from his head." Hun Hunahpu is one of these important vegetation gods.

According to the *Popol Vuh*, the most important sacred book still surviving of the Quiché Maya, Hun Hunahpu was the father of the Hero Twins, Xbalanque and Hunahpu and the Monkey Scribe twins Hun Batz and Hun Chuen. Hun Hunahpu and his brother, Vucab Hunahpu are defeated in a battle with the gods of death and are sacrificed in the underworld. In Mayan art the head of Hun Hunahpu is depicted resting in a tree that suddenly and magically is transformed into a gourd. The spittle from the head impregnates the maiden Xquic and she gives birth to the Hero Twins, who eventually defeat the gods of death and resurrect Hun Hunahpu and his brother. In some Mayan carvings, Hun Hunahpu's head is shown in a cacao tree and is depicted as turning into a cacao pod. Like

---

360. Ibid.
361. Doel, Fran & Geoff. *The Green Man in Britain.* Gloucestershire: Tempus Publishing Ltd. 2001, 103.
362. Rands, Robert L. "Some Manifestations of Water in Mesoamerican Art" in *Anthropological Papers Numbers 43-48, Smithsonian Institution Bureau of American Ethnology Bulletin 157.* Washington: US Government Printing Office 1955, 331-332.

the other Green Gods, Hun Hunahpu is a vegetation god. Miller and Taube note, "in many vessel scenes he emerges from the earth, much like planted corn sprouting out of the soil."[363] There are several things in this bit of lore that are also common among lore of the Green Man and myths of other cultures. Hun Hunahpu is decapitated, he is resurrected from the underworld, and he is intimately associated with trees and vegetation. He is a symbol of the renewal of life after death.

The corn or maize god is widespread throughout Native American and Mesoamerican culture. The importance of maize can hardly be overstated. "Man and maize and world," wrote Hartley Alexander, "are ultimately one inter-substantiate being."[364] To American Indians, the ear of corn and all of its kernels represented all the people of the earth and all of the things in the universe. Like corn, other forms of cereal crops were sacred to the Egyptians, Greeks, and Romans and to the Sumero-Semitic peoples who attributed cereal crops to Tammuz. Foremost, corn/cereal represents fertility and abundance.

It was not Tammuz however whom American Indians worshiped as the deity of corn. It was Mother Corn. Mother Corn was the source of wisdom and intelligence, the provider of sustenance, life-giver and guardian as well as the guide of humankind. Like the other Lords of the Wild, Mother Corn not only offered protection to man but to all animals, no less so. However, she also provides game for the hunt. Among the Arikara, it was said, "Father Heaven placed Mother Corn in authority over all things on this Earth. She moves between men and the Spirit Above from whom all things come."[365]

The Pueblo Indians, the Hopi and Navajo are famous for their Corn Dances but the Delaware also honor the Maize Mother with festival. According to lore "some childish abuse of the maize once provoked her [Maize Mother's] wrath, and she sent down a terrible sickness."[366] To appease the Maize Mother a nocturnal doll dance is performed, "in which the maize mother herself, in the form of a corn doll,[367] is fed with flesh and hominy and honoured in twelve dances, one

---

363.   Miller, Mary and Karl Taube. *An Illustrated Dictionary of the Gods and Symbols of Ancient Mexico and the Maya*. New York: Thames and Hudson 1993, 98.

364.   Alexander, Hartley Burr. *The World's Rim: Great Mysteries of the North American Indians*. Mineola: Dover Publications Inc., 1999, 78 (A reprint of the 1953 edition published by the University of Nebraska Press).

365.   Ibid., 31.

366.   Krickeberg, Walter & et al. *Pre-Columbian American Religions*. New York: Holt, Rinehart and Winston History of Religion Series 1969, 167.

for each month."[368] As part of the ceremony large figures in the form of the Maize Mother and of a bear are baked from maize flower. These are tossed crosswise between two rows of participants, who then take pieces of the figures home with them.

It is interesting to note that corn has a long association with marriage in other parts of the world, such as Great Britain. Thompson says, "the wedding or bride's cake is a survival of the symbolic corn-ears originally worn by the bride."[369] Thompson also says that in "later times" the cakes were scattered over the heads of the newly married couple after their return from church. It can be assumed that the corn cakes continued to preserve the sacredness of the act of marriage and associated fertility.

The Peruvian Indians also represented the Corn Mother in doll form. The doll, made from corn ears and leaves, was dressed in full female garb. The Peruvians believed that the doll "had the power of producing and giving birth to much maize."[370]

The Peruvian dolls were kept for a year but they were asked periodically how they felt, and if the doll indicated that it was becoming weak it would be burned and another made to take its place. In this way, the Maize Mother also became a sacrificial god, as were the male gods of vegetation in other parts of the world.

In Lakota belief, an ear of corn is much more. In the Hunka ceremony, it is used for "giving a particular relationship to two persons" — much as corn was used in wedding ceremonies in Britain in the 19th century. However, in this ceremony the relationship established is like father and son or brother and sister. The shaman secretly selects the ear of corn and he "subdues its...potency by his

---

367. Similar corn dolls used by the Delaware were also commonly made in Europe in the 19th century. Frazer wrote that in Perthshire "the last handful of corn is cut by the youngest girl...and is made into the rude form of a female doll, clad in paper dress, and checked with ribbons. It is called the Maiden, and is kept in the farmhouse, generally above the chimney,...sometimes till the Maiden of the next year is brought in." (The Golden Bough: The Roots of Religion and Folklore. New York: Avenel Books 1981, 345).

368. Krickeberg, op. cit.

369. Thompson, C.J.S. *The Hand of Destiny: Everyday Folklore and Superstitions.* London: Senate 1995, 61 (A reprint of the 1932 edition published by Rider & Company, London).

370. Frazer, op. cit. 351.

mystic powers and...compels it to do his will."[371] This ear of corn symbolizes the Great God — the Earth.

Corn Woman, also in Lakota tradition, acts as a guardian and facilitator of the spirit world. Corn Woman, called *Irriaku*, "maintains the connection between the non-human supernaturals and the tribe." [372] Irriaku is also "the heart of the people" and she appears in every tribal ceremony as a perfect ear of corn. According to Paula Gunn Allen who is not only a teacher of Native American studies but a Sioux Indian herself, "without the presence of her power, no ceremony can produce the power it is designed to create or release."[373]

Like other gods of the forest and vegetation, Corn Woman is the most important link between the spirit world and the world of humankind.

In the folklore of the Popoluca Indians of Veracruz, Mexico, it is a small boy who is recognized as the "Man of Crops." In the myth, the boy asked his father to kill him, saying that he did not want to live anymore but that he would be born again in the form of crops. "I am the one who is going to give food to all mankind, I am he who sprouts at the knees."[374] The Man of Crops is also prominent in Aztec, Tepecano and Tarascan mythology where, after he is buried, corn and tobacco grows from his grave. In contemporary Quiché mythology, crops spill from the body of Jesus immediately following his crucifixion. In these examples, it can be seen that the savior god is universally linked to vegetation with the sprouting of plants from the body of the fallen god.

Asherah

Until now, we have primarily focused on the male gods of vegetation. For one reason this is because only the male gods are universally known as sacrificial gods that must die for the sins of the world and are then reborn — mimicking the annual death and rebirth of nature. While we will continue to acknowledge the ties of trees and vegetation with goddesses, there is truly only one that needs

371. Walker, James R. *Lakota Belief and Ritual.* Lincoln: University of Nebraska Press 1991, 217.

372. Allen, Paula Gunn. *The Sacred Hoop: Recovering the Feminine in American Indian Traditions.* Boston: Beacon Press 1986, 17.

373. Ibid.

374. Bierhorst, John. *The Mythology of Mexico and Central America.* New York: William Morrow and Company Inc. 1990, 68.

to have some in-depth discussion. That one is Asherah. To the ancient Canaanites, it was Asherah who provided the continuation of all life.

Known by the names Astarte, Aphrodite, Isis, Hathor and Ishtar, in other parts of the world, Asherah, meaning "grove," was the Semitic name for the Great Goddess. She was also referred to as the Tree of Life and the Queen of Heaven. Asherah was foremost a Babylonian-Canaanite Goddess who, at one time, was also worshipped by the Hebrews as their chief deity. It was probably Solomon who introduced her to the Hebrews around 1000 BCE and installed her in the Temple of Jerusalem.[375] A tree or carved wooden pillar was erected in every temple to represent her. "It was a conventionalized or stylized tree," wrote Monica Sjöö, "perceived as she, and planted therefore at all altars and holy places. This *asherah* represented the Goddess as Urikittu, the green one, the Neolithic mother-daughter of all vegetation."[376] Asherah was worshipped from the Neolithic and Bronze Ages through the Early Iron Age as evidenced by plaques, amulets and the hundreds of figurines recovered in most every excavation undertaken in Palestine.[377]

The wooden posts, referred to as *asherah*, not only stood by the altars but also by the stone megaliths that were erected in the sanctuaries where the traditional religious rites were performed. These asherah not only represented the Goddess, but her spirit was believed to inhabit them as well. Asherah was so important to the Hebrews that her asherah pillars were prominently placed in the Temple of Jerusalem. Some researchers, such as Merlin Stone, believe that the asherah "were actually fig trees, the sycamore fig, the tree that was in Egypt considered to be the 'Body of the Goddess on Earth'."[378]

The Hebrews predominately worshipped Asherah from the earliest date of their occupation of Canaan until the destruction of Jerusalem almost 600 years later. The male god Yahweh was only superficially considered, and principally as a consort of Asherah. It was only by force that the monotheistic patriarchal priesthood replaced Asherah.[379] The monotheists slaughtered entire towns and the Bible provides evidence of the forces involved. In Deuteronomy 12:2, Yahweh

---

375. Patai, Raphael. *The Hebrew Goddess.* New York: Avon Books 1978, 23.
376. Sjöö, Monica & Barbara Mor. *The Great Cosmic Mother: Rediscovering the Religion of the Earth.* New York: Harper Collins 1991, 269.
377. James, E. O. *The Cult of the Mother-Goddess.* New York: Barnes & Noble Books 1994, 69.
378. Stone, op. cit 175.
379. Patai, op. cit 16.

is said to command the priests thusly: "You shall surely destroy all the places where the nations who you shall dispossess served their gods, upon the high mountains and upon the hills and under every green tree you shall tear down their pillars and burn their asherim with fire." According to James, the popular following of Asherah was so great, even after the butchery, that the standing of the patriarchal Yahweh was compromised: "Such was the strength of the Canaanite cult [of Asherah] that Yahweh from being a desert god was transformed virtually into a vegetation deity."[380]

The Green Man represents the collective history and meaning of these various gods, the most important of which always seem to end up manifesting as vegetation gods that represent, among other things, the link between humankind, the Earth, and all of life and creation.

CHAPTER 10. THE ORIGINS OF THE GREEN MAN

The Green Man image found in the cathedrals, churches and other public buildings of Europe predates Christianity by a thousand years. As noted in the previous chapter, he is found in Osiris in Egypt, Dionysus in Greece, Bacchus in Rome, John Barleycorn in England and the Maize Mother in Native America. The Green Man has also been associated with Robin Hood, St. George, and the Wild Men of Britain. Ultimately, the Green Man is the representative of the gods of vegetation, of life's renewal — of the power of male fertility and female life giving.

Noted scholar Ronald Hutton claims that the Green Man images are a product of the 12th century Renaissance based upon Christian metaphors, which "drew upon ancient ideas and images."[381] In fact, Mr. Hutton is probably correct to the extent that the image became fashionable during the Middle Ages as a metaphor of sin and excess. However, and I must underscore this *however*, the origin and popularity of the figure as a representative of vegetation, fertility and life is an ancient one based in pre-Christian lore. Many ancient Green Man artistic types have been found. Basford noted that the foliate head "originated in Roman art during the second half of the first century AD."[382] The more formal development of the leaf mask occurred in the second century. The European

---

380. James, op. cit 79

381. Hutton, Ronald. *The pagan Religions of the Ancient British Isles: Their Nature and Legacy.* Oxford: Blackwell Publishers Ltd. 1991, 316.

Green Man foliate mask may have originated in Roman art but older varieties are also found in Iraq, Bulgaria, Belgium, Cyprus, Turkey, France, Scotland, India, Indonesia, Norway, Italy, Sicily, the Middle East and Africa. Some examples of classic Green Man images include one from 138 CE (Baalbeck, Lebanon) and 150 CE (El Djem, Tunisia). These may trace their origins to Roman incursions.

Other independently derived Green Man images also exist in pre-Columbian Mexico and Pacific island areas. As Clive Hicks noted, "it is improbable that these are connected with Europe, so they can be seen as demonstrating a deep psychological association with the natural world inherent in the human mentality."[383]

While it is an open question whether the Green Man that is featured on so many church roof bosses was or was not specifically commissioned by the Church during the Middle Ages, what is more significant is the place that the Green Man has taken in cultural developments since that time, the continued rising popularity of his image, and his emergence in American architecture during the 18th, 19th and early 20th centuries.

Bill Yenne, in his book *Gothic Gargoyles*, wrote: "Out of...pagan beliefs came the notion that matter, mind, and spirit return to a primordial unity with God and the universe...Nature was a comfortable fit with theology....This pagan undercurrent was reflected in the art of the period more strongly than we generally realize."[384] Yenne goes on to say that the prevalence of the Green Man artistic renditions found in the various churches of Europe "is an example of the Church making itself relevant by designing its liturgy around that which was part of an established belief system."[385] In this case, a belief system rooted in ancient traditions and beliefs.

It may be surmised that the Green Man's identity, as well as that of the other gods of vegetation, grew from the close relationship that people had with nature and with plants, in particular, in the past. In ancient Greece and Rome, the root cutter, *herbas dividere*, developed an extensive knowledge of plants and their medicinal and spiritual uses. Whether to take plants at night or during the day, how and where they should be taken, as well as the ritual preparation to be

---

382. Basford, K.H. "The Quest for the Green Man," in *Symbols of Power*, edited by H.R.E. Davidson. Cambridge: D.S. Brewer Ltd. 1977, 103.

383. Hicks, Clive. *The Green Man: A Field Guide*. Helhoughton: COMPASSbooks 2000, 69.

384. Yenne, Bill. *Gothic Gargoyles*. New York: Barnes & Noble Books 2000, 20.

385. Ibid., 47.

performed before the act, were all-important considerations in the root cutter's life.

Richard Gordon mentions, "very often the plants that were of particular interest to root-cutters were those which possessed some striking natural feature, such as the glaring red 'eyes' of the open seed of the peony, or the stately spike of Celsia...or which were anomalous within the structure of rules through which these practitioners approached the natural world."[386] Recognizing the inherent "intelligence" of nature, and plants in particular, these root cutters carefully established a characteristic for each plant, which, in time, became a personality.

It may not be possible to assign a *date of birth* for the Green Man or, for that matter, a *place of birth*. Cassandra Eason implies that the Green Man and the associated festivals are directly linked to the Gypsy populations in Southern and Eastern Europe.[387] According to historian Christopher R. Fee, "the concept of the Green Man is hardly limited to Celtic culture; we can find similar concepts in folklore from around the world, from the sexual agricultural rites of pre-Classical Greece to the sacrifice of the Corn King of the Aztecs."[388] According to Fee, the Green Man in every culture and time shares certain fundamental attributes. These attributes are vegetation, vegetation deities, fertility and fertility rites, and an annual sacrifice or ritual death.[389] The fact that the Green Man is associated with powers of rain making and the growth of lush meadows indicates that his origin is a very old one.

There is some indication that the Green Men of Britain may have evolved from the various Roman and Mesopotamian "medusa" masks, which were common in the ancient world. The depictions of the Roman god Oceanus, or those of Sulis, are certainly very similar to the foliate head of the Green Man.

The similarity to the classic-featured Green Man is unmistakable. Basford writes, "The Bath medusa has...been compared with the frowning Okeanos (or Oceanus) mask...from Mildenhall. The Mildenhall Okeanos has a beard of sea

---

386. Gordon, Richard. "Imagining Greek and Roman Magic," in *Witchcraft and Magic in Europe: Ancient Greece and Rome*, edited by Bengt Ankarloo and Stuart Clark. Philadelphia: University of Pennsylvania Press 1999, 183.

387. Eason, Cassandra. *The Handbook of Ancient Wisdom*. New York: Sterling Publishing Co. 1997, 249.

388. Fee, Christopher R. and David A. Leeming. *Gods, Heroes, & Kings: The Battle for Mythic Britain*. Oxford: Oxford University Press 2001, 199.

389. Ibid.

The Bath "Medusa"

weed or acanthus...The penetrating, baleful glare...is a persistent though not invariable characteristic of the antique leaf masks. It must be recognized as a 'family trait,' and it was inherited by many of the medieval Green Men."[390]

The Green Man foliate masks that grace our churches and old secular buildings may be remnants of pagan processional masks that were common through the eighth century CE as part of annual Kalends celebrations held in honor of the ancient gods. Historian Ramsay MacMullen wrote of these "masked parades": "In the west in this and later periods the participants dressed up in masks representing Saturn also, along with Jupiter, Hercules, Diana, and, evidently, Cernunnos, favorite deer-headed deity among Celtic populations...Masks had been long familiar in religious parades in Rome and elsewhere..."[391]

---

390. Basford, (1977) op. cit, 104.

391. MacMullen, Ramsay. *Christianity & paganism in the Fourth to Eighth Centuries*. New Haven: Yale University Press 1997, 37.

The Green Man is found throughout world mythology and tradition from Osiris in Egypt, who is represented in many Egyptian temples by coffins filled with Nile mud and grass, to the Green Wolf of Normandy. The Green Wolf is represented by a man dressed in green that is ceremonially pursued, caught and, in pretense, flung into a raging fire.

The Green Man is certainly not restricted to the Celtic world and his motif and myth can be found around the world. The fact that it is most often the image of the Green Man's head that is found carved upon buildings in so many locations, according to medievalist Christopher Fee, shows that his tradition "overtly equates the head with the phallus, and the decapitation of a sacrificial victim with vegetative fertility and sexual fecundity."[392]

Gods of Vegetation

The Green Man almost certainly originated in the worship of Pan, the Great God, the universal god of nature. Like Pan, the Green Man is both playful and fearsome. *Panic* is a word derived from Pan and the fear that he could cause to those who threatened the life of the forests and valleys where he ruled.

While the majority of Green Man, or foliate head, carvings do appear during the Middle Ages,[393] the earliest European example found to date is the famous Pillar of St. Goar from Pfalzfeld, Germany. As noted previously, this carving is dated to the 5th century BCE and is a blend of Etruscan and Celtic influences.

Along with Pan, Dionysus, the Greek god of wine, was another manifestation of the Green Man. Not only was Dionysus a god of wine, he was also a god of vegetation with ivy, flowers, pine and fig trees sacred to him. Greek historian Walter F. Otto noted that while Dionysus "is called 'a god of vegetation'...it is obvious that he was known to reveal himself not in the plant world, as such, but in the life of certain specific plants, among which the vine is incomparably the most important."[394] We see that in the majority of Green Man representations the vine is also predominately the most important — emerging from the mouth

---

392. Fee, op. cit, 201.

393. It is certainly plausible that earlier works of art depicting Green Men were destroyed over the centuries either accidentally or intentionally. Thus far, however, few have been found.

394. Otto, Walter F. *Dionysus: Myth and Cult.* Trans. by Robert B. Palmer. Bloomington: Indiana University Press 1965, 49-50.

for the most part in what some believe represents language and the mysterious knowledge and wisdom of ancient power.[395]

The cult of Dionysus was well established in the Greek culture by the second millennium and may have come from Phrygia, which, interestingly, was the home of Mithra. Dionysus was the corn-spirit, like other gods of vegetation including Attis, Adonis, Geb and Osiris. He was also depicted in the form of the goat, like Pan, and the bull, like Apis. Dionysus was also a tree-god among other shapes, including a lion, bear, water, fire, snake and panther. He was a master of shape shifting.

Like Pan and his ability to cause *panic*, or feelings of madness, Dionysus is well known for the state of ecstatic madness he caused during rites often referred to as "orgiastic." The nature of Dionysus is one of both bliss and horror, creative wonder and savage destruction. Dionysus is known as the "mad god"; in this, he is seen as reflecting the true nature of the universe. He is associated with prophetic powers. It is almost as if the violent rituals, celebrated almost entirely by women, were a turning away from the civilized nature that humankind had supposedly undertaken — an act of rebellion perhaps or an acknowledgment of the yin/yang aspects of nature. Otto wrote, "He brought the primeval world along with him. This is the reason why his onslaught stripped mortals of all of their conventions, of everything that made them 'civilized,' and hurled them into life which is intoxicated by death at those moments when it glows with its greatest vitality, when it loves, procreates, gives birth, and celebrates the rites of spring."[396]

The death of the vegetation god is an almost universal part played out in the themes associated with his or her worship. Dionysus himself was ritually torn apart by some of his female followers, called "man renders," in an annual sacrifice. His reawakening in the spring, promising the renewal of life and procreation, was anxiously awaited. It is this same promise that other savior gods have provided to their followers, including Osiris, Mithra and Jesus.

God-sacrifice was also the theme of the Mayan gods Xochipilli and Xochiquetzal. Also known as the "Flower Prince," Xochipilli was a god of excess, as was Dionysus. He was recognized for his regenerative powers and creative energies. A maize god, Xochipilli was sacrificed during the growing season. His

395. Mann, Nicholas R. *His Story: Masculinity in the Post Patriarchal World*. St. Paul: Llewellyn Publications 1995, 152.
396. Otto, op. cit., 141.

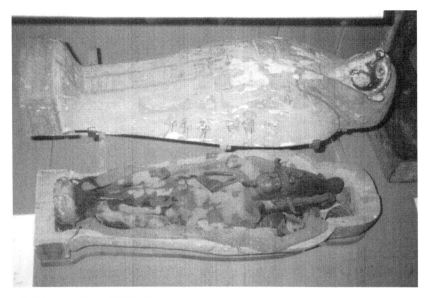

The Mummy of Osiris-British Museum

counterpart was Xochiquetzal, the "Flower Quetzal." She represented female sexual power, flowers and pleasure — and excess. She, like Xochipilli, also patronized creative energy and was sacrificed as a symbolic washing away of her people's sins. A carving of one such sacrificial figure at the Chichen-Itza Ball Court in Yucatan depicts a decapitated figure with vegetation sprouting from the severed neck.

Aztec vegetation gods included Tlaloque, Xipe Totec and Tlaloc. All of these were also gods of rain — obviously important in the connection with germinating seeds. This link is acknowledged by the importance played by the vegetation gods among the many Meso-American deities. It is common to see artistic renderings of maize gods in a foliated manner similar to the Green Man carvings in Europe. Maize sprouting from the heads of these gods and goddesses is a common feature among the Olmec vegetation deities. The emergence of these foliated representations in Olmec culture began around 1200 BCE.

The underlying symbolism to all of the Green Man-vegetation god myths is resurrection. "Resurrection" in this light means the pattern of creation and the renewal of life, the demise of crops followed by a renewal of life and greenness once again.

Sir James Frazer wrote, "in some parts of Bavaria...the festival of St. John's Fire usually lasted for fourteen days, ending on the second Sunday after Midsummer Day. On this last day the bonfire was left in charge of the children, while the older people retired to a wood. Here they encased a young fellow in leaves and twigs, who, thus disguised, went to the fire, scattered it, and trod it out. All the people present fled at the sight of him."[397] A certain mixture of pagan and Christian tradition can be seen in the St. John's Fire celebrations with the old Beltane fires and a hint of human sacrifices in evidence.

The widespread vegetation cults attest to the probability that the Green Man, in all of his guises, originated at the beginning of the agricultural age at least 7,000 years BCE. The symbolism inherent in the Green Man is a reflection of the archetypal lore of life-death-rebirth, the endless cycle seen so easily in vegetation.

Researcher Katy Jordan noted that the Green Man "certainly originated as a pagan woodland deity, but he was gradually taken over in the popular iconography of the Romanesque church. By the 13th century, he had become an image of the sin of *luxuria* (concupiscence or lust), his basic animal nature symbolised by the rampant and lush growth pouring from him."[398] Basford takes this a bit further, stating that the Green Man "represents the darkness of unredeemed nature as opposed to the shimmering light of Christian revelation."[399] It is probably this message that the Christian church wished to promote in the Middle Ages rather than the pagan message of life and renewal here on earth.

While this interpretation may have been common among the religious instructors of the day, Thirlie Grundy has developed an opposite interpretation for many of the Green Man images of that time. She notes, in her book *The Green Man of Carlisle Cathedral*, that many of the carvings show a Green Man actually breathing — inhaling and exhaling. The Green Man is a tree god, a *living* tree god. Grundy's explanation is that the Green Man was brought to England, or in this case specifically to Carlisle Cathedral, by medieval carvers who gave the carvings the characteristics of "a life-giving weather-god who breathed..."[400] His breathing was an attempt at cleansing the unclean medieval air. As will be seen

397. Frazer, Sir James. *The Golden Bough: A Study in Magic and Religion.* Hertfordshire: Wordsworth Editions 1993, 653.

398. Jordan, Katy. *The Haunted Landscape: Folklore, ghosts & legends of Wiltshire.* Bradford on Avon: Ex Libris Press 2000, 50.

399. Basford, Kathleen. *The Green Man.* Cambridge: D.S. Brewer 1978, 20.

400. Grundy, Thirlie. *The Green Man of Carlisle Cathedral.* Carlisle: The Studio 1998, 14.

later, many of the Green Man images carved in the 19th and 20th centuries in North America were also given this characteristic. The vegetation creeping from the Green Man's mouth was actually being *breathed into*, to give the vines life. It is this quality that defines nature and ultimately defines the Green Man. Hartley Alexander wrote: "Perhaps the most perfect image for nature is 'breath' — which can be wind, or soul, or breath of creation, or breath of life..."[401]

There are other views concerning the origins of the Green Man motif. Mercia MacDermott believes that the Green Man originated in India in the third century BCE in the form of the *makara*. The makara was a mythical creature combining the features of the crocodile, elephant and dolphin that "was believed to disgorge wonderful things, among them the 'Cosmic Tree' or 'Wish-fulfilling Tree', usually depicted as a kind of vine or tendril derived from the sacred lotus plant...."[402] Her argument is not persuasive, however, but only indicates that motifs analogous to the Green Man were universally created around the same time in many parts of the ancient world. The only "sure thing" we know is that the image was important throughout time and reappears off and on as an expression of art, imagination or religious thought. MacDermott does deviate somewhat from her statements that the Green Man was a meaningless piece of decoration with a further piece of clarification:

> Our journey of exploration has inexorably led us to the conclusion, that, in Christian Europe, the foliate head is primarily a decorative element, adapted from several more ancient sources and employed, as and when required, to convey a wide range of messages.[403]

Perhaps the largest and yet most ignored Green Man is in the guise of the Long Man of Wilmington. The Long Man is a 240-feet-long figure of a man carved from the chalk on Windover Hill in Wilmington, England. He is ancient. Part of the ground near his left shoulder is comprised of a Neolithic long barrow and Bronze Age bowl barrows (burial mounds). Researcher Paul Newman believes that the origins of this giant "are essentially Celtic, like those of the Cerne Giant, and relate to the cult of Lugh or Lugus, in which the principles of light and fertility are yoked to meditation and balanced judgment."[404]

401. Alexander, Hartley Burr. *The World's Rim: Great Mysteries of the North American Indian.* Mineola: Dover Publications, Inc. 1999, 100.

402. MacDermott, Mercia. *Explore Green Men.* Loughborough: Explore Books/Heart of Albion Press 2003, 170.

403. Ibid., 193.

404. Newman, Paul. *Lost Gods of Albion: The Chalk Hill-Figures of Britain.* Gloucestershire: Wrens Park Publishing 2000, 150.

Contemporary Druid leader Philip Carr-Gomm believes that this giant figure is "actually a Green Man....[H]e was a god who appeared on the hillside only under certain conditions. Up until the nineteenth century, he was often known as the Green Man of Wilmington.

"Covered in grass, the Green God would appear only at early morning or late evening on certain days when there was sufficient sun at the right angle."[405]

Because this ancient and mysterious figure has been altered so many times over the years none of us may ever know his true origins or meaning. I doubt, however, if the Long Man would be disappointed to learn that he is considered simultaneously a Celtic figure of light and fertility as well as a representative of the Green Man: the Green Man who has become, at least since the Middle Ages, synonymous with life and rebirth.

CHAPTER 11. ST. GEORGE: CHRISTIAN DRAGON SLAYER OR PAGAN GREEN MAN?

The gods of the Old and New World include a number of characters with various powers, secrets and origins. India has several thousand individual gods and goddesses which rule the minutest aspect of life — from the rains and the flow of the water to the operation of machinery to luck and fertility. Western culture has for the most part reduced this number down to one — but one with thousands of personalities, purposes and origins. The two cultures are not that different from each other in this regard. Is the animist, who thanks a god or spirit for helping him survive another day, very different from the American high school or college football player who stops after a touchdown, kneels on the playing field, and thanks God for the point, or from musicians who accept awards but give God credit for their talent and success?

My point in saying this is that followers of all sorts of religions tend to relate to their deities in the same way. It used to be the practice to cajole and even threaten the gods to ensure delivery of the desired outcome or event. The gods people worship today have evolved directly from those worshiped by our ancient ancestors thousands and thousands of years ago.

And what, for example, is St. George, really? He certainly is not considered a god. However, he does figure prominently in Christian mythology as the slayer of the demon-dragon and the protector of the faith from pagan ideology. A

405. Carr-Gomm, Philip. *The Druid Way.* Shaftesbury: Element Books Limited 1993, 85.

simple answer is that St. George was created in the 4th century CE, as were most of the early Catholic saints, from a pagan origin. Estonian folklorist Mall Hiiemäe wrote of St. George:

> Perhaps the richness of the tradition accumulated on St. George's Day should rather be viewed in the light of the fact that the Greek form Georgius means a ploughman, a cultivator of land. And when trying to divine the ancient predecessor of the holiday, one should better consider such tradition that is connected with spring-time vegetation as well as the concentration of special customs on certain pre-Christian dates to mark the awakening of nature and the arrival of spring.[406]

St. George's Day has been celebrated all over Europe and Britain, figuring prominently in the various rituals of spring. St. George has also been called Green George — the spirit of spring — throughout that part of the world. Barbara Walker directly links Green George, or St. George, to the Green Man. She says, "His image was common in old church carvings, a human head surrounded by leaves or looking out of a tree trunk."[407]

The importance of St. George in Eastern European countries should not be missed. Russian proverbs such as *"George will bring spring"* and *"There is no spring without George"* are common, as are similar ones in other Slavic countries. Finnish sayings of *"St. George comes with his fish basket"* alternate with others that indicate that he brings grasses. What George is, is fertility. He is the fertility of green plants, fish, game and people. He is directly associated with the ability of people to survive and to provide for themselves. This is nowhere more evident than in France, where statues of St. George were carried through the cherry orchards of Anjou to ensure a good crop.

East European lore also states that the earth of winter is poisonous and cannot be sat or walked upon before St. George's Day. It is on St. George's Day that the earth is reborn and is once again alive and pure.[408] Frazer tells us "amongst the Slavs of Carinthia, on St. George's Day...the young people deck with flowers and garlands a tree which has been felled on the eve of the festival. The tree is then carried in procession, accompanied with music and joyful acclamations, the chief figure in the procession being the Green George...."[409] Other

---

406. Hiiemäe, Mall. "Some Possible Origins of St. George's Day Customs and Beliefs" in *Folklore*, Vol. 1, June 1996, published by the Institute of Estonian Languages, Tartu.

407. Walker, Barbara G. *The Women's Encyclopedia of Myths and Secrets*. Edison: Castle Books 1996, 339.

408. Hiiemäe, op. cit.

409. Frazer, Sir James. *The Golden Bough: A Study in Magic and Religion*. Hertfordshire: Wordsworth Editions Ltd. 1993, 126.

rituals of St. George's Day include, in the Ukraine, the blessing of crops where, after a benediction is given by a priest, couples would lie down in the fields and roll over the newly sprouted shoots. In Southern Slavonia, childless women used to hang a chemise on a fruitful tree on St. George's Eve, hoping that a "creature" would sleep in it overnight or at least tread through it. The next morning the woman would put the chemise on once again, in the hopes that her desires for a child would be fulfilled in the next few months.[410]

In the 19th and early 20th centuries, women hoping to become pregnant sought out shrines of St. George. "In Syria," wrote Frazer, "it is still believed that even dead saints can beget children on barren women, who accordingly resort to their shrines in order to obtain the wish of their hearts....But the saint who enjoys the highest reputation in this respect is St. George. He reveals himself at his shrines which are scattered all over the country."[411]

In England St. George is an important part of the annual Mummers Play. This event, normally held around Christmas, Easter or All Souls Night[412] has been part of the local landscape since the 14th century or earlier. George Long in his important book published in the early 20th century, *The Folklore Calendar*, said this old folk drama "has been continuously carried on every Christmas since the time of the Crusades,"[413] and that it obviously contains "traces of prehistoric paganism." Mummers plays are, according to Long, "the *only* survival of the pre-Reformation folk drama."[414] Christmas, Easter and All Souls Night are important dates to examine. Obviously, Christmas is the Christian celebration of the birth of Jesus, but it basically coincides with the birth date of many other Savior Gods including Attis, Adonis, Dionysus, Osiris and the Syrian Baal, and marks the winter solstice.

Easter is named for Eostre or Ostara — Goddess of Spring and the celebration of the rebirth of vegetation. It too has a dual nature, for Christians view Easter as the rising of Jesus from the dead and a promise of rebirth and new life.

---

410. Ibid. 120.
411. Frazer, Sir. J. G. *Adonis: A Study in the History of Oriental Religion.* London: Watts & Company 1932, 60.
412. O'Hanlon, Maggie. *Customs & Traditions in Britain.* Hampshire: Pitkin Unichrome 2000, 9.
413. Long, George. *The Folklore Calendar.* London: Senate 1996, 217. A reprint of the 1930 edition published by Philip Allan, London.
414. Ibid., 219.

All Souls Night is, of course, Halloween, the pagan New Year. The origin for these Mummers plays, according to John Matthews, probably date from a pre-Christian society dominated by male-oriented rituals.[415] The Morris Dance, which figures prominently in the Mummers plays, "grew out of folk-memories of older, ritual acts," says Matthews, "preserved in this way against the encroachment of Christianity."[416]

The Mummer Plays have been popular folk celebrations for at least 300 years and probably far longer, and the Sword Dances are folk festivals that occur around Christmas and are known for the green leafed "Wilde Mann" and other green festooned figures such as the Burry Man who are an integral part of the celebrations. As with all folkways, the play has changed over time and it is now a two-part event. The first part of the play is known as the "Hero Combat" and the second is the "Sword Dance." "The Mummers plays recorded over the past 300 years,"[417] wrote Fran and Geoff Doel, "have largely been intended for performance at the Christmas period and so have the Sword Dance Plays of the northeast of England…The swords of the dancers link into a magical symbol…They pretend to draw the swords together to decapitate…the victim symbolically dying and reviving."[418]

The death and revival theme of the event is directly related to the rebirth and renewal of life afforded in the spring. The many bits of folklore from around the world associated with St. George's Day give credence that this was, at one time, a very significant event celebrated in many cultures in the ages preceding Christianity. Ronald Hutton notes that the Mummers' Plays have been recorded in 824 different English communities, and while the "earliest definite one dates from the 1730s…the centerpiece of the action, a combat between champions in which one is killed and then revived, is an enactment of a theme so common and widespread that it must be archaic."[419]

415. Matthews, John. *The Quest for the Green Man.* Wheaton: Quest Books 2001, 124.

416. Matthews, John. *Robin Hood: Green Lord of the Wildwood.* Glastonbury: Gothic Image Publications 1993, 117.

417. While the Doels refer to the plays "recorded over the past 300 years," in reality, the plays date to a much earlier time. Historically the plays have been observed and recorded for over 800 years.

418. Doel, Fran and Geoff. *The Green Man in Britain.* Gloucestershire: Tempus Publishing Ltd. 2001, 81.

419. Hutton, Ronald. *The pagan Religions of the Ancient British Isles: Their Nature and Legacy.* Oxford: Blackwell Publishers Ltd. 1993, 328.

Janet and Colin Bord link the appearance of St. George in the Mummers' Plays with the Green Man. "The theme [of the Mummers] is generally the same," they wrote, "as in the Green Man or Green George ceremony of May Day, that is, of death and rebirth of nature... These mummers' plays had their origins in the same pagan times as the Green Man rituals when human sacrifice was part of the annual round of life, and in mankind's attempt to regain the favour of the gods who seemed to have deserted them."[420]

The ancient origin of the Day is indicated by the many Estonian customs associated with it. According to Hiiemäe, "more than one tenth of the reports concerning St. George's Day customs in Estonia have something to do with snakes." One would think that the image of George slaying the dragon would render snakes as the counterpart of evil. However, it is to the contrary in Estonian lore. The snakes, according to Hiiemäe, are "used in repelling and preventive magic to help the cattle thrive and people fare well and also to cure people's diseases..."[421] It would appear that snakes are not indicative of evil but of good — as long as the snake used in the ritual was killed before St. George's Day.

Various other traditional rituals of Estonia and Eastern Europe have played some part in the creation of St. George's Day. Hiiemäe notes, "Interesting reports come from North-East Estonia where the cattle-magic practiced on St. George's Day has merged with some traits of a women's holiday dating back to the tribal era."[422] Other pagan holidays/festivals that have merged with St. George's Day include Ploughing Day and the Shedding of Yellow Leaves celebration. The festival day of the pagan god Pergrubius,[423] god of flowers and all plants, falls on April 23' which is the church calendar day for St. George.

Even though St. George continues to be an important folk-hero, appearing throughout the Old World in various festivals to mark important dates, the Church began to refer to him as "the imaginary saint" because he "was so shamelessly involved in fertility rites."[424]

---

420. Bord, Janet and Colin. *Mysterious Britain: Ancient Secrets of Britain and Ireland.* London: Thorsons 1995, 270.

421. Hiiemäe, op. cit.

422. Ibid.

423. Pergrubius was worshipped in several East European countries. In Poland, the cult of Pergrubius was absorbed into the Catholic church's "St. George's Flower Month" festival, dedicated to St. Florian.

424. Walker, op. cit

Another more direct link to the Green Man image is circumstantial. In some Bulgarian icons of St. George, he is shown with a "Medusa head" on his breastplate — however, the "Medusa" is in reality a face with two vine tendrils coiled on either side. Whatever George's true origins are, it cannot be denied that he is intricately linked to nature's resurrection every spring and the abundance of plant and animal life that results. He is part of the daily life and ritual of many peoples around the world that view him as the bringer of fertility and the continuation of life on earth. He is, in this way, the Green Man.

CHAPTER 12. THE GREEN MAN IN MYTH

When we hear the word "mythology," we think of stories, fables, and fairy tales. Nevertheless, myth is not make-believe. Myth is based on true events and real people — somewhat exaggerated over time, true — but not *fairy tales.* Mircea Eliade defined "myth" as "'living' in the sense that it supplies models for human behavior and, by that very fact, gives meaning and value to life."[425] It was only with the predominance of Christian thinking that myth came to mean "fiction" and "illusion," and worse, as "falsehood." Eliade noted that myth came "to denote 'what cannot really exist'" in our contemporary society.[426] The mythology of the Green Man is a living mythology. The "meaning and value" it gives to our lives is fluid and continues to unfold and evolve for us.

The story of Gawain and the Green Knight, which is really a poem, was written in the 14th century — a time when many of the foliate heads were being carved on the cathedrals of Europe. Since the time of Gawain and the Green Knight, a variety of myths and legends of a more contemporary setting have originated. Some of these legends (some that can be defined as "urban legends") have appeared in the later part of the 20th century — at a time when the foliate head has again become "popular," occurring in mainstream society via jewelry, wall plaques, statuary and garden decorations. In this chapter, we will look at a few of the older as well as more recent legends of the Green Man. Before we enter the realm of myth and legend, let us consider the importance of *green.* Is the color itself important in our study? Does the color alone symbolize the underlying meaning of the Green Man?

425. Eliade, Mircea. *Myth and Reality.* New York: Harper Torchbooks 1963, 2.
426. Ibid., 1.

The Significance of Green

Green has been known for untold ages as the color of the fairy. Green was so universally recognized as the color of the fairy that many in Scotland refused to wear it as to do so would be to invite the anger of the fairy folk. "Greenies" and "greencoaties" were common euphemisms used in Britain for the fairy. The Green Man as the woodland deity is obviously closely associated with the forest fairy-folk. Green was a color shunned by many as being associated with evil fairies and witches. But why green? Green is associated with nature, with ripening life and with fertility, paganism and the supernatural — things that the Church could not control. Perhaps more importantly, green symbolized not only enchantment but also divine beings. Green is also a sacred color of many religious traditions. David Catherine wrote, "Much like Sufism, which associates the colour green to a realization of Wholeness/God, Tibetan culture sees the colour green as a container for all other colours."[427]

During the formation of Christianity, nature was seen to exist for the pleasure and consumption of man. Man was regarded as supreme over nature. That nature should exist, as an entity unto itself, with powers beyond those of man, was a thought that put fear into many. Later, uncontrolled nature came to be seen as evil and anything associated with nature was seen in a similar way. At one time, "by imitative magic," wrote Barbara G. Walker, "wearing green was supposed to encourage Mother Earth to clothe herself in the green of abundant crops."[428] But green, which represented the power and fertile life of nature, slowly came to be associated with pagans, whom the Christian church considered their enemy; and the enemy is necessarily portrayed as evil, bent on the torment of humanity. Thus, green was eventually associated with the dead, witches and sexual promiscuity. Thus fairies, who were considered mischievous entities of the underworld, part of the Old Race which inhabited many parts of the world prior to man's arrival, became, if not outright evil, close relatives of evil. Green became, over time, associated with bad luck. This is well illustrated by 19th century writer Patrick Graham. Graham wrote of the fairy, which he called "the men of peace," that inhabited the Scottish Highlands: "The men of

---

427. Catherine, David. "The Green Fingerprint: Exploring a critical signature in the quest for the authentic Self". Unpublished paper copyright 2004 by Ufudu Medicinal Arts, South Africa, 8.

428. Walker, Barbara G. *The Women's Encyclopedia of Myths and Secrets.* Edison: Castle Books 1983, 355.

peace, are believed to be always dressed in green; and are supposed to take offence, when any of mortal race presume to wear their favourite colour. The celebrated Viscount of Dundee, was dressed in green, when he commanded at the Battle of Killicrankie; and to this circumstance the Highlanders ascribe the disastrous event of that day. It is still accounted peculiarly ominous to any person of *his name,* to assume this sacred colour."[429] Graham also notes that the color green "was probably the appropriate dress of the Druidical Order...in the Battle with the Fingallians, which, according to tradition, finally decided the fortunes of the Druidical Order, their Standard was Green."[430] The Radfords note, "the colour green is so allied throughout Europe with luck and protection from the tree spirits, that it is...strange to find it regarded at all as an unlucky colour."[431] This bit of propaganda concerning the unluckiness of green was so entrenched in the minds of Europeans in the early 20th century that one "cultured man" was heard to say that the pre-World War I troubles in England all stemmed from the introduction of a green halfpenny stamp.[432] Popular superstition about the color green was abundant in the 19th century. The December 28, 1850 issue of the English periodical *Notes and Queries* reported, "In a parish adjoining Dartmoor is a green fairy ring of considerable size, within which a black hen and chickens are occasionally seen at nightfall." Black hens were often considered as embodiments of evil.

To wear green was, simply put, asking for trouble. To wear green was to put oneself in the power of the Fairy.

Green as a color was more fundamentally associated, however, with the symbolism of new growth and it is through this association which the fairy have their link. However, it is that fundamental link that humankind has lost over the centuries and that has been reestablished through the Green Man, the Wild Huntsman and the other legends and images of the super-natural. Green is, according to the Doels, an "extension to the natural world — and the supernatural in both its 'Otherworld' and afterlife elements." [433]

---

429. Graham, Patrick. *Sketches Descriptive of the Picturesque Scenery of Perthshire.* Edinburgh 1810, 107-108.

430. Ibid.

431. Radford, Edwin and Mona A. *Encyclopaedia of Superstitions.* New York: The Philosophical Library 1949, 137.

432. Ibid.

433. Doel, Fran & Geoff. *The Green Man in Britain.* Gloucestershire: Tempus Publishing Ltd. 2001, 25.

Brian Stone, a Reader in English Literature at the Open University, succinctly defines the importance of the color of green in regard to the Green Knight: "It surprises me that no critic has picked up one very important medieval theological reference to green as the colour of truth...evergreen...is the colour assigned to ever-living and eternal truth."[434]

It may be of interest however to note that the Celtic word for "green," *glas*, can also mean "gray," or as Professor Norma Goodrich noted, the "Green Man" may portray the "gray man of death or winter" in some aspects.[435]

Green was also the color of the Egyptian gods Geb and Osiris — in both cases symbolizing their roles as gods of fertility and vegetation. Geb was the Egyptian Earth god, consort of the sky goddess Nut, and father of Osiris. Osiris brought the knowledge of agriculture and civilization to the people as did the green god Quetzalcoatl — the Mayan-Aztec god of learning, civilization, agriculture, the calendar and resurrection. The characteristics of Osiris and Quetzalcoatl are practically identical. Quetzalcoatl is also depicted as a great green snake.

Sir Gawain and the Green Knight

One of the best-known stories of the 14th century is that of the nephew of King Arthur, Sir Gawain. Written during the peak of popularity of the Green Man stone and woodcarvings, the author of this famous poem remains unknown but is believed to have been a resident of northwestern England. The poet is also a sophisticated and talented alliterative stylist, adept in the style that was common during the older Anglo-Saxon period. The poetic story, as summarized by Richard Cavendish:

> At Camelot on New Year's Day there rode into Arthur's hall a gigantic green warrior on a towering horse, holding a holly branch in one hand and an immense battle-axe in the other. His skin was green, his hair was green, and even his horse was green. He had come to play what he called a game. Any champion who dared could strike him one blow with the axe, on condition that a year later the champion submits to a return blow from the Green Knight. Gawain took up the challenge and struck the Green Knight a blow that cut his head clean off his shoulders and sent it rolling to the floor. The Green Knight calmly picked up his head by the hair and turned the face towards Gawain. The eyelids opened and the mouth spoke, telling Gawain to meet him for the return blow a year later at the Green Chapel.[436]

---

434. Stone, Brian. "The Common Enemy of Man," in *Sir Gawain and the Green Knight*, trans. by Brian Stone. London: Penguin Books 1974, 123.

435. Goodrich, Norma Lorre. *Merlin.* New York: Harper Perennial 1988, 234.

The year passed and Gawain set out on his journey to the Green Chapel to meet the gigantic Green Knight.

> After a long journey he came to a noble castle, where he was welcomed by the jovial Sir Bercilak and his lovely young wife. He stayed there until New Year's Day, royally entertained by Bercilak and, though sorely tempted, resisting the persistent attempts of Bercilak's wife to seduce him.

> On New Years Day Gawain went as he said he would to the Green Chapel. There "the Green Knight appeared and Gawain bravely bared his neck for a stroke of the axe. The Green Knight raised the axe high, but struck Gawain only a glancing blow, which nicked his skin. He then explained that he was Sir Bercilak, transformed into the Green Knight by the magic of Morgan le Fay, who had planned the whole adventure in the hope of discrediting the Round Table. Gawain had been spared because he had honorably refrained from making love to Bercilak's wife and had shown himself to be the most faultless knight in the world.

An interesting note about the Green Chapel, according to J.D. Wakefield, is that it was not a structure but rather a green mound situated in a valley beside a stream of bubbling water. Wakefield believes that the Green Chapel was, in reality, Silbury Hill — a sacred man-made mound in Cornwall not far from West Kennett Long Barrow and Avebury — two other ancient sacred sites. [437] Some researchers believe that the Green Chapel was symbolic of a Fairy Mound.

How do we associate the Green Knight to the Green Man? This was obviously a test for Gawain, and one he passed, but this is also a story of "truth-bringing" through a mixture of pagan ritual and the confused teachings of medieval Christianity. The poem also is an alliterative telling of the turning of the year, taking place at a time between two winters, which signifies a time of death of vibrant vegetation, and then a changing back to life through renewed growth, and then again, a return to death. The Green Knight is beheaded, and through his sacrifice he shows that life still goes on and, as John Matthews notes, "he challenges us to honor the sacrifice he makes every winter."[438] In addition, according to Matthews, the poem tells us that "one of the gifts of the Green Man is that he instructs us in how to face our deepest fears and conquer them. In this way he becomes a companion as well as a challenger, a dual role that is present in the archetype in virtually all of its manifestations."[439]

---

436. Cavendish, Richard. "Lancelot and Gawain," in *Legends of the World*. New York: Barnes & Noble Books 1994, 243.

437. Wakefield, J.D. *Legendary Landscapes: Secrets of Ancient Wiltshire Revealed*. Marlborough: Nod Press 1999, 95-96.

438. Matthews, John. *The Quest for the Green Man*. Wheaton; Quest Books 2001, 88.

Other associations with the Green Man are found in the Green Knight's long hair and beard, both green of course. His beard "is like a bush...his long green hair covers his chest and back...down to his elbows. He carries a holly branch in one hand..."[440]

As the poem reads:

Men gaped at the hue of him
Ingrained in garb and mien,
A fellow fiercely grim,
And all a glittering green.
And garments of green girt the fellow about —
And verily his vesture was all vivid green,
So were the bars on his belt and the brilliants set
In ravishing array on the rich accouterments
About himself and his saddle on silken work.
...Yes, garbed all in green was the gallant rider,
And the hair of his head was the same hue as his horse... [441]

Brian Stone, in his essay on the Green Knight, also discusses this mixture of the Green Knight's character:

> ...the Green Knight's combination of greenness, hairiness, energy, earthiness and mainly rough, imperative speech incline us irrevocably to think of two common medieval types, one an outcast and the other a rural deity. The wild man of the woods, the "wodwose," was often an outlaw who...had developed sub-human habits and the fierce unpredictable behavior of a wild beast. The green man, on the other hand, was a personification of spring, a mythological supernatural being who persists to this day in English folk dance and in the name of many pubs.[442]

The Green Knight is a mixture of the heroic tales of knights, of Christian value teaching and of the lore of the pre-Christian god of vegetation and the Wild Men. The tale of the Green Knight continues into "modern" times through the festivals of the Mummer Plays. I do not believe that we can interpret the Green Knight's actions in this poem as easily as Matthews seems to. *Sir Gawain and the Green Knight* does indicate that the underlying archetype was equally

---

439. Ibid. 90-91.
440. Doel, op. cit 79.
441. Stone, Brian, editor. *Sir Gawain and the Green Knight*. London: Penguin Books 1974, 26, 27.
442. Ibid., 122.

important in the 14th century to the literate and peasant classes in England, through storytelling and carved images, as he is universally important today as exhibited through carvings, novels and other forms of expression.

Professor Christopher Fee believes that the poem is "concerned with decapitation and fertility, and these concerns have important implications regarding comparative British mythology. The Celtic incarnation of the Green Man motif is reflected in this poem's treatment of the relationship between the beheading of the Green Knight and the changing of the seasons...."[443]

Littleton and Malcor noted that the "Green Knight may derive from Cernunnos, the god of abundance and forests,"[444] which would seem to directly link the mysterious knight to the Green Man and the gods of vegetation.

Robin Hood, Christianized Green Man?

It was Lady Raglan, the woman who is said to have given the name "Green Man" to the foliate head,[445] who first theorized that the Green Man was the folk-hero Robin Hood. Although Robin was pretty much the invention of an early balladeer, in the 14th century Robin was pictured as the May King, and "essentially a vegetation sacral hero..." as historian E.O. James wrote.[446] John Matthews noted that from the 15th century until the end of the 17th century Robin Hood ruled over the May Day Games. These games were intimately associated with the May King and Queen (Maid Marian) and the Green Man.[447] It was the introduction of Robin into the May Day Games that, according to Matthews, "represented the entrance of a forest law into the realm of the city and the everyday,"[448] just as the image of the Green Man brought the spirit of the forest into the Christian church, which had for so long been in combat with nature.

The very presence of Robin on May Day was viewed by the Church as a threat. Anthropologist Margaret Murray[449] wrote that "the cult of Robin Hood was widespread both geographically and in time, which suggests that he was

---

443. Fee, Christopher R. *Gods, Heroes, & Kings: The Battle for Mythic Britain*. Oxford: Oxford University Press 2001, 201.

444. Littleton, C. Scott & Linda A. Malcor. "Gawain and the Green Knight" in *Heroes of the Dawn: Celtic Myth*. London: Duncan Baird Publishers 1996, 114.

445. See Chapter Sixteen for a further discussion on this subject.

446. James. E.O. *Seasonal Feasts & Festivals*. London: Thames & Hudson 1961.

447. Matthews, John. *Robin Hood: Green Lord of the Wildwood*. Glastonbury: Gothic Image Publications 1993, 81.

448. Ibid., 85.

more than a local hero in the places where his legend occurs....Robin and his band were a constituent part of the May-day ceremonies, they had special dances and always wore the fairies' colour, green."[450] The very nature of Robin's death, says Murray, is reflective of his role as a sacrificial king who dies and is reborn. He is bled by his cousin, a prioress of a convent, who lets his wound bleed freely until he succumbs. However, his death is not unexpected, as his route to the convent is lined with people already morning his passing.[451] The May Day Games recreated the life and death of Robin and during the games, wrote Carol Ballard, "Robin would die and come back to life; this was believed to encourage good crops and to ensure the return of summer."[452] It should be noted, however, that the Green Man was never a part of the May Games so a direct connection cannot be made. The dominance of the Church, however, during that time in history may have forced the Green Man image to stay inside ecclesiastical structures.

Robin Hood is also associated with the woodland spirit Robin Good-fellow, also known as Puck in Shakespeare's *A Midsummer Night's Dream.* Carol Ballard believes that Shakespeare's play was inspired by the many Green Man images present in England in that era.[453] In a broader sense, Robin was much the same as Pan, the Lord of the Wild. According to Barbara Walker, "by force of arms he maintained a heathen preserve in the wildwood, a sanctuary for heretics and others persecuted by the church...Like the Greeks' Pan, Robin defended unspoiled land against the encroachment of towns."[454]

The Church, following its long established practice of incorporating pagan traditions into its fold, did so with the May Day Games as well. "In such a way," Walker reports, "did the church ingest pagan ceremonials by sponsorship, and eventually deprive them of serious meaning."[455] The followers of Robin and the

---

449. Murray's research has been disputed since the publication of her book *The God of the Witches,* however her ideas do create some room for discussion on the Robin-Green Man subject.

450. Murray, Margaret A. *The God of the Witches.* Oxford: Oxford University Press 1952, 41.

451. Ibid.

452. Ballard, Carol. *The Green Man: The Shakespeare Connection.* Warwickshire: Self published 1999, 9.

453. Ballard, op. cit.

454. Walker, Barbara. *The Women's Encyclopedia of Myths and Secrets.* Edison: Castle Books 1983, 858-859.

455. Ibid., 859.

Church leaders were seriously at odds during the 16th and 17th century. Keith Thomas noted that one Christian scholar, in 1608, "observed that they [the people] certainly knew more about Robin Hood than they did about the stories of the Bible."[456]

The Green Man of Fingest

The Green Man of Fingest was in reality a ghost. As Daphne Phillips reports, in 1320 Henry Burghersh was named bishop of Lincoln, and he was granted 300 acres of land for the development of a park as well as a large "extent" of land which surrounded the Manor of Fingest, as "free warren" — or hunting rights — for the bishop. However, this large tract of land had been in common use by the villagers; they had worked it, raising beef and mutton, to pay taxes to the crown. Over sixty families had depended on the use of this land for their livelihoods. When the bishop took control of the manor, only a third of the land remained available for the villagers to use. Phillips notes, "The bishop, not surprisingly, had 'many a bitter curse in his lifetime and after his death"[457] some twenty years later.

Legend had it that soon after his death the bishop was seen as a "keeper in a short green coat with...bow, quiver of arrows and horn by his side." He was, by his offensive actions in life, doomed to be the park keeper until the land was again returned up to the people. Not long after this the "banks and pales [were] thrown down and the ditches...filled up again," the land was once again open for public use. Is this the end of the ghost stories of the bishop? No. As recent as 1898 it was recorded that the ghost was still to be seen in the churchyard, dressed in the green keepers dress. He is seen in the role of a protector of the land and it is thought that the legends of the ghostly bishop have been reformatted as a more recent version of the Lord of the Wild, or, as Phillips believes, "a god (converted) into a repentant bishop."

The Islamic Legend of Khidr

According to legend, Alexander the Great happened to obtain a copy of Adam's will, which mentioned that God had created a magical spring behind Mt. Oaf, the mountainous barrier around the world, which was located in the Land

---

456. Thomas, Keith. *Religion and the Decline of Magic.* London: Penguin Books 1971, 195.

457. Phillips, Daphne. "The Green Man of Fingest," in *Strange* Buckinghamshire, www.cleaverproperty.co.uk/strange'bucks/fingest.html 11/15/2000.

of Darkness. The water of this spring "was whiter than milk, colder than ice, sweeter than honey, softer than butter and sweeter smelling than musk."[458] It also granted eternal life to those who drank from it. Alexander's guide Khidr, taking Alexander's army with him, entered the Land of Darkness and found the spring. He bathed in the water, drank of its sweetness, and became immortal. However, when he attempted to show Alexander his find, it had become lost once again. Another version of this legend states that Khidr fell into the Well of Life, gained immortality and became the Green Man.[459] Khidr is regarded among the Sufi followers as the Guide to the Sufi Path and is said to appear before Sufi adepts, in their sleep or in person, to help them on their way. Khidr has also been equated with St. George and Elias, having lived these lives through reincarnation.

Khidr was also, in legend, a companion to Moses. Khidr's name, according to lore, is an Arabic term meaning "green" or "verdant" and he was often referred to as "The Green One" or the "Green Ancient." It is said that even the rock upon which Khidr prayed turned green.[460] Like the Green Man, Khidr "is perceived as a representative of nature and as a source of supernatural wisdom who lives both inside and outside time and is therefore immortal."[461] According to Islamic scholar Irfan Omar, "Khidr literally means 'The Green One', representing freshness of spirit and eternal liveliness, green symbolizing the freshness of knowledge' drawn out of the living sources of life." Omar also writes, "the color green has also been related to Khidr's disappearing 'into the "green landscape."'"[462] Sufi writer Shawkat M. Toorawa states that although Khidr is a prophet, "for Sufis he is above all a Friend of God...able to perform wonders as a matter of routine. They sky and sea obey his will...He is able to appear anywhere and everywhere, at all times, for all time."[463]

Toorawa notes that the Alexander Romance states that after Khidr falls, or jumps, into the Well of Life, "'all the flesh of his body became bluish-green and his garments likewise'. In the Ethiopian version of the Romance, he is told: 'You

---

458. Elwell-Sutton, L.P. "The Islamic World: The Two Horned One," in *Legends of the World.* Edited by Richard Cavendish. New York: Barnes & Noble Books 1994, 116.

459. Ibid.

460. Ibid.

461. Matthews, op. cit. 30.

462. Omar, Irfan. "Khidr in the Islamic Tradition" in *The Muslim World* Vol. LXXXIII, No. 3-4 July — October, 1993.

463. Toorawa, Shawkat M. "Khidr: The History of a Ubiquitous Master" in *Sufi Selected Article*, Issue Number 30, Published by Khaniqahi Mimatullahi Publications 2000.

are Khidr: wherever your feet touch, the earth will become green'. His greenness suggests links to St. Gregory and St. George and echoes, if distantly, Zachariah, 6: 12: 'Behold the man whose name is The Branch'."[464]

Is Khidr the Green Man? Yes, he is one manifestation of the Green Men of the world linking the people of that region to nature and fertility and the rebirth of life.

The Green Man of Hughenden

The Green Man remains alive in the imagination of many, and has reportedly physically manifested himself in England as late as 1986. An article in the *South Bucks Star* newspaper on September 26, 1986 entitled, "Phantom of the Forest," read:

> A ghostly figure dressed in green startled two motorists as they drove past a crematorium just before midnight.
>
> The apparition suddenly loomed up at the side of the road sending shivers down the spine of driver Mark Nursey and his girlfriend Allyson Buleptt, who was in the car behind.
>
> Mark, of Hepplewhite Close, High Wycombe, said: "The most uncanny thing was the way it stood. It seemed to be wearing what I can only describe as a big green jumper. I couldn't make out the head or hands. It seemed to be stooping but was about 5ft 11ins tall and well built."

The article goes on to theorize on the origin of the apparition:

> One theory is the figure was the spirit of the forest, a green man, as depicted on a number of pub signs in the Chilterns. He is also related to Herne the Hunter, spirit of the forest as depicted on TV's *Robin of Sherwood*.

The October 17 edition of the *South Bucks Star* saw an additional account of the "phantom":

> Another witness of the phantom of the forest has recalled his terrifying ordeal. The seven-foot tall green ghost was seen by warehouseman Phil Mullett just yards from where 21-year-old Mark Nursey saw the figure on Four Ashes Road, Cryers Hill, near High Wycombe.
>
> Phil said: "It gave me quite a shock to read it (the previous report in the Star). The account was so close to my own. It was about 9.30pm when I drove into Four Ashes Road and on turning my car lights on full I saw this green person appear from the right hand side of the road. It drifted out to the centre of the road and turned towards me. It waved its arms, not to frighten but as if to warn me to keep back. It drifted into the hedge on the other side of the road but as I got closer it came out

---

464. Ibid.

again to the centre, turned and lifted its arms. I knew I was going to hit it. I think I cried out or shouted something."

According to the news account, Mr. Mullett did hit it but when he got out of the car to check, there was nothing to see. He described the apparition as "bright green but appeared to have no legs or hands. The body was solid and it stood about seven foot tall. Instead of a face there was just a misty grey round shape."

Green Children

One report of "Green Children" has often been repeated over the years. The earliest account given is that of Thomas Keightley in his 1878 publication *The Fairy Mythology*.[465] Keightley notes that this story was "as quoted by Picart in his Notes on William of Newbridge. We could not find it in the Collection of Histories, etc., by Martenes and Durand, — the only place where, to our knowledge, this chronicler's works are printed."

The story, in its entirety:

> "ANOTHER wonderful thing," says Ralph of Coggeshall, "happened in Suffolk, at St. Mary's of the Wolf-pits. A boy and his sister were found by the inhabitants of that place near the mouth of a pit which is there, who had the form of all their limbs like to those of other men, but they differed in the colour of their skin from all the people of our habitable world; for the whole surface of their skin was tinged of a green colour. No one could understand their speech. When they were brought as curiosities to the house of a certain knight, Sir Richard de Caine, at Wikes, they wept bitterly. Bread and other victuals were set before them, but they would touch none of them, though they were tormented by great hunger, as the girl afterwards acknowledged. At length, when some beans just cut, with their stalks, were brought into the house, they made signs, with great avidity, that they should be given to them. When they were brought, they opened the stalks instead of the pods, thinking the beans were in the hollow of them; but not finding them there, they began to weep anew. When those who were present saw this, they opened the pods, and showed them the naked beans. They fed on these with great delight, and for a long time tasted no other food. The boy, however, was always languid and depressed, and he died within a short time. The girl enjoyed continual good health; and becoming accustomed to various kinds of food, lost completely that green colour, and gradually recovered the sanguine habit of her entire body. She was afterwards regenerated by the layer of holy baptism, and lived for many years in the service of that knight (as I have frequently heard from him and his family), and was rather loose and wanton in her conduct. Being frequently asked about the people of her country, she asserted that the inhabitants, and all they had in that country, were of a green colour; and that they saw no sun, but enjoyed a degree of light like what is

---

465. Keightley, Thomas. *The Fairy Mythology: Illustrative of the Romance and Superstition of Various Countries*. London: G. Bell Publishers 1878, 281-283.

after sunset. Being asked how she came into this country with the aforesaid boy, she replied, that as they were following their flocks, they came to a certain cavern, on entering which they heard a delightful sound of bells; ravished by whose sweetness, they went for a long time wandering on through the cavern, until they came to its mouth. When they came out of it, they were struck senseless by the excessive light of the sun, and the unusual temperature of the air; and they thus lay for a long time. Being terrified by the noise of those who came on them, they wished to fly, but they could not find the entrance of the cavern before they were caught."

This story is also told by William of Newbridge, who places it in the reign of King Stephen. He says he long hesitated to believe it, but he was at length overcome by the weight of evidence. According to him, the place where the children appeared was about four or five miles from Bury St. Edmund's: they came in harvest-time out of the Wolf-pits; they both lost their green hue, and were baptised, and learned English. The boy, who was the younger, died; but the girl married a man at Lenna, and lived many years. They said their country was called St. Martin's Land, as that saint was chiefly worshiped there; that the people were Christians, and had churches; that the sun did not rise there, but that there was a bright country which could be seen from theirs, being divided from it by a very broad river.

This story is interesting on several counts. The hidden world through which the children traveled through a huge cavern is reminiscent of those legends of passages to the Underworld through sacred wells and caves.[466] An unknown race of green-skinned people whose total diet consisted of vegetable matter is a mixture of fairy lore and lore associated with the Wild Folk. That Keightley's account claims that the children's country was Christian and that they worshipped St. Martin is obviously a Christian elaboration of a possibly older tale. One similar group of earth spirits are the *Daome-Shi*, a subterranean form of fairy that "dwell in burning mountains, or occupy themselves in mining, and the storing of treasure" who also dressed in green.[467]

Green Women of the Woods

Legends of Wild Men and Wild Women are abundant around the world. While the Wild Man may be more directly linked to the Green Man archetype, the Wild Woman is also an important, and ancient, link to the primordial Mother Earth. The Green Woman, the Wild Woman, is seen in numerous carvings in both the Old and the New World. Alexander Porteous wrote that "Wood-Wives," another name for the Wild Women, "frequented the old sacred forests or groves, and apparently it had been they who had formed the court or

466. Varner, Gary R. *Sacred Wells: A Study in the History, Meaning, & Mythology of Holy Wells and Waters.* Baltimore: PublishAmerica Publishers 2002.

467. Bonwick, James. *Irish Druids and Old Irish Religions.* New York: Barnes & Noble Books 1986, 90 (A reprint of the 1894 edition).

escort of the ancient gods when they sat enthroned on the trees. These Wood-Wives were principally found in southern Germany, but varieties of them are mentioned in northern Germany and Scandinavia. They were the quarry of the Wild Huntsman but were saved from him if they could reach a tree with a cross on it."[468] In fact, versions of such entities exist in most folklore around the world.

This story is another Christianized version of an ancient tale. The Wood-Wives are spirits of the forest, free spirits of nature. The Wood-Wives have many of the characteristics given to the fairy[469] and elves. They often give gold for food or kindness and may cause innumerable disruptions of human life through rapid changes in weather or other mischief. Porteous notes, "very often the colour of these spirits was green, and their skin of a mossy texture..."[470]

Some of these wood spirits were known to possess the secrets of herbal medicine and protected various species of trees. Matthews wrote, "They appear frequently as gentle spirits of trees and woodland, dressed in leaves, their flowing hair contrasting with their wizened faces."[471] These female wood spirits are not depicted as often in architectural motifs as the Green Man, but they are there. Chesca Porter, writing in John Matthews' book *Robin Hood: Green Lord of the Wildwood*,[472] believes that the ancient *Sheila-na-Gigs*[473] carved in many of the old churches of France and England are representatives of the Wild Women and are "possibly a medieval manifestation of the goddess of life and death, a reflection of the feminine power of the land itself." "These figures," Matthews writes, "who

---

468. Porteous, Alexander. *The Lore of the Forest: Myths and Legends.* London: Senate Publishers 1996, 91 (A reprint of the 1928 publication *Forest Folklore* published by George Allen & Unwin, London).

469. Fairies were not always the diminutive and mischievous, green-clad folk of legend. Originally, they were the People of Danu, the Tuath-de-Danaan who were the legendary, magical and learned inhabitants of Ireland. After the Milesians gained control of the island, they became gods and over time became what we now regard as the Fey, or Fairies. Many of the kings and queens of the Tuath-de-Danaan became the Old Ones, the Gods and Goddesses of Ireland. The Dagda, the Good God, was one of their kings and Boann, his wife, one of their great Goddesses. After the Tuath were defeated by the Milesians, the Dagda became the King of the Fairies and the Fey melted back into the earth, living in the many Fairy mounds and other Otherworld locations.

470. Porteous, op. cit, 90.

471. Matthews, op. cit., 110.

472. Matthews, John. *Robin Hood: Green Lord of the Wildwood.* Glastonbury: Gothic Image Publications 1993, 201.

473. It is also spelled "Sheela-na-gig" and is believed to be a corruption of an Irish term for "loose women".

display their genitalia, are recognized to have been connected to pre-Christian fertility rites. The fact that those which have survived are found on churches may well be for the same reason that foliate heads are found there — the Church wanted to show that it had absorbed (and therefore conquered) pagan beliefs."[474]

To any who have seen the Sheila figures, Matthews' statement that they are "connected to pre-Christian fertility rites" seems hardly plausible. Looking more like figures from concentration camps, these bald, emaciated female figures are generally depicted as showing off giant genitalia. Researcher Katy Jordan notes that academic studies indicate that these figures are "carefully chosen depictions of the grossness of the sins of the flesh"[475] and that their presence on church walls throughout Europe may have been more as totems to turn away evil[476] rather than ancient pornography. As Mercia MacDermott so aptly writes, "far from being a fertility goddess, the female exhibitionist is an *anti*-fertility image intended to arouse disgust in the beholder and to foster the idea that sex is sordid and sinful."[477] However, the Sheilas may also represent the ancient pagan hag-goddesses, left by stone-carvers who, more likely than not, were carving ancient symbols of their past whose meaning had been long forgotten — similar to the foliate masks. Many of the Sheila-na-Gigs have been destroyed over the years due to their overt sexual connotation and their contemporary linkage to Goddess worship.

Feminine-faced Green Women carvings are rare; however, there are many carvings of female hybrid creatures that appear to be sprouting from the stalks of plants, their lower bodies actually part of the vegetation. These are as meaningful as the imaginative Green Man foliate-heads, which are more common. These carvings of female human-plant beings are symbolic of our link to nature in its primitive and innocent beauty and Mother Earth's life-giving force.

A fine example of a Green Woman carving is that of the Spring Maiden created during the 14th century at Exeter Cathedral. Other examples are located at Brioude, France and Ashby Folville in Leicestershire. Another Green Woman

474. Ibid., 107.

475. Jordan, Katy. *The Haunted Landscape: Folklore, ghosts & legends of Wiltshire.* Bradford on Avon: Ex Libris Press 2000, 48.

476. Representations of female genitalia were used at one time as effective preventative measures against evil.

477. MacDermott, Mercia. *Explore Green Men.* Loughborough: Heart if Albion Press 2003, 132.

carving can be found at Shepherdswell Church in Kent, which dates back to 944 CE. Green Women were also goddesses. The Libyan goddess Neith is depicted with a green face as well as the symbols of fertility, the bow and arrow, which also represent lightning and rain. Likewise, Green Demeter was the goddess of growing corn — an obvious symbol of fertility and renewed life.

The Wild Man

The legendary Wild Man most likely is based in reality. During the Middle Ages, a sub-culture existed on the fringes of European society made up of outlaws and social outcasts. At times, such individuals made their way into the towns and cities and the Wild Man–Wild Folk stories began. At the same time, the terms were also applied to the mythical race of dwarves, who were also called "Moss-Folk." One folklorist wrote, "they are considered to be dwarfs, and they live in communities. They are grey and old-looking, and are hideously over-grown with moss, giving them a hairy appearance."[478] These Moss Folk weave the moss of the forests and protect it with a vengeance. They do help some people with their knowledge of the healing plants and herbs and they help crops to grow. Other Wild Men were described as "often of gigantic proportions, dwell in woods or mountains, and originally were no doubt closely connected with the spirits of trees...From head to foot they are clothed in moss, or covered with rough shaggy hair, their long locks floating behind them in the wind."[479] In folklore these Wild Men are sometimes helpful to humans in that they will locate lost cattle and have the ability to treat the illnesses of cattle, but, according to Philpot, they are "more often mischievous, having the propensity for stealing the milk and carrying off the children of the peasants."[480]

There is another aspect of the Wild Man as a creature removed from accepted society that is more closely associated with the Green Man. Lady Raglan was instrumental in erroneously connecting the Green Man with the Wild Man creature — for they are two entirely different beings. The Wild Man subculture came to represent those things rejected by the "civilized" elements — those being natural elements found in animal and vegetable life as well as those

---

478. Porteous, op. cit 93.
479. Philpot, Mrs. J.H. *The Sacred Tree in Religion and Myth.* Mineola: Dover Publications Inc. 2004, 68 (A reprint of the 1897 edition published by Macmillan and Co., Limited, London).
480. Ibid.

more "primitive" aspects of humanity. These very basic characteristics of nature came to be those most feared by the Christian society of the day. "For much of the Middle Ages, hairy, cannibalistic, sexually omnivorous wild men and women had represented the antithesis of the civilized Christian," wrote British historian Simon Schama.[481] The many illustrations of the Wild Man of the Middle Ages show a naked individual completely covered in long, shaggy hair with only the face, hands, elbows (and the breasts of the female) exposed. Other illustrations show this very same individual covered in leaves instead of hair or fur. Matthews believes that the Wild Man "expresses an aspect of the Green Man that is angry" ...angry due to humankind's denial of the *rightness* of nature, and angry due to the attempts to dominate nature by Christian civilizations which promote the "divine right" of man to subdue the wild.

Schama believes that society itself transformed the wild folk into this guardian of nature. "[B]eginning in the later part of the fifteenth century...wild men were made over into exemplars of the virtuous and natural life."[482] Over the next hundred years, the wild man was "turned into conspicuously gentler creatures."[483]

The wild man became the symbol of popular discontent with the burgeoning cities and court society; he was, in a sense, a response of nature towards this unnatural existence and the destruction of the Wild Wood.

In North America, the Wild Man is present in the ancient legends of Big Foot and Sasquatch — huge human-like figures covered in long hair and leaves. Nineteenth century American folklore tells of a family of Big Foot who attacked a group of gold miners in their California cabin one evening, destroying the building and tearing the men apart. Was this a response to the encroachment of "civilized" man? The characteristics of the two are very similar and they react in the same way. As Matthews writes of the Wild Man, "he can only dwell in such wild spots and avoids those places tamed by humankind, retreating ever deeper into the wilderness to escape the excesses of civilization — its cruelty, greed, and hypocrisy."[484] So too do these mythic figures in the North American lore.

It is not only in North America that stories of these mysterious wood-folk are found. Among the Yupa Indians, living in Colombia and Venezuela a similar nature spirit is spoken of. Called the Mashíramu, or "Bush Spirit," he is described

---

481. Schama, Simon. *Landscape and Memory.* New York: Vintage Books 1995, 97.
482. Ibid.
483. Ibid.
484. Matthews, John. *Quest for the Green Man,* op. cit 110.

as being covered with hair and its feet are turned backwards. This creature is called a "devastating demon," to be greatly feared.[485] Another Yupa spirit is the Karau, the Spirit of the Night. It too is covered with hair, has very large teeth and very cold hands. The Karau is said to rape women, kill, and eat his victims.[486]

The Wild Man and Wild Woman were known among the Nehalem Tillamook Indians in Oregon as well. "The Wild Woman," wrote ethnographer Elizabeth Jacobs "was one of the most important of the supernatural beings. She was a large woman and lived in the forest."[487] Described as having "long beautiful hair and wearing lots of dentalia," Wild Woman was believed to be spiritually connected with the spruce tree. She could make people sick and die, cause insanity or simply make a tree fall on someone. Those who were in her favor, however, would be granted supernatural powers to diagnose illnesses and cure them, or would be endowed with special skill to make beautiful baskets.

The Wild Man, on the other hand, is an ugly giant who also lives in the forest. He as well causes sickness or grants certain powers and skills.[488]

Clive Hicks noted that the Wild Men and Wild Woman "are not necessarily malevolent and are depicted as helping humanity in some cases...The wild man represents an asset in each of us, the whole reservoir of qualities with which each of us is endowed..."[489] Again, we are faced with a paradoxical image as so often is the case in myth and legend.

Little Green Men

The Great Basin of California and Nevada is a wonderful country. At first glance, it is devoid of life, littered with rock outcrops, brush, a few cactus, sand, and mountain ranges. Closer up it is an amazing thing to see. Mysterious places decorated with rock art thousands of years old seem to be in every direction. The spirituality of the place is awe-inspiring. Indian folklore and mythology concerned about supernatural beings such as "rock babies" or "water babies" are abundant. One of these stories is of the Little Green Men. Described as two feet tall and armed with a bow and arrow, the Little Green Men are the guardian

---

485. Wilbert, Johannes. *Yupa Folktales.* Los Angeles: Latin American Center, University of California 1974, 139.
486. Ibid., 138.
487. Jacobs, Elizabeth D. *The Nehalem Tillamook: An Ethnography.* Corvallis: Oregon State University Press 2003, 190.
488. Ibid., 182.
489. Hicks, Clive. *The Green Man: A Field Guide.* Helhoughton: COMPASSbooks 2000, 7.

spirits of shamans who have received their power purely through supernatural agents.[490] What is striking, though, when exploring these stories, is how similar they are to other myths of fairy-folk from around the world. The similarity between these small beings, their appearances, their powers, their influence is much more than coincidental.

CHAPTER 13. A DISCUSSION OF THE VALIDITY OF THE GREEN MAN MYTH

The last few years have seen a boon in the number of books published on the Green Man. It has also seen an increased amount of words printed to dispute the Green Man's symbolism and perceived history — much of it as presented here. I will discuss the points presented by others to invalidate the Green Man myth in this chapter.

Historian Ronald Hutton argues effectively for the rather late development of the Green Man motif and as a Christian endeavor — not as a pagan survival. However, his argument is somewhat muddied when he states that the culture of the 12th century Renaissance, which he claims produced the images, "was a Christian movement, even though it drew upon ancient ideas and images."[491] His reasoning is technically correct but does not detract from the hypothesis that the Green Man, in fact, is based on ancient pagan traditions. Christianity, as a whole, is based on such pagan traditions and borrows heavily upon them. Hutton also wrote that the Wild Man was a figure of the Christian Middle Ages — even though, says Hutton, he "was based on ancient models."[492] Hutton's distinctions are vague and unnecessary. The actual workmanship used to create most of the Green Man images in Britain was, admittedly, from the Renaissance — but the underlying inspiration was indeed based "upon ancient ideas and images." Most of the earlier examples known were created in Classical Rome, and the motif was carried to distant parts of the ancient world by the Roman army and then, in later times, by Christians along pilgrim routes. Even the motif used by the Romans, however, most assuredly had a beginning in a far earlier culture.

---

490. Eliade, Mircea. *Shamanism: Archaic Techniques of Ecstasy.* Princeton: Princeton University Press 1964, 102.

491. Hutton, Ronald. *The pagan Religions of the Ancient British Isles: Their Nature and Legacy.* Oxford: Blackwell Publishers LTD.1993, 316.

492. Ibid., 310.

That being said, the meaning of the Green Man has not been altered significantly. Hutton has missed this important aspect. Regardless whether a Christian bishop employed the artisans during the Middle Ages, the fundamental quality and pre-Christian meaning of the Green Men continued to exist, to flourish and to regenerate. Early documents indicate that, while Church officials may have employed the artisans responsible for the Green Man images, they did not necessarily approve of them or even know what they represented. St. Bernard of Clairvaux complained to the Abbot of St. Thierry in 1125, "What mean those ridiculous [carved] monstrosities in the court of cloisters?"[493] Grundy discounts Hutton's assumption that the carvings were Christian symbols of evil and sin, writing, "taking into account St. Bernard's unfamiliarity with the carved imagery, it can...be anticipated that the subject-matter had little to do with Christian doctrine but much to do with the carvers themselves."[494]

The carvings produced by these craftsmen undoubtedly reflect their own experiences, values, traditions and beliefs. The twentieth century stonemasons responsible for the gargoyles and grotesques present on the Washington National Cathedral are not so different from their 12th-century brothers. "Wrought from personal experience and handcrafted with the tools and skills of their trade," notes folklorist Marjorie Hunt, "the stone carvers' freehand carvings are quintessential expressions of the spirit of freedom and responsibility that pervades their work — poignant, powerful statements of individual creativity and shared cultural values."[495] Stone carvers today, as they did in the past, share "esoteric" knowledge among themselves, knowledge which surfaces in their carvings.

Kathleen Basford also believed that the Green Man image found on so many cathedrals and other ecclesiastical structures represented punishment rather than life. Writing in her book *The Green Man*, she noted, "although the Green Man was a much loved motif I think it is very unlikely that he was revered as a symbol of the renewal of life in springtime"[496] that Lady Raglan had proposed.

---

493. Grundy, Thirlie. *Going in Search of the Green Man in Cumbria.* Cumbria: Thumbprint 2000, 5.

494. Ibid., 6.

495. Hunt, Marjorie. *The Stone Carvers: Master Craftsmen of Washington National Cathedral.* Washington: Smithsonian Institution Press 1999, 136.

496. Basford, Kathleen. *The Green Man.* Cambridge: D.S. Brewer 1978, 20.

The Green Man, according to Basford, "represents the darkness of unre-deemed nature" and "the root of all evil."[497] While the Green Man does have a dual nature, it is certainly not evil but illustrates the very characteristics of nature — both of death and life and mankind's fate if it chooses to abuse nature rather than live within the bounds of nature's rules.

MacDermott states that early environmentalists erroneously proclaimed the Green Man image as a symbol for their cause. MacDermott goes on to say that the many "attractive, imaginative and emotive things" which the Green Man has been called "could not possibly have represented...the context of earlier cen-turies. Medieval Christians," she writes, "did not identify themselves with untamed Nature, and would not have understood a desire to do so."[498] I agree with this statement, as far as it goes. But while the Green Man, the foliate head, is found in Christian artwork, it did not originate as part of Christian artwork. A "Christian country" did not necessarily equate to a Christian population. The rural folk kept many, if not most, of their traditional folkways — including or even especially when it came to arts and crafts. As shown previously the image is a far older one, and was used extensively by the Romans and other ancient cul-tures around the world in their religious iconography. It is an image that reso-nated with the popular imagination and was incorporated in Christian architecture for various reasons — some intentional and others not. To state that the foliate head was solely the creation of the Christian Church in Christian Europe is a vast over-simplification.

It is perhaps our concept of "God" and "good and evil" which dictates for each of us what the Green Man represents. Those who lived, or still live, in a "pagan" society, or who value the powers of the natural world rather than viewing nature as man's adversary, will see the message of life, fertility, and renewal in the Green Man's leafy visage. Much more importantly, the Green Man image shows humanity's close relationship to nature — the leaf and vine growing from or into the Green Man's face is the very life-blood that humans rely on. To sever those vines or to pluck the leaves from the face only creates a mortal wound.

Some writers seem to believe that cultural change caused by the stresses of societal evolution leads to changes in popular folklore — in effect creating "one

---

497. Ibid., 21.

498. MacDermott, Mercia. *Explore Green Men.* Loughborough: Explore Books/Heart of Albion Press 2003, 192.

more veneer on the ever-changing nature of these 'traditions'" that creates a false history and a pre-conceived meaning that is blindly accepted by those not educated in the sciences.[499] Certainly, society and its related traditions do constantly change. But that is as it should be, in reflection of changing collective or shared needs. If a certain aspect of history, art or religion has in recent times become "paganized," it suggests that some segments of modern society sense that something has been missing in today's culture and civilization. This fresh look at pagan traditions is a sign of a broad search for meaning — a meaning that can only be satisfied by those primal feelings and symbols that were so abundant in the dim past.

With the destruction of religious iconography during the Reformation, the Green Man image became even more popular, migrating from the church to the secular world. "Deprived of their traditional homes," wrote Mercia MacDermott, "foliate heads re-appeared in all manner of secular settings from lintels to door-knockers."[500] The 18th and 19th centuries saw a veritable flood of Green Man images on secular buildings around the world. Whereas at one time they figured predominately in ecclesiastical motifs, they now became widespread on government, financial, educational structures, and even apartment buildings. Regardless of its many possible meanings in a Church setting, the Green Man is valued today as a symbol of life and renewal and humanity's connection with nature.

Researcher Carol Ballard introduces an interesting theory in her booklet, *The Green Man: The Shakespeare Connection.* She believes the many Green Man figures that can still be seen today in the area where William Shakespeare was raised and lived into adulthood indirectly make their way into some of his plays, particularly *A Midsummer Night's Dream.* According to Ballard, John Shakespeare, William's father, "was instrumental in defacing and covering wall paintings in the Guild Chapel," the year of William's birth. These acts became the contribution of John Shakespeare to the Protestant Reformation's destruction of religious symbolism. "The fact," Ballard wrote, "that his own father was involved in the destruction of images, could well have made iconography such as those pertaining to the pagan world take on an accentuated significance in Shakespeare's mind."[501] Thus, we find the Green Man being transformed from the ecclesiastic

499. Trubshaw, Bob. "paganism in British Folk Customs". In *At the Edge*, No. 3 1996.
500. MacDermott, Mercia. *Explore Green Men.* Loughborough: Explore Books/Heart of Albion Press 2003.

world and its illuminated manuscripts to the secular world as part of society's daily entertainment through drama and dance.

It seems that there is wide disagreement over most aspects connected to the Green Man. Does he represent life, fertility and the promise of rebirth or is he a symbol of man's fallen nature, lust, sin and the promise that life is only temporary? Such disagreement is reflective of the mystery of the origins and meanings of this symbol and it shows that the Green Man is, like most other religious symbols, something that will never be completely accepted or agreed upon by all people. Indeed, all spiritual symbols and ideals retain a level of mystery; their complex and profound nature is what makes them effective.

Mercia MacDermott does, however, come through with an excellent synopsis of the issue. "Perhaps what we are now witnessing," she writes, "is simply the latest round — and the first to be documented — in an often repeated, periodic rediscovery of the symbolic potential of an ancient decorative motif."[502]

CHAPTER 14. THE GREEN MAN AND THE CHURCH

Carvings of Green Men in North America tend to be architectural motifs on public buildings such as post offices, banks and apartment buildings rather than church architecture. This is contrary to those carvings in Britain where a majority, but not all, are found on (and in) church buildings. During the Middle Ages, and before, the buildings that were designed and built to last were places of power — those being castles and fortresses of the government and churches. We are familiar with many of the grotesque figures of gargoyles found on many of the cathedrals; and it is on and in these magnificent structures too that we still can find carvings of Green Men. As we have discussed, the reasons for their inclusion on Christian shrines have been debated for years. They could be pagan survivals, which were either incorporated by the early church architects to show their conquest of pagan beliefs or were carved by stonemasons intending to show that their pagan beliefs had *not* been vanquished. Or, the numerous carved foliate heads found in churches may represent the continuation of the ancient Celtic head cult into the Christian era. Or the Green Man motif may have con-

---

501. Ballard, Carol. *The Green Man: The Shakespeare Connection.* Warwickshire: Self Published 1999, 11.
502. MacDermott, op. cit., 192.

tinued to be popular simply as a survival of classical art and constitute a fondness of style rather than substance of meaning.[503]

Researcher Clive Hicks wrote, "Commentators have found no mention of the Green Man in Medieval texts,[504] and the image seems to have been used in a wholly intuitive way, accepted but not explained."[505] While many of the carvings, according to Hicks, were intended to be purely decorative, he also believes that a great many were the result "of a deep, but probably intuitive, sense of symbolism."[506] Carol Ballard has a similar view, writing in her booklet *The Green Man: The Shakespeare Connection:* "rarely, if ever, can the Green Man be said to be a purely decorative ornament devoid of meaning."[507]

Basford agreed, proclaiming "Rarely if ever can the Green Man be considered a 'meaningless' ornament or an empty echo."[508]

There is also some indication that in some instances the Christian church directly amalgamated the Green Man to the Madonna and Child, and to Jesus in particular. Hicks noted in his book, *The Green Man: A Field Guide,* that "one boss in the vault of the Lady Chapel in Ely might be seen as a green Virgin and Child, and another, at Lincoln, as a green Christ. Two of the most important we discovered were from Exeter Cathedral, where a choir corbel shows the Madonna and Child surrounded by the foliage pouring from the mouth of a Green Man, and from Freiburg im Breisgau, where the Easter Sepulcher, containing a carved figure of Christ in the tomb, is framed by weeping green men." According to Hicks, "these were clearly intentional iconography, not customary decoration, not pagan survivals, not warnings against sin."

However, C.J.P. Cave, a celebrated architectural photographer of British cathedrals, wrote, "In various parts of the cathedral [of Exeter] we find heads with stems of plants coming out of their mouths. This motif is very common

503. MacDermott, Mercia. *Explore Green Men.* Loughborough: Explore Books/Heart of Albion Press 2003.

504. While the Green Men may not have been written of in early texts their images were used in some illuminated manuscripts in the 10th century.

505. Hicks, Clive. *The Green Man: A Field Guide.* Helhoughton: COMPASSbooks 2000, 8-9. Hicks' statement is true as far as specific commentaries written during that time, however, as noted in Chapter Eight, there are some manuscripts from this time that included the motif in their illustrations.

506. Ibid. 9.

507. Ballard, Carol. *The Green Man: The Shakespeare Connection.* Warwickshire: Self published 1999, 6.

508. Basford, Kathleen. *The Green Man.* Cambridge: D.S. Brewer 1978, 21.

from Norman times to the end of the Gothic period, and I suppose that it may be a survival from tree worship which had come down through the Middle Ages, just as Jack-in-the-Green has come down almost to our own days."[509]

Nicholas Mann, writing in *His Story: Masculinity in the Post-Patriarchal World*, notes that it may seem ironic that the Green Man, a very pagan symbol, "makes his most frequent appearances in ecclesiastical architecture." However, Mann believes that "in this case, the denial of a chthonic and daemonic immanent power by the Church...has led to its most vital expression in the elements of wood and stone which form the places of worship of the Church. There is irony in this, a quality much loved by the Green Man."[510]

When did the carvings of the Green Men first appear in British ecclesiastical architecture? The evidence is that they first appeared in large numbers in the late Norman period, from the late 12th to the early 16th centuries.[511] The Doels note that the popularity of foliate head carvings was most evident in the 14th and 15th centuries, following the Black Death. This would certainly make sense with the symbolism of life and fertility being associated with the Green Man — an intuitive response to the grotesque death that killed over a third of the population in Europe. Basford writes that the "history and development of the Green Man in the Church can...be followed continuously from the fourth or fifth century. Though pagan in origin, the motif evolved within the Church and, during the Middle Ages, became part of its symbolic language."[512]

The Green Man may be identified more directly with Sylvanus, the Roman "country god', the god of the oak. Thirlie Grundy, writing in her little book *The Green Man in Northumberland and County Durham*, notes that during the Middle Ages when the large stone churches began to replace the small wooden ones, stonemasons did not exist. It was the wood carvers who were called upon to fashion the extensive and ornate stonework. "On finding themselves in charge of stonebuilding projects," asserts Grundy, the woodcarvers "had summoned the aid of their most trustworthy ally — the powerful, spiritual god of the oak, or today's enigmatic Green Man."[513] Sylvanus, also known as the "woodland god," was a Roman-Celtic tree deity of ancient Britain. Basford wrote of a leaf mask carving

---

509. Cave, C.J.P. *Medieval Carvings in Exeter Cathedral.* London: Penguin Books 1953, 12.

510. Mann, Nicholas R. *His Story: Masculinity in the Post-Patriarchal World.* St. Paul: Llewellyn Publications 1995, 143.

511. Doel, Fran & Geoff. *The Green Man in Britain.* Gloucestershire: Tempus Publishing Ltd. 2001, 37.

512. Basford 1978, op. cit., 19.

on a fountain at the Abbey of Saint-Denis, which today is a 20-minute ride from Paris. Dating back to 1200 CE the fountain has a series of heads carved on the basin, each head with the name of a particular deity engraved over it. The one Green Man face represented is named "Silvan."[514] An altar dedicated to him was set up in Yorkshire, on Scargill Moor, by the occupying Roman army.[515]

The concept of the woodland god, the foliate head or Green Man, appears to have followed the Roman armies as they trekked through conquered lands, eventually adopted by the early Christians who aided in the Green Man's spread along trade and pilgrim routes. While early Christian authorities may have used the Green Man image to induce the pagan community to go to church, it is also possible that the early Christian faith did not have a clear definition between the ancient pagan traditions and the new Christian faith, which so heavily borrowed from the past. Because of this lack of definition, the two traditions became fused together — pagan and Christian — co-existing in the same religious structures for hundreds of years. As researcher John Timpson wrote, "maybe in those days no one was quite sure they [the pagan gods] wouldn't make a comeback — so these medieval craftsmen were just hedging their bets."[516]

William Anderson, however, believed that the incorporation of the Green Man motif into church architecture and art was perhaps unconsciously intentional: "...the missionary saints needed to bring the greatest source of living power on earth under the guidance of Christ: the power that is in grass and leaf and sap on which all living things depend. Though they knew that demonic forces dwelt among the works of Nature, they had at the same time to assert the goodness of creation, and there arose a dualism between their fear of the demonic and the beauty and usefulness of God's work."[517]

Green Man researcher Mike Harding has estimated that there are five times the number of Green Man figures in Exeter Cathedral as there are images of Jesus. This would certainly imply that they held an important function and

---

513.   Grundy, Thirlie. *The Green Man in Northumberland and County Durham.* Carlisle Cumbria: Thumbprint 2001, 3.

514.   Basford 1978, op. cit. 15.

515.   Hutton, Ronald. *The pagan Religions of the Ancient British Isles: Their Nature and Legacy.* Oxford: Blackwell Publishers Ltd 1991, 208.

516.   Timpson, John. *Timpson's Leylines: A Layman Tracking the Ley's.* London: Cassell & Co. 2000, 29.

517.   Anderson, William. *Green Man: The Archetype of our Oneness with the Earth.* London: Harper Collins 1990, 54.

spiritual place in the Christian church for a significant period of time prior to the Reformation.

One notable boss at Exeter is that of a woman within a mass of vines, holding the stems in her hands. Cave believes that many of these carvings were not done under Church authority, but rather by craftsmen that "may in such bosses easily have given rein to their humour, knowing that as soon as the work was done it would pass unnoticed from the floor of the church...."[518] Other images that may be thought strange in Christian churches, unless one takes into account the then contemporary mixture of folk-religion, paganism and Christianity, include wild men and centaurs. Cave notes that early legend "explains the human part of the centaur as a type of Christ."[519]

One way or another the early Church apparently was comfortable with pagan imagery, as can be seen with the tomb of Saint Abre in the Church of Saint-Hilaire-le-Grand in Poitiers. The tomb, dating from the 4th or 5th century C.E., is decorated with a variety of pagan themes including dolphins, and a foliate head. Basford notes, "it is a curious carving, quite unlike the Hellenistic leaf masks. The head is surrounded by contiguous and overlapping leaves which may represent the hair and beard, while large sprays of stylized foliage and flowers spring from the nostrils and extend on either side of the head, like fantastic moustaches."[520] It is this carving, according to Basford, which may be the prototype of the Green Man images of the medieval period. The foliate head at Saint Abre is the earliest known example of the "disgorger of vegetation" in Europe.[521] It was from this same area in France that the Gothic style of Green Man developed.[522]

For approximately three hundred years, between the 10th and 12th centuries, the foliate mask began to change, to represent evil and sin — in fact, the foliate head became part of the exclusive realm of demonology. To this day, many examples of these demon masks exist — including some in the United States. The 13th century reversed this trend with a delightful focus on the lifelike and natural quality of the carved leaves. The obvious struggle between nature and man is shown in many of the Green Man images during the 13th to 15th centuries.

518. Cave, op. cit., 18.
519. Ibid., 22.
520. Basford, K. H. "Quest for the Green Man," in *Symbols of Power*. Edited by H.R. Ellis Davidson. Cambridge: D.S. Brewer Ltd. 1977, 107.
521. Anderson, William. op. cit. 46.
522. Harte, Jeremy. *The Green Man*. Andover: Pitkin Unichrome Ltd 2001, 2.

Myth and images of the Green Man certainly influenced the art of the Florentine Renaissance.[523] Fifteenth-century artist Sandro Botticelli (1444-1510) painted for the Medici family for half of his life. He was allowed much artistic freedom by Lorenzo Medici, who was influenced by Christian Neo-platonism, which tried to reconcile classical (pagan) and Christian views. Botticelli's *La Primavera*, painted around 1478, is perhaps his most famous painting incorporating pagan themes in the Christian Neo-platonism philosophy. However, *La Primavera*, like Botticelli's *Birth of Venus*, has remained somewhat a mystery. According to Jean Seznec, "their ultimate secret has not yet been penetrated — or rather, their secrets, for it is our belief that they hide several layers of allegorical meaning."[524]

The most striking aspect of *La Primavera*, a painting depicting Venus attended by Mercury, the Three Graces, Flora, Cupid and others, is the appearance of a flowering vine flowing from the mouth of a wood nymph. According to Robert Coughlan, this painting is an allegory of spring that "takes place on a flowered plain, backed by a forest where trees bloom and bear fruit at the same time." [525] Even though the painting, while appearing pagan in theme, "is a Christian painting"[526] reflecting the Neo-Platonist philosophy of the time, this would be one of the last paintings to incorporate the symbiotic themes of Nature and humans being linked physically together. The vine gushing from the nymph's mouth surely was inspired by the foliate masks found around Botticelli's environment and the concept struck a cord with him. Nowhere could a finer example of the meaning of rebirth and regeneration be found than in such a depiction.

With the overthrow of the Medici court by French armies, things changed. The arrival of the Dominican monk Savonarola ended Botticelli's artistic license. It was "the reforming priest-dictator," according to Helen Gardner's *Art Through the Ages*, "who denounced the paganism of the Medici and their artists, philoso-

---

523. Likewise, "Christian literature in...learned language was permeated by the allusions, thought, symbolism, mythology, and esthetic of the pagan past, inevitably" notes Ramsay MacMullen in his book *Christianity & paganism in the Fourth to Eighth Centuries*, pg. 147. It is not difficult to see how easily art was also influenced by these "pagan" qualities.

524. Seznec, Jean. *The Survival of the pagan Gods: The Mythological Tradition and Its Place in Renaissance Humanism and Art.* New York: Harper Torchbooks/The Bollingen Library 1961,112.

525. Coughlan, Robert. *The World of Michelangelo 1475-1564.* New York: Time-Life Books 1966, 53.

526. Ibid.

phers, and poets"[527] and who caused the decline of Florentine culture. Botticelli turned his talents to painting safer Christian subjects.

Some foliate heads were the work of Michelangelo, appearing on the tombs of Pope Julius II in Rome and on the Medici Chapel in Florence. Many historical figures in Britain have Green Man images as part of their tombs dating back to the Renaissance and, in fact, it may be due to the influence of the Renaissance that finally got the Green Man out of the church and into secular architecture. Along with the forced insistence of Reformation leaders, that classic religious imagery no longer had a place in ecclesiastical buildings. An ivory helmet owned by George II (1722-60) is decorated with a foliate mask on each side, along with the Royal Coat of Arms and a winged dragon. It would seem that, to the King, the foliate mask was symbolic of power as well as of rebirth and renewal.

The artisans employed to construct and decorate the early churches were, says Grundy, "chosen for their skills rather than for their Christian beliefs."[528] "On finding themselves in charge of stone-building projects" Grundy writes, "...they had summoned the aid of their most trustworthy ally — the powerful, spiritual god of the oak, or today's enigmatic Green Man."[529] We must be thankful to the Church for the survival of the Green Man image into the 21st century. It appears that this struggle, at least as shown in contemporary Green Man art, has changed to one of a symbiotic relationship between humankind and nature. The foliate head has given birth to such garden ornaments as leafy children, birdbaths and other items which embrace life and the spirits of nature.

CHAPTER 15. THE SECULAR IMAGE OF THE GREEN MAN

The Green Man appears in as many different forms as he does in as many locations. I have found him looking down on the busy traffic of Dublin, Cardiff, London, San Diego, Sacramento, San Francisco, Astoria and Corvallis, Oregon

---

527. Gardner, Helen. *Art Through the Ages, Fifth Edition.* New York: Harcourt, Brace & World, Inc. 1970, 443.

528. Grundy, Thirlie. *Going in Search of the Green Man in Cumbria.* Cumbria: Thumbprint 2000, 5.

529. Grundy, Thirlie. *The Green Man in Northumberland and County Durham.* Cumbria: Thumbprint 2001, 3.

with faces filled with glee, mischief, horror, humor and stoicism. His moods are many and his expressions endless.

Images of the Green Man take a variety of forms. Some are more gargoyle-like than human, others more demonic and yet others are of fantastical beasts or reminiscent of the whimsical fairy spirits. In this chapter, I will examine and compare the various images around the world with those in the United States and examine the widely varied designs that are found throughout the world.

These intricate carvings may be based in ancient nature worship, as the earliest concepts of the form of the Green Man image evolved in later centuries. Carvings of tree spirits and tree gods have been universally crafted. Philpot writes of an ancient 3,000-year-old banyan-tree in India that, at least into the 17th century, was sacred to the Hindu religion. "On its trunk" she writes, "at a little distance from the ground a head has been roughly carved, painted in gay colours, and furnished with gold and silver eyes. This simulacrum was constantly adorned with fresh foliage and flowers, the withered leaves which they replaced being distributed amongst the pilgrims as pious souvenirs."[530]

Clive Hicks [531] has determined that there are three types of images in Europe. The first are those of the Roman type, in which the foliage forms the face. This type is found in amazing sculptures from Dublin to Istanbul and many old European cities in between. This ancient style is also reproduced in some very nice examples of more recent vintage, including a Roman-style foliate head on a 19th-century corbel at St. Peter's in Wiltshire.

Kathleen Basford, writing about another foliate face located at St. Mary's, near Cambridge, believed that the Roman style "is a delightful 'now you see it, now you don't' fantasy. It is, however, pure ornament."[532]

The second form, according to Hicks, is that of the face itself generating the foliage. This may be the most common style, being prevalent in England,

530. Philpot, Mrs. J. H. *The Sacred Tree in Religion and Myth.* Mineola: Dover Publications Inc 2004, 35 (A reprint of the 1897 edition published by Macmillan and Co. Ltd, New York & London).

531. Hicks, Clive. *The Green Man: A Field Guide.* Helhoughton: COMPASSbooks 2000, 8. Note also that Janet and Colin Board in their 1982 book, *Earth Rites*, noted that the foliate head carvings had variations in their design. First, according to the Bords, "a human face peeps out through foliage," second, "a human face is formed in foliage, usually shown by the hair and edges of the face being carved as foliage," and third, "a face sprouts foliage from the mouth (most often), or sometimes from the nose, eyes, or ears." (pg. 87)

532. Basford, K.H. "Quest for the Green Man," in *Symbols of Power.* Edited by H.R. Ellis Davidson. Cambridge: D.S. Brewer Ltd. 1977, 118.

France and North America. This style appears as the earliest in Christian architecture on a tomb in Poitiers, France, that dates from 400 CE. Hicks notes the
second form is the most common among architecture dating to the Middle Ages.

And, finally, the third form of Green Man image is that of a carved face set
in among the leaves and foliage — these faces simply inhabit the area and are not
part of the vegetation itself.

There are many examples of all three Green Man types in Europe. During
the Middle Ages it is apparent that the second form is the most prevalent. In the
United States, there are no Green Men associated with churches as far as the
author has been able to determine; and all three Green Man styles are equally
represented on public buildings in American cities.

Other vegetative figures, which expand on the three types noted above,
are found around the world. The hybrid human-plant combinations where the
top half is of a human man or woman and the lower half is vegetative seem to be
the most common. The hybrid figure below is from Bolivia.

Hybrid figure from Bolivia

Dublin Foliate Men

England, Ireland and Wales

Perhaps the most varied forms of Green Man images in the world are located in the British Isles. They vary from obviously noble human faces with leaves growing as hair and beards to ghostly semi-foliate heads to rather abstract, almost comical faces.

The photo below depicts classic, purely foliated Green Men. This Dublin building sported several such faces overlooking the entryway. Mercia Mac-Dermott noted in her study *Explore Green Men*, "the frequent occurrence of foliate heads over, or flanking domestic doorways and windows, suggests that some people may have regarded them as auspicious or protective, as well as decorative."[533]

Two other Green Man doorway decorations, also in Dublin, are shown associated with serpent motifs.

---

533. MacDermott, Mercia. *Explore Green Men.* Loughborough: Explore Books/Heart of Albion Press 2003, 68.

A Noble Dublin Green Man

Dublin Green Men with Serpent Motifs

However, the classic noble head is also present in Dublin. If one looks closely, this bearded face is sprouting leaves, not hair.

Even though the vast majority of Green Men are found on and in churches throughout Britain, I have located a surprising number of them also on the sides of buildings devoted to government, royalty and business.

My observations are contrary to those of Kathleen Basford, who stated that the Green Man is rarely found on secular buildings. Rare they are not — one just has to look outside the church, rather than inside!

Britain has a fascinating variety of Green Men figures. They are featured on castle walls, lampposts in shopping areas, on 16th-century gates, doorframes and corner supports of buildings. Many have a phantom look to them as if they are spirits emerging from their concrete and brick tombs. I have found none of them discussed or depicted in any other reference on British Green Men.

Two of these phantom Green Men appear on a gate constructed in 1841 on Earls' Court in the Kensington area of London.

More devilish-like Green Men are located a block away on Kensington

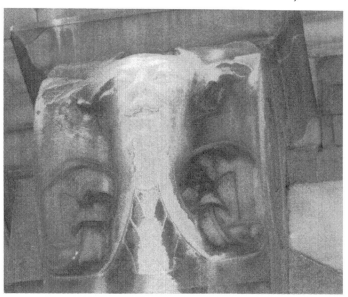

The Ghostly Earl's Court Green Man

High Street, a large shopping district. For a whole block there are Green Men spaced approximately every twenty feet decorating several building supports. As the Green Men located on the gate and those along the shopping lane were constructed in the first half of the 19th century, they may reflect some of the changes in British society and attitudes under Queen Victoria.

One of the magnificent cathedrals in England which sports not only Green Men but other pagan motifs as well as Christian ones, is Norwich. Built and rebuilt from the 12th to the 16th centuries, Norwich Cathedral has several

One of the Kensington High Street Green Men

hundred roof bosses hand carved by master masons and woodcarvers; many of the later ones seem to relate Biblical fables. The earliest examples, however, are of Green Men, dragons, a profusion of foliate carvings, mermaids and hybrid creatures. Historian Martial Rose noted, "the earliest carvings are of leaves and flowers. Subsequently, figures of Green Men, dragons and griffins appear as neighbors to the saints and martyrs. Pre-Christian and Christian symbols inhabit the same bay, cheek by jowl."[534] However, while the Green Men were abundant during the early phases of construction, "by the mid- to late-fifteenth century they have been confined to areas not generally scrutinized, as though suppressed by the Christian story which has made itself manifest elsewhere."[535] Nevertheless, even among the truly Christian symbols one finds those with an obvious linking to the earlier, pagan ones. "In the carving of the Crucifixion," writes Rose, "foliage springs from all the extremities of the cross as though the body of Christ gives life to the dead wood."[536] During the Reformation, when

534. Rose, Martial and Julia Hedgecoe. *Stories in Stone: The Medieval Roof Carvings of Norwich Cathedral.* New York: Thames and Hudson 1997, 10.
535. Ibid. 63.
536. Ibid. 31.

practically every form of religious image, as well as folk-ritual, dance and music, was eliminated by the Puritans, religious images in churches were particularly vulnerable. However, at Norwich, while the "Passion sequence shows evidence of deliberate damage, many other bosses of animals, of foliage, or of a pagan nature, bear little witness of the vandal's hand."[537] MacDermott argues that the survival of the Green Man image in Catholic churches during the Reformation was due to their being simply "non-controversial, arousing no passions and offending no one."[538] They survived, she says, because "of their Classical connections and decorative potential, aided and abetted by fashion."[539]

Other, more traditionally foliated heads abound in Cardiff, Wales. Here again they are not sequestered in churches but are located on public governmental and financial buildings. But again, they seem to have a feeling of despair and pain reminiscent of those medieval carvings that were so reflective of the anguish of the Black Death.

Cardiff, Wales Grimacing Foliate Head

---

537. Ibid. 34.

538. MacDermott, Mercia. *Explore Green Men.* Loughborough: Explore Books/Heart of Albion Press 2003, 69.

539. Ibid., 70.

Green Man with Pigeons

Welsh Green Man with Fangs

A few Green Man masks actually show humor. The Gates at Hampton Court Palace, the home of Thomas Wolsey, who became Lord Chancellor in 1515 under Henry VIII, include a serious-faced Green Man and a dog-like, whimsical creature also sporting vegetation and a royal crown.

Hampton Court's Green Man and Crowned Whimsical Creature

The Green Man in America

Although it is associated commonly with medieval churches, the Green Man as a remnant of ancient, possibly pre-historic, cultures can be found throughout the world, in wildly sculpted artifacts. The Green Man is also found in areas with far less religious meaning in architecture associated more with the mundane, everyday lives of common people. Unfortunately, the Green Man image has many times been miss-identified — making his discovery that much more difficult. One example of this is the "cherubic capitals" on the Duluth Central High School in Duluth, Minnesota.[540] Built in 1891-92, these fine examples of human faces peering out of vines and leaves have eluded their real place in American architectural motifs. Like most "contemporary" architecture

---

540. Wrenn, Tony P. and Elizabeth D. Mulloy/The National Trust for Historic Preservation. *America's Forgotten Architecture*. New York: Pantheon Books 1976, 227.

sporting the Green Man, the Duluth Central High School was built during a time in history when a the Green Man resurgence was in full swing.

As I previously mentioned, a few years ago, while I was researching an article on the Green Man, I found to my amazement and delight examples of the Green Man in architectural art from the late 19th and early 20th centuries in modern American cities. These sculptures are found from New York to Des Moines to San Francisco. The Green Man is also appearing in popular wind chime motifs, birdbaths, garden stones, statuary and jewelry. It seems the more "modern" American culture becomes, the more these ancient pagan symbols become part of the mainstream. What is it that draws us to these mythical representations? Why are they becoming so prevalent once more in a society that seems at first glance more interested in the latest CD or computer software than in the mystical realm? The Green Man has survived for hundreds, if not thousands, of years, modified through time to fit the needs and spirit of the individuals who populate those times. Kathleen Basford wrote that the Green Man "provides an illustration of how an inherited or traditional theme can evolve and diversify as it is exposed to different cultural climates and as it interests and catches the imagination of the particular individuals who use it."[541]

The Green Man in America, as an image from the distant past, is found primarily on the "sides of political and financial buildings," writes Anthony Clifton, "from the nineteenth century onward. In this context, he seems to assert the stability and perpetuation of these institutions. He reassures the public that the balance of power in their society is natural and will contribute to their prosperity and to the continuance of their lifeways."[542]

The Green Man in Manhattan

One would expect the east coast and New York in particular to be the home of many of the early Green Man carvings in the United States. Undoubtedly, many of the Irish and English immigrants brought with them their artistic talents and traditions, which were put to good use in many of the old buildings that still exist. Some of those are found in the architecture of one particular street in Manhattan: East 85th Street. East Eighty-fifth Street boasts a

---

541. Basford, op. cit 102.
542. Clifton, Anthony. "The Hidden Green Men of Iowa," American Witch and pagan, Summer Solstice 1998. www.americanwitchandpagan.com/articles/summer1998article2.html.

series of brown stone apartment buildings built during the 1800s, which sport an amazing variety of Green Man carvings.

One of the most impressive related carvings is that of a fantastic dragon with vegetation sprouting from its mouth. While nothing of comparable style has been found in Europe, mystical Green Beasts, including dragons, do appear in St. Edmund's Church in Sedgefield, Durham Cathedral, and Hexham Abbey. One such "fruitful dragon" exists in Sampford Courtney Church, Devon. The Sampford dragon as well disgorges foliage and fruit from its mouth. In Christian iconography, the dragon represents the devil, death and darkness. In the pre/non-Christian world, the dragon symbolized life and spirit, supernatural strength, knowledge and power. The Bords, writing of dragon motifs, note: "bunches of grapes, a potent fertility symbol, are often part of these dragon carvings, and to us these symbols express the idea that whatever the dominant creed and dogma, the fertility and renewal of man and earth are inextricably linked, and this knowledge will be at the root of any effective religious practice."[543] Dragons were both revered and feared as they could either rejuvenate or destroy the earth.

Manhattan Green Dragon

Another fine carving is that of a nicely depicted Green Man with horns and two of the older scroll-type forms that appear to originate in the ears; these scroll forms characterize some of the 5th-century images. Similar scroll forms are found

---

543. Bord, Janet and Colin. *Earth Rites: Fertility Practices in Pre-Industrial Britain.* London: Granada Publishing Ltd. 1982, 90-91.

on the Pillar of St. Goar from Hunsrück, Germany, and a stone figure from Holzgerlingen, dating from the 3rd to 4th century BCE, also in Germany.

Scrolled-horned Green Man

This horned Green Man does not conform to any of those "typical" styles that Hicks categorizes but rather seems related to an older pre-cursor of the three most common Green Man images. It is obviously a mixture of images which depict Pan and Cernunnos, and the pre-foliate style of the Middle Ages. Horned Green Men were utilized in Church architectural motifs but did not represent Pan or agrarian ideals. Basford noted that while many Green Man images included luxurious vines and leafy tendrils, "the demon nature of the motif was not, however, forgotten. A horned leaf demon appears in the corner of the lintel of the portal of Saint-Urbain in Troyes, and is placed immediately beneath a dramatic representation of the Jaws of Hell."[544] While Basford sees a "demonic nature" of the vine, others see something else. Archaeologist Marija Gimbutas noted that sacred energy, symbolic of the continuity of life, was the purpose for such artistic symbols of snakes, spirals, vines, growing trees and phalluses since pre-historic times.[545]

---

544. Basford, Kathleen. *The Green Man.* Cambridge: D.S. Brewer 1978, 17.
545. Gimbutas, Marija. *The Language of the Goddess.* San Francisco: HarperSanFrancisco 1991, 121.

Another of the New York Green Men is more reminiscent of Hick's second style, wherein the foliage gushes from the mouth, eyes and ears. In this example, thick vines grow from the mouth and appear to originate in the corners of the eyes. These are most common in the 12th- to 15th-century carvings in Great Britain.

Green Man with Foliage Growing from the Mouth

Other Manhattan examples include a highly stylized Green Man showing a bold Celtic countenance with his beard, eyebrows and mustache composed of vegetation. This again is a modified "style two" carving, and is similar to one located in Sacramento, California, dating from 1914, as well as several in Exeter Cathedral from the 13th century. It does not have any vegetation originating from its mouth, nose or eyes — the leaves simply make up what would be the hair, mustache and beard.   An entirely different style of Green Man also located in this area of Manhattan is a large sculpture of a grimacing countenance with decidedly non-benevolent features. Though somewhat reminiscent of a sculpture at Salamanca Cathedral, in Spain, this Manhattan example is quite unusual in its appearance.

"Grimacing" Green Man

California and Oregon's Green Men

California is known as one of those rare places where you can find more of everything and more varieties of "everything" than elsewhere. From vast wealth to abject poverty, from the beautiful sunsets spreading over the sea to the stark sunrises over its deserts — California embraces a full range of the pleasant, unusual, not so pleasant, and outright bizarre features. I first discovered for myself that the Green Man image was alive and well in California while I was walking on K Street in Sacramento. For some reason I stopped and looked up, and there beheld a cheery, full cheeked and horned Green Man smiling down at me. Adorning a Victorian era office building constructed in 1899, the Horned Green Man is striking in its similarity to a figure discovered in the 1970s at a site on the Bosporus. Kathleen Basford, in her paper *Quest for the Green Man*, wrote that the Bosporus figure was "a rather fleshy featured Okeanos[546] with an elaborate coiffure of stylised foliage which branches out on either side of the head in 'ram horn' spirals. Leaves grow out of the folds of the cheeks and at each side of the full-lipped mouth...He is a glowering, profoundly perplexed creature."[547]

---

546. Okeanus, or Oceanus, was the Greek God of the Sea and the oldest of the original twelve Titans. Although he was known as the God of the Primordial Sea he was often depicted as an old man with a long beard and the horns of a bull.

547. Basford, op. cit., 110.

Horned Green Man, Sacramento

It is perplexing that the Sacramento figure created in 1899 could so closely resemble an ancient carving so far away; it is highly improbable that the artist could have seen the image discovered near Turkey, yet they seem more similar than pure coincidence would allow. Is this an example of universal, ancestral memory or symbolic image that all human races retain? Or is this figure simply an expression in art that periodically resurfaces when such expressions lend themselves to a certain time?

I have been unable to locate anything similar to this figure in European Green Man art. With his ram horns and foliate characteristics, this Green Man is a fine example that combines pagan elements.

Two additional horned Green Man figures can be seen on the City Hall building a few blocks away and in Sacramento's Old Town. All three carvings are of distinctly different styles and features. The City Hall figure has a maritime feel to it with a heavy rope feature coiled behind the Green Man's head.

In Sacramento's Old Town, historic buildings from the Gold Rush days dating back to the 1840s evoke scenes of the horse-drawn wagons along the waterfront. One of these buildings has two Green Men situated high above the second story windows. This is another type of horned Green Man that seems to be fairly common in Sacramento.

The Maritime Green Man

A Horned Green Man in Old Town

A few blocks to the south, on 10th Street between K and L streets, is another fine example of Green Man sculpture very similar to one of the Manhattan styles mentioned previously. This figure, with its hair, beard and mustache composed of leaves, adorns the entryway of an apartment building dating to 1914.

A variety of Green Man images decorate this location, formerly the El Cortez Apartments at 1110 10th Street in Sacramento, directly across from the state capital building. Four of the foliate heads are similar, but not identical. There are slight differences in expression as well as hair and moustache design. There is also a variety of smaller images on upper floors. Recently the entire building was painted, and I was shocked to see that the Green Men were also painted — they are slightly beige, now, rather than their original dark coloring. The natural dark stone color is no more, but the foliate heads look content in their new paint.

Thirlie Grundy notes, "The only visible difference between a living god and a dead one was that one breathed and the other did not."[548] But, she finds, the Green Man, as a tree god, does breath — at least as depicted in many of the images found in Britain and in the United States. Grundy observed that some of the Green Men have mouths open, either inhaling or exhaling. In Grundy's symbolism, all of the El Cortez Apartment figures are inhaling and thus representatives of a living god. This is also true for many of the Manhattan figures.

"Breathing" Green Man

---

548. Grundy, Thirlie. *The Green Man of Carlisle Cathedral.* Carlisle: The Studio 1998, 6.

The El Cortez "Inhaler"

As previously mentioned, not all images of the Green Man archetype are male or only of foliated heads. Human figures, both male and female, are depicted rising out of vegetation as if the legs are made of leaves or vines. At Brioude Basilica, in Auvergne, France, several carvings of men and women apparently show the figures transformed from humans to plants. William Anderson wrote of the Brioude figures: "there is an extraordinary carving of a naked man whose legs turn into twisting branches with leaves."[549]

Prendall wrote, "at Brioude, there is a mermaidlike figure with her tail split to the crotch, reminiscent of Yacu Mama in Quichuan Amazonia, tails covered with branchlets and leaves instead of scales and fins."[550] While William Anderson believed that the Brioude style figures were a subtle warning from the Church against lust, he also wrote that the second century CE carvings of the half-human, half-vegetation beings "arise from a desire to anthropomorphize vegetation — to draw out the hidden intelligence in plant forms and to give them human forms and faces...."[551] I found a figure very similar to the Brioude

549. Anderson, William. *The Green Man: The Archetype of Our Oneness With the Earth.* London and San Francisco: Harper Collins 1990, 74.

550. Perndell, Dale. *Pharmako/Poeia: Plant Powers, Poisons and Herbcraft.* San Francisco: Mercury House 1995, 216.

551. Anderson, op. cit. 45.

carvings on a 1930s building in Sacramento — while uncommon, it is evidently present around the world.

A Brioude Style Green Man, Sacramento

And what about Green Women? They may appear more often in American architecture than anywhere else. The female form sprouting out of stalks of leaves is a common motif in early 20th century architectural style, and they do not always appear in sculptured form. One painted Green Woman image, her head and face framed by twisting vines, is located in the State Library Building in Sacramento. There are also the more traditional depictions of foliate women showing the nude form of a woman with her legs either part of, or entirely hidden by, leafy scrollwork. Many of these are examples of pseudo-Greek sculpture typical of early 20th-century Romanticism. The Green Man is, however, predominately male as are the Vegetation Deities. Why is this so? One researcher believes "that the Green Man is taking a part which is a protective part for, for example, the female forest or the Earth Mother."[552]

It has been suggested that the Green Man image is a symbol of Freemasonry. While this would seem improbable, the façade of the Masonic Temple in Sacramento is populated with several Green Men. The various figures are part of window frames and serve as support for the front entry canopy. The canopy cables are held tight in the Green Man's mouth. This building, located at 1123 J Street, was constructed in 1918.

The Masonic Temple building is a wealth of interesting images of pagan symbolism. Angelic children sitting atop rams, snakes, sea life and other sym-

---

552. Susan Clifford as quoted in *The Green Man in Britain* by Fran & Geoff Doel. Gloucestershire: Tempus Publishing Ltd. 2001, 22.

Masonic Temple Green Man

bolic animals decorate the first floor while the Green Men appear to dominate the upper floors. On the 12th Street side of the building, eight different and distinct Green Man masks adorn the second floor windows.

12th Street Green Men

San Francisco and San Diego have a few Green Men — and Women — as well. San Diego's include a series of carvings found on an office building near the famous Horton Plaza shopping district not far from the Gas Lamp quarter. These figures, both male and female, show the typical scrolling found on so many carvings with vines and leaves surrounding the heads. These faces are all laughing, with a rather leering look to them.

"Leering" San Diego Green Man

A number of Bacchus-style figures, both male and female, were carved on the San Francisco City Hall a century ago. These solemn-looking figures were decorated with oak and grape leaves. While the mythic tales of the Green focus on the male Green Man, we must not lose sight of the powers that the divine feminine wield in nature. The Green Woman is an important reflection of the creative, life renewing and sustaining forces of nature. The fact that so few female carvings are found, and those mostly in the United States, probably reflects the dominant role of males and the fact that male images were more readily accepted during the early Christian period up through the Middle Ages. Female carvings were easily labeled as tempting and sinful.

Not to be outdone is San Francisco. San Francisco has a block of classic Green Men between Powell Street and the Embarcadero; two that caught my eye were located on the second story of the City Hall. A Green Man and a Green Woman, in the Bacchus style, calmly peer down upon the crowds lingering in the park across the street.

Bacchus Style Green Woman

San Francisco Green Man in the Bacchus Style

Approximately 200 miles southeast of San Francisco is the City of Hanford. Located in Kings County in the San Joaquin Valley half way between Monterey and Yosemite National Park in California's rich agricultural land, Hanford is a surprisingly clean, well organized, and beautiful town that has succeeded in preserving much of its historic architecture and Victorian style buildings. One building that deserves mention is the Kings County Courthouse, also known as the William Wilcox building. Built in 1896-97, this large stone

His Green Woman Companion

structure has a beautiful stained glass window over its main entryway. What is remarkable about this window is that the subject is the Green Man. Built during the same era as many of the other buildings using the Green Man motif, this courthouse has not previously been mentioned as an example of preserved architecture that so aptly incorporates the Green Man. It is fortunate for the 50,000 residents of Hanford that this building and many others in the city were preserved from demolition in the 1970s.

Kings County Courthouse Green Man Window

Like California, Oregon has its own share of Green Men, albeit not as many. Oregon is smaller, with few large cities and, for the most part, it is still pristine; its forests, mountains and seashores have retained their ancient beauty and ties to nature. In many places around the United States, it seems there are more Green Men to make up for the loss of the wilderness — to remind all of us of what once was. Oregon retains much of its natural openness and quality and the awe of Nature. Nature at her best is everywhere you care to look. However, even here the environment struggles and the Green Man is present to watch over it and to remind us of our responsibilities. Horned Green Men appear to be a common form in the United States. One such example is located in Corvallis, a university town about 50 miles east of the Pacific Ocean, above the main entryway of the 1888 Benton County Courthouse. There is no record remaining as to the original purpose or intended meaning for this image.

The Corvallis, Oregon Green Man

Another 200 miles northwest of Corvallis is the oldest American settlement west of the Rocky Mountains — the village of Astoria. Known as the winter encampment of the Lewis and Clark Discovery Expedition, Astoria is a small town near the mouth of the Columbia River; it boasts a large harbor for oil tankers, cargo ships and fishing boats. Separated from the state of Washington by the Columbia River, Astoria is a quaint town with many Victorian homes. Approximately five blocks south of the river on 12th and Commercial Street is the Liberty Theatre. The original building burned to the ground in 1922 and was rebuilt in 1924. The "new" Liberty boasts three Green Men on the outside façade as well as two large plaques on the inside portico of human figures rising from vegetation. While the Liberty building is listed on the National Register of Historic Places, it is in desperate need of cosmetic repairs. Two of the three Green Men are reminiscent of Pan and, in fact, they hold Panpipes and have horns sprouting from their heads. This mixture of the Green Man motif and Pan, the god of Nature, is certainly a logical one.

Above the entryway of the Liberty Theatre, twenty feet above the ground, is a bust of a man with his hair comprised of leaves and fruit around his neck. This is another fine example of a Bacchus styled figure.

In the theatre's alcove is a fine carving of the ancient half-human, half-plant hybrid discussed previously. Common from Bolivia to Europe, the Medi-

Astoria's Pan Type Green Man

terranean and the United States, William Anderson wrote that the carvings of these hybrid figures "arise from a desire to anthropomorphize vegetation — to draw out the hidden intelligence in plant forms and to give them human forms and faces..."

The Green Men of Iowa

While New York and California would seem to contain the majority of Green Men, they are not exclusive and Green Men are even found in the

A Bacchus Style Green Man at the Liberty Theatre

Astoria's Hybrid Human-Plant Being

heartland of America. In fact, Iowa has an unusual collection. The Polk County courthouse, located in downtown Des Moines, has 28 carved faces on its outside walls. Writer Jan Fleming states that the variety and number of the carved faces are "unmatched anywhere in the United States."[553]

While many of the carved images on the courthouse appear to be mere caricatures of historic figures, some of the images do show the more traditional visage of the foliate Green Man. In 1998, Fleming began a Farmers' Market in a square near the courthouse with a roving "Jack in the Green" figure, Gaelic music and other celebratory items more common in the older festivals of Britain.

A Green Man and a Green Woman also decorate the Johnson County courthouse in Iowa City. The beautiful scrollwork on this building is more reminiscent of the British-Celtic motifs than the Polk County courthouse carvings and brings a more solemn feeling to the building.

Iowa Green Man (photos courtesy of Sharon Sommerfelt)

Iowa Green Woman

---

553. Clifton op. cit.

The Green Man Elsewhere

The Green Man also appears sometimes where you least expect him to. I have found his image carved on furniture from the eighteen and nineteen hundreds — further attesting to the fact that the Green Man was not only a religious symbol utilized by the Church but for the "common man" as well. I recently obtained a magnificent oak rocking chair dating to the beginning of the 20th century that has an amazing carving of a Green Man on the back. This ferocious-looking creature is peering out of a midst of flowing oak leaves and vines befitting the Green Man. To the best of my knowledge, this is a highly unusual piece, and the designer and/or original owner must have been particularly intrigued with the meanings of the Green Man image. This carving probably originated in the Boston area and may have been crafted by immigrant Irish wood carvers who understood the complexities of the Green Man.

While rare in the United States, furniture such as this was popular in the Renaissance and into the 18th century in Europe. "They appear," writes Mac-Dermott, "on some ornate black and gold chairs, made in Venice about 1590....While these Venetian heads are human in aspect, snarling animal heads were popular as decoration on massive seventeenth-century English furniture, such as chairs and sideboards."[554]

Aside from furniture, reproductions of many of ancient carvings can be purchased from such places as the Tower of London gift shop as well as from the many catalogue companies and Renaissance Faires held around the world. It is rare to find a gift shop or garden shop today that does not have a Green Man piece. While it is possible that one of his early meanings was to warn of the evils of sin and the transitory nature of life on earth, today most viewers focus on his aspect as a representative of nature and the vibrancy of life — which is where I feel his true spirit has always resided.

CHAPTER 16. WHAT'S IN A NAME? THE ORIGINS OF THE TERM "GREEN MAN"

Lady J. Raglan took credit in 1939 for coining the term "the Green Man." "It is now about eight years ago," Raglan wrote, "since my attention was first drawn by the Revd. J. Griffith...to a curious carving. It is a man's face, with oak leaves

---

554. MacDermott, op. cit., 58.

The Green Man Chair, ca. 1900-1920

growing from the mouth and ears, and completely encircling the head. Mr. Griffith suggested that it was intended to symbolise the spirit of inspiration, but it seemed to me certain that it was a man and not a spirit, and moreover that it was a 'Green Man,' so I named it...."[555] Raglan was also credited with assigning the Green Man term to the Jack-in-the-Green, the May King and Robin Good-fellow. While Raglan may have been among the first to assign the "Green Man" name to the foliate head carvings, the name had been in use for sometime. Dione Fortune, founder of the Western Esoteric Tradition, used the term three years earlier in her 1936 novel, *The Goat Foot God*: "I suppose you know who the Green Man is? He's Pan...He's Jack-In-The-Green, the wood-spirit — ."[556] Did Lady

555. Raglan, Lady J. "The 'Green Man' in Church Architecture". In *Folklore* #50 (1939), 45.
556. Fortune, Dione. *The Goat Foot God.* York Beach: Samuel Wiser, Inc. 1980, 165. A reprint of the 1936 edition.

Raglan get the idea from Dione Fortune's book? We can only wonder; but it seems certain that Dione Fortune was the first to use the name in popular literature and she should receive credit for doing so.

There is substantial evidence, moreover, that the term "Green Man" was in use much earlier than Lady Raglan's claim or Dione Fortune's use of the term in *The Goat Foot God*. "Green-men" was a term in common use at least as early as the 1500s in various plays and pageants. Brandon S. Centerwall quotes Robert Amerie's 1610 publication, *Chesters Triumph in Honor of Her Prince*, describing these pageant Green Men:

> Two disguised, called Greene-men, their habit Embroydred and Stitch'd on with Ivie-leaves with blacke-side, (3) having hanging to their shoulders, a huge black shaggie Hayre, Savage-like, with Ivie Garlands upon their heads....[557]

The fact that the term and costuming was obviously well-entrenched in British pageantry and folklore in the 16th century indicates that his image and name were also well known among the general population — and it is an error to credit Lady Raglan, or Dione Fortune for that matter, with the creation of the moniker.

Centerwall and others attack the older notion that the Green Man was a representation of the spirit of nature, fertility and rebirth by illustrating the entertainment value of the figure in 16th century pageants. This seems to be an ill-conceived argument. Obvious similarities include the Passion Plays, which draw throngs of Christians who view these pageants as not only reverent reflections but also as entertainment; the plays do not in any way detract from the original meanings of Jesus for Christians around the world. The two must be viewed as separate issues. Centerwall himself appears to vacillate in his reasoning. "Although originally intended to represent the Green Man of church architecture," he writes, "by the latter half of the sixteenth century the pageant Green Men had lost all earlier significance, having evolved into a popular species of whiffer whose antics suggested bacchanalian revelry."[558]

While it was entertaining, in the 16th century, the origins of the Green Man are certainly much older, and the deeper meanings must be sought in its earlier manifestations. It is unfortunate that so much effort has been put into disproving the origins and meanings of the Green Man by using isolated and friv-

---

557. Centerwall, Brandon S. "The name of the Green Man," In *Folklore*, January 1, 1997, V. 108, 27.

558. Ibid., 32.

olous events in social history that were created 2000 years after the first carvings of the foliate head appeared.

AFTERWORD

The Green Man is a universal figure and one that continues to play an important, if sometimes subconscious, role in our relationship with nature. Current literature treats the Green Man only as a fixture on ecclesiastical architecture, reflective of ancient pagan traditions or perhaps as Christian warnings against sin. This book, and the photographs that illustrate it, prove that Green Man images appear around the world and on more secular buildings than has been acknowledged previously. This is important because it shows that the Green Man belongs to all people, of every class, and every religious tradition.

The history of the Green Man in Britain is a long one. Even if he is utilized primarily as a decorative motif, his arrival in the United States and other countries gives us the occasion to renew his meaning, and allows us to look to his image as a reminder, leading us all back to nature and to the knowledge that we must take responsibility for protecting and nurturing our wildernesses.

First and foremost, the Green Man beckons to each of us to once again embrace nature. Most of the problems that beset the world are caused by human failures. Mass starvation, warfare, pollution, toxic waste, many diseases and the extermination of thousands of forms of life have all been created or abetted by human activity.

What can we do to reverse this trend? Brian Branston hit it on the head when he wrote, "those individuals who take practical steps to make their peace with Nature in what they eat and drink, in how they think, sleep and behave — these peace-makers shall inherit the earth. In effect, we have to stop regarding ourselves as things apart — Man as opposed to animals and plants, or Man in vacuous space without what the botanists call a habitat. We have to reach a symbiotic relationship with all else in the world, living or dead."[559]

The debate over the origins and meanings of this ancient motif has not diminished. It is doubtful that all of the many researchers and writers will ever agree. Is the Green Man a depiction of an ancient nature god or simply an artistic metaphor, based on Christian doctrine? William Anderson wrote: "The Green Man, as a composite of leaves and a man's head, symbolizes the union of · humanity and the vegetable world. He knows and utters the secret laws of Nature. When an image of great power such as the Green Man returns...after a long absence, the purpose of its return is not only to revive forgotten memories but to present fresh truths and emotions necessary to fulfilling the potentialities of the future."[560] Jeremy Harte, on the other hand, wrote "The Green Man began as a grotesque: it is we who have made him into a god."[561]

However that may be, he seems to represent a god as enduring as many others throughout history and one that continues to gain strength and popularity in troubled times.

559. Branston, Brian. *The Lost Gods of England.* New York: Oxford University Press 1974, 201.

560. Anderson, op. cit., 14.

561. Harte, Jeremy. *The Green Man: The Pitkin Guide.* Andover: Pitkin Unichrome Ltd. 2001, 18.

APPENDIX A
AN ANALYSIS OF THE ELEMENTS IN THE GREEN MAN MOTIF

The foliate head, the mask of the Green Man, is comprised of various symbolic motifs. Vines, leaves of various trees, certain expression types, the disgorging of leafy tendrils from the eyes, mouth and ears all make up the Green Man image. All of these items are important symbolisms in religious thought in both the pagan and Christian traditions.

VINES

Vines are depicted on religious statuary and reliefs throughout time — including the foliate head of the Green Man. Vines represent fertility, the Tree of Life and life itself. The vine is symbolic of deities as well. Jesus referred to himself as the "True Vine" in John 15: "I am the true vine, and my Father is the husbandman." In Egypt the vine was sacred to Osiris, in Greece and Rome to Dionysus and Bacchus, and in Sumer to Tammuz. The vine is intimately associated with these Dying Gods and the promise of life reborn.

The symbol of Dionysus is the ivy vine. A life-sized mask of Dionysus located at Icaria, states Otto, "is wreathed with ivy."[562] In Greek mythology ivy

---

562. Otto, Walter F. *Dionysus: Myth and Cult.* Bloomington: Indiana University Press 1965, 153.

191

"appeared simultaneously with the birth of Dionysus."[563] Ivy is symbolic of eternal life — growing green even during the winter season.

LEAVES

Leaves denote fertility, growth and renewal. Green leaves are symbolic of life renewed. Cooper notes, "Crowns of leaves symbolize divinity or triumph and victory. In Chinese symbolism the leaves of the Cosmic Tree represent all beings in the universe."[564]

Leaves are also closely associated with prophecy and, according to Porteous, "ancient magicians used to encircle their heads with leaves so as to obtain wisdom."[565] Perhaps the foliate head is representative of the wisdom that is obtainable by all of us if we would only surround ourselves with those things that stimulate fertile thoughts! Because the Green Man is sometimes equated with knowledge, the leafy appendages to the masks add to this symbolic characteristic.

Leaves were also believed to have souls or to be inhabited by intelligent beings, and like some trees, were believed to be responsible for the creation of life. Porteous noted, "Some of the ancient writers tell of wonderful trees whose leaves produced animals and even serpents, and in one case the leaves as they fell off became changed into butterflies."[566]

In many Green Man sculptures, the leaves are those of the acanthus, which is widely symbolic of life and rebirth in the Mediterranean world. It also represents immortality but, in the Christian tradition, the acanthus thorns represent sin and the pain associated with the punishment of sin. "The influential scholar Hrabanus Maurus (784-856)," wrote Anderson, "had identified the [acanthus] leaf with sin, especially with sexual sin, and this probably gave a further licence to the portrayal of vegetation."[567]

---

563. Ibid.

564. Cooper, J.C. *An Illustrated Encyclopaedia of Traditional Symbols.* New York: Thames and Hudson 1978, 96.

565. Porteous, Alexander. *The Lore of the Forest: Myths and Legends.* London: Senate Publishers 1996, 252. A reprint of the 1928 publication *Forest Folklore* published by George Allen & Unwin, London.

566. Ibid., 253.

567. Anderson, William. *Green Man: The Archetype of our Oness with the Earth.* London: Harper Collins 1990, 64.

Acanthus certainly are not the "leaf of choice," however, for the Green Man image. Hawthorn, oak, ranunculus, potentilla, hops, rose and ivy make up the majority of the plants present in the carvings. Not all leaves or flowers that are present on the foliate head have a known magical or even much of a folkloric meaning. The maple leaf is an example. The decorative beauty of the maple leaf must have been a deciding factor in the stone carver's choice. However, although the leaf had little folkloric value, the tree had more. The maple tree was believed to be an "old age giver." There is an old saying, "A child passed through a maple tree will live long." According to Edwin and Mona Radford, "As late as the nineteenth century, this belief held its ground in many rural areas of the country. The passing had to be through the branches of the maple. And passed through the branches all the babies of the village were."[568] Perhaps the carving of the maple leaf as part of the foliate head was intentional after all as it represents time and longevity.

HORNS

While horns are common on many American Green Man images, they are relatively rare in Britain. One example that does exist is the 12th-century carving on a pillar capital located at St. Michael's church in Herefordshire. This figure has the typical vegetable disgorgement but also two horns on its head that recall the classic image of Satan. Other British Green Men sport outgrowths that are reminiscent of horns but are composed of vines or other vegetable matter.

A foliate head on the west font of the church of Notre-Dame-la-Grand in Poitiers, France, does have classic horns that seem to grow from the middle of the forehead. This one is also on a 12th-century church.

One of the Kensington High Street Green Men mentioned in Chapter 15 also has horns but is from a much more recent age — the 18th century.

Horns are commonly linked to gods of nature and vegetation, such as Pan, Cernunnos, Dionysus and Hathor. Horns represent supernatural power; divinity; virility and fertility, and abundance.

---

568. Radford, Edwin and Mona A. *Encyclopaedia of Superstitions.* New York: The Philosophical Library 1949, 168.

FACE TYPES

As previously noted, there are three distinct Green Man types that have evolved over time. The first are those of the Roman type in which the foliage forms, or rather "generates," the face. This type is found in and around Dublin, Ireland, London, Istanbul and old cities on the European continent. A very nice example reproducing the Roman-style foliate head is found on a 19th century corbel at St. Peter's in Wiltshire.

The second form, according to Hicks, is that of the face itself generating the foliage. Lastly, the third form of Green Man image is that of a carved face set in among the leaves and foliage. There are many expressions carved into the Green Man face that are reflective of the religious attitudes and the particular time in history when the images were created. It is these images that cause so much disagreement about the intent of the motif in general.

The earliest forms of Green Men show expressions of calm and quiet dignity. As the Christian church became the dominant force in the Western world, the images began to change to reflect not dignity but suffering. Some of this can be explained by the simple fact that during part of this time the plague was ravaging the populace and death became more "normal" than life. Some writers, such as Basford, note, "the Green Man can be at once both beautiful and sinister."[569] It would seem that our own beliefs color our perceptions of the images, and the meaning changed over time. Basford finds the Green Man to be representative of "demonic character" and the "uneasy or actually hostile relationship" between humans and nature.[570] The teachings of the Church during the 14th and 15th centuries did promote this idea and the intentional portrayal of nature as an enemy rather than as a friend of humankind resulted in many of the grotesque images of the Green Man that Basford refers to. Where a given researcher chooses to place his emphasis may be more a reflection of the researcher's own religious beliefs than a reflection of the aggregate history of Green Man images.

Many of the Green Man faces show an intent entirely different to the nature-as-adversary view. Here, he is a message of life and humor, not suffering and evil. Thirlie Grundy effectively argues that many of the Green Man carvings depict the archetype as breathing both in and out — indicating that they are

569. Basford, Kathleen. *The Green Man.* Cambridge: D.S. Brewer 1978, 19.
570. Ibid.

carvings of a "living, breathing tree-god...[a] smiling god."[571] The Green Man carved into the French tomb of St. Hilaire-le-Grand dating to 400 CE is the earliest known example of the breathing Green Man.

APPENDIX B: TIMELINE OF THE GREEN MAN MOTIF

Before Common Era				Common Era			
12000-7000BCE[a]	1200 BCE	500 BCE	400 BCE	50-100 CE	400 CE	700 CE	1000-1200 CE
Possible date of origin of vegetation gods in early agrarian society	Foliate masks Appear in Olmec carvings	Pillar of St. Goar Pfalzfeld, Germany (Earliest known use in Europe)	Foliate masks appear in India	Foliate masks appear in Roman art. They were further developed and widely used by 200 CE	Tomb of Saint Abre in the Church of Saint-Hilaire-le-Grand in Poitiers, decorated with foliate heads.	Foliate masks used in Kalends celebrations	Foliate heads widely used in Norman-Christian churches as symbols of sin
1300s CE	1478 CE	1500-1800 CE	1870-1920CE	1840-1930CE			1970- present
The epic poem, "The Green Knight" written. Foliate heads take on a delightful natural appearance	Sandro Botticelli paints La Primavera depicting a nymph with foliage growing from her mouth in the classic foliate head motif	Foliate heads used widely in art and architecture throughout Italy, Europe and Britain.	A "Green Man revival" starts as part of the Palladian and Renaissance Revival movement in British architecture	Foliate head carvings used in secular American architecture from New York to the West Coast			A resurgence in the Green Man motif takes place. Green Man designs are used in jewelry, garden and household decorations

a. Scientific journals have gradually gotten away from using BC and AD in discussing dates and have switched to BCE (Before Current Era), CE (Current Era) and BP (before present). I have used those terms in this book, as they generally give a broader and more accurate sense of time when discussing prehistoric and historic sites.

---

571. Grundy, Thirlie. *Going in Search of the Green Man in Cumbria.* Carlisle: Thumbprint 2000, 14.

About the Author

Gary R. Varner has lectured and written several articles and books on folklore and early religions, including *Sacred Wells: A Study in the History, Meaning, and Mythology of Holy Wells & Waters; Water of Life — Water of Death: The Folklore & Mythology of Sacred Water;* and *Menhirs, Dolmen, and Circles of Stone: The Folklore and Magic of Sacred Stone.*

He is a member of the Oregon Writers Colony, the American Folklore Society and the Joseph Campbell Foundation. Varner writes about ancient traditions and how those traditions, along with their folklore and mythology, continue to play an important part in contemporary society. He is listed in *Who's Who in America* and *Who's Who in the World* reference works.

BIBLIOGRAPHY

Alexander, Hartley Burr. *The World's Rim: Great Mysteries of the North American Indians.* Mineola: Dover Publications Inc., 1999. A reprint of the 1953 edition published by the University of Nebraska Press.

Alexander, Marc. *A Companion to the Folklore, Myth & Customs of Britain.* Gloucestershire: Sutton Publishing Limited, 2002.

Allen, Paula Gunn. *The Sacred Hoop: Recovering the Feminine in American Indian Traditions.* Boston: Beacon Press, 1986.

Anderson, Johannes C. *Myths and Legends of the Polynesians.* Rutland: Charles E. Tuttle Company Publishers, 1969.

Anderson, M.D. *History and Imagery in British Churches.* London: John Murray Ltd., 1971.

Anderson, William. *The Green Man: The Archetype of Our Oneness with the Earth.* London: Harper Collins, 1990.

Andrews, Tamra. *A Dictionary of Nature Myths: Legends of the Earth, Sea, and Sky.* Oxford: Oxford University Press, 1998.

Anon. *Celtic Mythology.* New Lanark: Geddes & Grosset, 1999.

Anon. *The Spirit World.* Alexandria: Time-Life Books, 1992.

Arrowsmith, Nancy and George Moorse. *A Field Guide to the Little People.* London: Macmillan Company, 1977.

Ash, Steve. "Bacchus and Isis in Britain: Romano-British Mysteries and their descendants. A cultural, social, spiritual, political and psychological multiple perspective." www.angelfire.com/aka/Forum/Bl ONE.htm July 11, 2004.

Aubrey, John. "Remaines of Genilisme and Judaisme" in *Folklore Society*, No. IV 1881.

Ballard, Carol. *The Green Man: The Shakespeare Connection.* Warwickshire: self published, 1999.

Basford, K. H. "Quest for the Green Man," in *Symbols of Power.* Edited by H. R. Ellis Davidson. Cambridge: D.S. Brewer Ltd., 1977.

Basford, Kathleen. *The Green Man.* Cambridge: D.S. Brewer, 1978.

Bates, Brian. "Sacred Trees" in *Resurgence Magazine* #181, March/April, 1997.

Beckham, Stephen Dow. "Coos, Lower Umpqua, and Siuslaw: Traditional Religious Practices" in *Native American Religious Practices and Uses, Siuslaw National Forest.* Eugene: Heritage Research Associates Report No. 7(3), September 20, 1982 .

Beckwith, Martha. *Hawaiian Mythology.* Honolulu: University of Hawaii Press1970. A reprint of the 1940 edition published by Yale University Press..

Bierhorst, John. *The Mythology of Mexico and Central America.* New York: William Morrow and Company, Inc., 1990 .

Bilson, Charles. *Vestiges of paganism in Leicestershire.* Loughborough: Heart of Albion Press, 1994. A reprint of the 1911 article appearing in *Memorials of old Leicestershire* published by George Allen, London.

Black, William George. *Folk-Medicine: A Chapter in the History of Culture.* London: Publications of the Folk-Lore Society #12, 1883.

Bonwick, James. *Irish Druids and Old Irish Religions.* New York: Barnes & Noble Books, 1986 (A reprint of the 1894 edition).

Bord, Janet and Colin. *Earth Rites: Fertility Practices in Pre-Industrial Britain.* London: Granada Publishing Ltd., 1982.

Bord, Janet and Colin. *Mysterious Britain: Ancient Secrets of Britain and Ireland.* London: Thorsons, 1995.

Branston, Brian. *The Lost Gods of England.* New York: Oxford University Press, 1974 .

Brewster, Harry. *The River Gods of Greece: Myths and Mountain Waters in the Hellenic World.* London: I.B. Tauris Publishers, 1997.

Bridwood, George. *Symbolism of the East and West.* London: George Redway, 1900.

Budge, E.A. Wallis. *Cleopatra's Needles and Other Egyptian Obelisks.* New York: Dover Publications, Inc., 1990. A reprint of the 1926 edition published by the Religious Tract Society, London..

Budge, Sir Wallis. *Egyptian Religion.* New York: Bell Publishing Company, 1959.

Burkert, Walter. *Ancient Mystery Cults.* Cambridge: Harvard University Press, 1987

Burns, Charlotte Sophia. *The Handbook of Folklore.* London: Senate, 1996. A reprint of the, 1914 edition published by Sidgwick & Jackson Ltd., London.

Bury, J.B., *A History of Greece to the Death of Alexander the Great.* New York: The Modern Library, no date.

Cantero, Antonio. "Occult Healing Practices in French Canada" in *Canadian Medical Association Journal,* New Series 20, (1929), pgs 303-306.

Carmichael, Joel. *The Birth of Christianity: Reality and Myth.* New York: Dorset Press, 1989.

Carr-Gomm, Philip. *The Druid Way.* Shaftesbury: Element Books Limited, 1993.

Catherine, David. "The Green Fingerprint: Exploring a critical signature in the quest for the authentic self." Unpublished paper copyright, 2004 by Ufudu Medicinal Arts, South Africa.

Cave, C.J.P. *Medieval Carvings in Exeter Cathedral.* London: Penguin Books, 1953.

Cavendish, Richard. "Lancelot and Gawain," in *Legends of the World.* New York: Barnes & Noble Books, 1994.

Centerwall, Brandon S. "The name of the Green Man." In *Folklore,* January 1, 1997, V.108, pgs. 25-34.

Cizmár, Josef. *Lidové lékarství v Ceskoslovensku. Vol. 1 & 2.* Czechoslovakia: Melantrich, A.S., 1946.

Clark, Ella E. "Indian Thanksgiving in the Pacific Northwest," in *Oregon Historical Quarterly* Vol. LXI, Number 4, December 1960, 437-461.

Clifton, Anthony. "The Hidden Green Men of Iowa," American Witch and pagan, Summer Solstice, 1998. www.americanwitchandpagan.com.

Cooper, J.C. *An Illustrated Encyclopaedia of Traditional Symbols.* London: Thames & Hudson Ltd., 1978.

Coughlan, Robert. *The World of Michelangelo 1475-1564.* New York: Time-Life Books, 1966.

Cumont, Franz. *Oriental Religions in Roman paganism.* New York: Dover Publications, 1956. A reprint of the 1911 edition published by C. Routledge & Sons, Ltd..

Cunliff, Barry. *The Ancient Celts.* New York: Oxford University Press, 1997.

D'Alviella, The Count Goblet. *The Migration of Symbols.* New York: University Books, 1956. A reprint of the 1894 edition..

Darby, George E. "Indian Medicine in British Columbia" in *The Canadian Medical Association Journal* #28, 1933, 433-438.

Davidson, H.R. Ellis. *Gods and Myths of the Viking Age.* New York: Bell Publishing Company, 1981.

Davidson, H.R. Ellis. *Myths and Symbols in pagan Europe: Early Scandinavian and Celtic Religions.* Syracuse: Syracuse University Press, 1988.

Day, Brian. *Chronicle of Celtic Folk Customs.* London: Hamlyn, 2000.

Doel, Fran & Geoff. *The Green Man in Britain.* Gloucestershire: Tempus Publishing Ltd., 2001.

Eason, Cassandra. *The Handbook of Ancient Wisdom.* New York: Sterling Publishing Co., 1997.

Eisler, Riane. *The Chalice & The Blade: Our History, Our Future.* San Francisco: HarperSanFrancisco, 1987.

Eliade, Mircea. *Rites and Symbols of Initiation: The Mysteries of Birth and Rebirth.* New York: Harper & Row, Publishers, 1958.

Eliade, Mircea. *Myth and Reality.* New York: Harper Torchbooks, 1963.

Eliade, Mircea. *Shamanism: Archaic Techniques of Ecstasy.* Princeton; Princeton University Press, 1964.

Ellis, Peter Berresford. *The Ancient World of the Celts.* New York: Barnes & Noble Books, 1998.

Elwell-Sutton, L.P. "The Islamic World: The Two Horned One," in *Legends of the World.* Edited by Richard Cavendish. New York: Barnes & Noble Books, 1994.

Ely, Talfourd. *The Gods of Greece and Rome.* Mineola: Dover Publications Inc., 2003. A reprint of the 1891 publication..

Evans, E. Estyn. *Irish Folk Ways.* Mineola: Dover Publications Inc., 2000. A reprint of the 1957 edition published by Routledge & Kegan Paul Ltd., London..

Evans-Wentz, W.Y. *The Fairy-Faith in Celtic Countries.* Mineola: Dover Publications Inc., 2002. A reprint of the 1911 edition published by Henry Frowde, London..

Fee, Christopher R. *Gods, Heroes, & Kings: The Battle for Mythic Britain.* Oxford: Oxford University Press, 2001.

Fiske, John. *Myths and Myth-Makers: Old Tales and Superstitions.* Boston: Houghton, Mifflin and Company, 1881.

Fortune, Dione. *The Goat Foot God.* York Beach: Samuel Wiser, Inc., 1980. A reprint of the 1936 edition..

Franklin, Anna. *The Illustrated Encyclopaedia of Fairies.* London: Paper Tiger/Chrysalis Books, 2004.

Frazer, James G. *The Golden Bough: The Roots of Religion and Folklore.* New York: Avenel Books, 1981. A reprint of the 1890 two-volume edition of *The Golden Bough: A Study in Comparative Religion* published by Macmillan Company Ltd., London..

Frazer, Sir. J. G. *Adonis: A Study in the History of Oriental Religion.* London: Watts & Co., 1932.

Frazer, Sir James. *The Golden Bough: A Study in Magic and Religion.* Hertfordshire: Wordsworth Editions, 1993.

Gadgill, M.D. Subash Chandran. "Sacred Groves and Sacred Trees of Uttara Kannada" in *Lifestyle and Ecology,* edited by Baidyanath Saraswati. New Delhi: Indira Gandhi National Centre for the Arts, 1998.

Gardner, Helen. *Art Through the Ages, Fifth Edition.* New York: Harcourt, Brace & World, Inc., 1970.

Gimbutas, Marija. *The Language of the Goddess.* San Francisco: HarperSanFrancisco, 1991.

Gordon, Richard. "Imagining Greek and Roman Magic," in *Witchcraft and Magic in Europe: Ancient Greece and Rome,* edited by Bengt Ankarloo and Stuart Clark. Philadelphia: University of Pennsylvania Press, 1999.

Graham, Patrick. *Sketches Descriptive of the Picturesque Scenery of Perthshire.* Edinburgh 1810.

Graves, Robert. *The White Goddess.* New York: The Noonday Press, 1948.

Green, Miranda J. *The World of the Druids.* London: Thames and Hudson, 1997.

Grundy, Thirlie. *The Green Man of Carlisle Cathedral.* Carlisle: The Studio, 1998.

Grundy, Thirlie. *Going in Search of the Green Man in Cumbria.* Cumbria: Thumbprint,, 2000.

Grundy, Thirlie. *The Green Man in Northumberland and County Durham.* Carlisle Cumbria: Thumbprint, 2001.

Hallam, Elizabeth. *Gods and Goddesses.* New York: Macmillan, 1996.

Hand, Wayland D. editor, *American Folk Medicine: A Symposium.* Berkeley: University of California Press 1976.

Hand, Wayland D. *Magical Medicine: The Folkloric Component of Medicine in the Folk Belief, Custom, and Ritual of the Peoples of Europe and America.* Berkeley: University of California Press, 1980.

Harte, Jeremy. *The Green Man.* Andover: Pitkin Unichrome Ltd, 2001.

Hicks, Clive. *The Green Man: A Field Guide.* Helhoughton: COMPASSbooks, 2000.

Hiiemäe, Mall. "Some Possible Origins of St. George's Day Customs and Beliefs" in *Folklore,* Vol. 1, June, 1996, published by the Institute of Estonian Languages, Tartu.

Hoeller, Stephan A. *The Gnostic Jung and the Seven Sermons to the Dead.* Wheaton: The Theosophical Publishing House, 1982.

Howells, William. *The Heathens: Primitive Man and His Religions.* Garden City: Anchor Books, 1962.

Hunt, Marjorie. *The Stone Carvers: Master Craftsmen of Washington National Cathedral.* Washington: Smithsonian Institution Press, 1999.

Hutton, Ronald. *The pagan Religions of the Ancient British Isles: Their Nature and Legacy.* Oxford: Blackwell Publishers Ltd, 1991.

Inwards, Richard. *Weather Lore.* London: Senate, 1994. A reprint of the 1893 edition published by Elliot Stock, London.

Jacobs, Elizabeth D. *The Nehalem Tillamook: An Ethnography.* Corvallis: Oregon State University Press, 2003.

James, E. O. *The Cult of the Mother-Goddess.* New York: Barnes & Noble Books, 1994.

Jones, Prudence & Nigel Pennick. *A History of pagan Europe.* New York: Barnes & Noble Books, 1995.

Jordan, Katy. *The Haunted Landscape: Folklore, ghosts & legends of Wiltshire.* Bradford on Avon: Ex Libris Press, 2000.

Keightley, Thomas. *The Fairy Mythology: Illustrative of the Romance and Superstition of Various Countries.* London: G. Bell Publishers 1878.

Kluckhohn, Clyde and Dorothea Leighton. *The Navaho.* Garden City: Doubleday & Company Inc./The Natural History Museum, 1962 .

Koch, William E. "Hunting Beliefs and Customs from Kansas" in *Western Folklore*, Vol. XXIV, July, 1965, Number 3. Published by the California Folklore Society, UCLA, pg. 165-175.

Kostof. Spiro. *A History of Architecture: Settings and Ritual.* Oxford: Oxford University Press, 1985 .

Krickeberg, Walter & et al. *Pre-Columbian American Religions.* New York: Holt, Rinehart and Winston History of Religion Series, 1969.

Leeming, David Adams. *The World of Myth.* New York: Oxford University Press, 1990.

Leland, Charles G. *Etruscan Roman Remains.* Blaine: Phoenix Publishing Inc., n/d. A reprint of the 1892 edition..

Lesley, Craig. *River Song.* New York: Picador USA, 1989.

Lintrop, Aado. "The Great Oak and Brother-Sister" in *Folklore*, Vol. 16 Published by the Folk Belief and Media Group of ELM, Tartu, Estonia, 2001, pages 34-56.

Littleton, C. Scott & Linda A. Malcor. "Gawain and the Green Knight" in *Heroes of the Dawn: Celtic Myth.* London: Duncan Baird Publishers, 1996.

Long, George. *The Folklore Calendar.* London: Senate, 1996. A reprint of the, 1930 edition published by Philip Allan, London.

MacCulloch, J.A. *The Religion of the Ancient Celts.* Mineola: Dover Publications, Inc., 2003. A reprint of the, 1911 publication from T. & T. Clark, Edinburgh.

MacDermott, Mercia. *Explore Green Men.* Loughborough: Explore Books/Heart of Albion Press, 2003.

Mack, Carol K. and Dinah Mack. *A Field Guide to Demons, Fairies, Fallen Angels, and Other Subversive Spirits.* New York: Owl Books, 1998.

Mackenzie, Donald A. *Crete & Pre-Hellenic Myths and Legends.* London: Senate, 1995 (A reprint of the, 1917 publication by the Gresham Publishing Company, London).

Mackenzie, Donald A. *Ancient Man in Britain.* London: Senate, 1996. A reprint of the, 1922 edition by Blackie & Son Limited, London.

MacMullen, Ramsay. *Christianity & paganism in the Fourth to Eighth Centuries.* New Haven: Yale University Press, 1997.

Mandeville, Sir John. *The Travels of Sir John Mandeville.* Trans. by C.W.R.D. Moseley. London: Penguin Books, 1983. A translation of the 1356 publication.

Mann, Nicholas R. *His Story: Masculinity in the Post-Patriarchal World.* St. Paul: Llewellyn Publications, 1995.

Matthews, John. *Robin Hood: Green Lord of the Wildwood.* Glastonbury: Gothic Image Publications, 1993.

Matthews, John. *The Quest for the Green Man.* Wheaton: Quest Books, 2001.

Mbiti, John S. *African Religions and Philosophy.* Garden City: Anchor Books, 1970.

Millar, Ronald. *The Green Man: Companion and Gazetteer.* East Sussex: S.B. Publications, 1997.

Miller, Mary and Karl Taube. *An Illustrated Dictionary of the Gods and Symbols of Ancient Mexico and the Maya.* New York: Thames and Hudson, 1993 .

Moony, James. *The Ghost-Dance Religion and the Sioux Outbreak of 1890.* Chicago: The University of Chicago Press, 1965. A reprint of Part 2 of the *Fourteenth Annual Report of the Bureau of Ethnology to the Secretary of the Smithsonian Institution, 1892-93.* Washington: Government Printing Office 1896.

Mooney, James. *Myths of the Cherokee.* New York: Dover Publications Inc., 1995. A reprint of the *Nineteenth Annual Report of the Bureau of American Ethnology 1897-98* published in1900 by the Smithsonian Institution, Washington.

Murray, Margaret A. *The God of the Witches.* Oxford: Oxford University Press, 1952.

Neumann, Eric. *The Great Mother: An Analysis of the Archetype.* Princeton: Princeton University Press, 1963.

Newman, Paul. *Lost Gods of Albion: The Chalk Hill-Figures of Britain.* Gloucestershire: Wrens Park Publishing, 2000.

Newman, Philip L. *Knowing the Gururumba.* New York: Holt, Rinehart and Winston Case Studies in Cultural Anthropology, 1965.

O'Grady, Joan. *The Prince of Darkness: The Devil in History, Religion and the Human Psyche.* New York: Barnes and Noble Books, 1989.

O'Hanlon, Maggie. *Customs & Traditions in Britain.* Hampshire: Pitkin Unichrome, 2000.

Otto, Walter F. *Dionysus: Myth and Cult.* Trans. by Robert B. Palmer. Bloomington: Indiana University Press, 1965.

Owen, Gale R. *Rites and Religions of the Anglo-Saxons.* Dorset Press, 1985.

Patai, Raphael. *The Hebrew Goddess.* New York: Avon Books, 1978.

Pendell, Dale. *Pharmako/Poeia: Plant Powers, Poisons and Herbcraft.* San Francisco: Mercury House, 1995.

Pennick, Nigel. *Celtic Sacred Landscapes.* New York: Thames and Hudson, 1996.

Philips, David E. *Legendary Connecticut: Traditional Tales from the Nutmeg State.* Willimantic: Curbstone Press, 1992.

Phillips, Charles & Michael Kerrigan. *Forests of the Vampire: Slavic Myth.* New York: Barnes & Noble Books, 1999.

Phillips, Daphne. "The Green Man of Fingest," in *Strange Buckinghamshire,* www.cleaverproperty.co.uk/strange'bucks/fingest.html 11/15/2000.

Philpot, Mrs. J. H. *The Sacred Tree in Religion and Myth*. Mineola: Dover Publications Inc., 2004. A reprint of the 1897 edition published by Macmillan and Co. Ltd, New York & London.

Piggott, Juliet. *Japanese Mythology*. New York: Peter Bedrick Books, 1982.

Porteous, Alexander. *The Lore of the Forest: Myths and Legends*. London: Senate Publishers, 1996. A reprint of the, 1928 publication *Forest Folklore* published by George Allen & Unwin, London.

Powers, Stephen. *Tribes of California*. Berkeley: University of California Press, 1976. A reprint of the 1877 publication *Contributions to North American Ethnology, Vol. III* published by the Department of Interior, Government Printing Office, Washington, D.C.

Radford, Edwin and Mona A. *Encyclopaedia of Superstitions*. New York: The Philosophical Library, 1949.

Raglan, Lady J. "The 'Green Man' in Church Architecture." In *Folklore* #50 (1939), pgs 45-57.

Randolph, Vance. *Ozark Magic and Folklore*. New York: Dover Publications, 1964. A reprint of *Ozark Superstitions* published by Columbia University Press, 1947.

Rands, Robert L. "Some Manifestations of Water in Mesoamerican Art" in *Anthropological Papers Numbers 43-48, Smithsonian Institution Bureau of American Ethnology Bulletin 157*. Washington: US Government Printing Office, 1955, pgs 265-393.

Ringgren, Helmer. *Religions of the Ancient Near East*. Philadelphia: The Westminster Press, 1973.

Rose, Martial and Julia Hedgecoe. *Stories in Stone: The Medieval Roof Carvings of Norwich Cathedral*. New York: Thames and Hudson, 1997.

Rothery, Andrew. "The Science of the Green Man." http://www.ecopsychology.org/ezine/green_man.html. August 9,, 2004.

Rutherford, Ward. *Celtic Lore: The history of the Druids and their timeless traditions*. London: Aquarian/Thorsons, 1993.

Sackett, S.J. "More Folk Medicine from Western Kansas" in *Western Folklore* #23, 1964. Published by the California Folklore Society, UCLA .

Sahi, Jyoti. *The Child and the Serpent: Reflections on Popular Indian Symbols*. London: Arkana, 1980.

Schama, Simon. *Landscape and Memory*. New York: Vintage Books, 1995.

Seznec, Jean. *The Survival of the pagan Gods: The Mythological Tradition and Its Place in Renaissance Humanism and Art*. New York: Harper Torchbooks/The Bollingen Library, 1961.

Sitwell, Sacheverell. *Gothic Europe*. New York: Holt, Rinehart and Winston, 1969, 64.

Sjöö, Monica & Barbara Mor. *The Great Cosmic Mother: Rediscovering the Religion of the Earth.* New York: Harper Collins, 1991.

Skinner, Charles M. *Myths and Legends of Flowers, Trees, Fruits, and Plants In All Ages and In All Climes.* Philadelphia: J.B. Lippincott Company, 1911.

Skinner, Fred Gladstone. *Myths and Legends of the Ancient Near East.* New York: Barnes and Noble Books, 1970.

Spence, Lewis. *Ancient Egyptian Myths and Legends.* New York: Dover Publications, Inc., 1990. A reprint of the 1915 edition.

St. Pierre, Mark and Tilda Long Soldier. *Walking in the Sacred Manner.* New York: Touchstone Books, 1995.

Stewart, R. J. *Celtic Gods Celtic Goddesses.* London: Blandford, 1990.

Stone, Brian, editor. *Sir Gawain and the Green Knight.* London: Penguin Books, 1974.

Stone, Brian. "The Common Enemy of Man," in *Sir Gawain and the Green Knight*, trans. by Brian Stone. London: Penguin Books, 1974.

Stone, Merlin. *When God Was A Woman.* New York: Barnes & Noble Books, 1993.

Teit, James A. "The Salishan Tribes of the Western Plateaus," edited by Franz Boas, in *45th Annual Report, 1927-28*, Bureau of American Ethnology. Washington: Smithsonian Institution.

Thomas, Keith. *Religion and the Decline of Magic.* London: Penguin Books, 1971.

Thompson, C.J.S. *The Hand of Destiny: Everyday Folklore and Superstitions.* London: Senate, 1995. A reprint of the, 1932 edition published by Rider & Company, London.

Timpson, John. *Timpson's Leylines: A Layman Tracking the Ley's.* London: Cassell & Co., 2000.

Toorawa, Shawkat M. "Khidr: The History of a Ubiquitous Master" in *Sufi Selected Articles*, Issue Number 30, Published by Khaniqahi Mimatullahi Publications, 2000.

Trubshaw, Bob. "Paganism in British Folk Customs." In *At the Edge*, No. 3, 1996.

Varner, Gary R. *Essays in Contemporary paganism.* San Jose: Writers Club Press, Inc., 2000.

Varner, Gary R. *Sacred Wells: A Study in the History, Meaning & Mythology of Holy Wells and Waters.* Baltimore: Publish America, 2002.

Wakefield, J.D. *Legendary Landscapes: Secrets of Ancient Wiltshire Revealed.* Marlborough: Nod Press, 1999.

Walker, Barbara G. *The Women's Encyclopedia of Myths and Secrets.* Edison: Castle Books, 1983.

Walker, James R. *Lakota Belief and Ritual.* Lincoln: University of Nebraska Press, 1991.

Wilbert, Johannes. *Yupa Folktales.* Los Angeles: Latin American Studies Volume 24, Latin American Center, UCLA, 1974.

Wilde, Lady. *Irish Cures, Mystic Charms & Superstitions.* New York: Sterling Publishing Company, Inc., 1991.

Wilkinson, Richard H. *The Complete Gods and Goddesses of Ancient Egypt.* London: Thames & Hudson Ltd., 2003.

Wintemberg, W. J. *Folk-Lore of Waterloo County, Ontario.* Ontario: National Museum of Canada, Bulletin No. 116, Anthropological Series No. 28, 1950.

Wrenn, Tony P. and Elizabeth D. Mulloy/The National Trust for Historic Preservation. *America's Forgotten Architecture.* New York: Pantheon Books, 1976.

Yenne, Bill. *Gothic Gargoyles.* New York: Barnes & Noble Books, 2000.

Zimmer, Heinrich. *Myths and Symbols in Indian Art and Civilization.* Edited by Joseph Campbell. Princeton: Princeton University Press, 1946.

INDEX

Made in the USA
Lexington, KY
10 February 2013